TECHNICAL STANDARDS

An Introduction for Librarians

second edition

TECHNICAL STANDARDS

An Introduction for Librarians

second edition

Walt Crawford

G.K. Hall & Co.

70 Lincoln Street, Boston, Massachusetts

First published 1991
by G.K. Hall & Co.
70 Lincoln Street
Boston, Massachusetts 02111

10 9 8 7 6 5 4 3 2 1

Library of Congress Cataloging-in-Publication Data

Crawford, Walt.
    Technical standards: an introduction for libraries /
  Walt Crawford. – 2nd edition.
      p. cm.
  Includes bibliographical references and index.
  ISBN 0-8161-1950-3 (hc) ISBN 0-8161-1951-1 (pbk)
  1. Library science – Technological innovations – Standards.
  2. Information technology – Standards. I. Title.
Z678.85.C7 1991
020'.285 – dc20
                                             91-7306
                                             CIP

The paper used in this publication meets the minimum requirements of
American National Standard for Information Sciences – Permanence of
Paper for Printed Library Materials. ANSI Z39.48-1984.   ∞™
MANUFACTURED IN THE UNITED STATES OF AMERICA

Contents

List of Figures

Preface

When an American National Standard or International Standard reaches age five, it must be reviewed by the body that created it (according to American National Standards Institute and International Organization for Standardization procedures). The review can lead to reaffirmation, revision, or withdrawal. It seems reasonable that a book about standards should go through the same process. I wrote the first edition of *Technical Standards: An Introduction for Librarians* in 1985; it appeared in 1986. Thus, 1990 marks the first five years of the book.

I started work on my first book because I felt strongly that the topic, the U.S. machine-readable formats for bibliographic records (MARC), needed a good, nontechnical, book-length introduction. Others convinced me that the library field would benefit by a nontechnical introduction to technical standards. After all, I'd already written one book; how hard could it be to do another one?

I have long since forgiven those who made that argument. People apparently found the book useful. Library interest and activity in technical standards have grown substantially since 1986, with the National Information Standards Organization (NISO) becoming a healthy, vital institution.

My interest and activity in technical standards have continued in a variety of sometimes peculiar ways. In 1988 I agreed to serve as the founding editor for a new NISO publication to replace the old, increasingly irregular *Voice of Z39*. Creating and editing *Information Standards Quarterly* is a considerable pleasure and keeps me aware of the activity within NISO. Given that background, I found it obvious that this volume should be either revised or withdrawn.. People within NISO argued for revision, and G.K. Hall agreed to a second edition. I hope that the profession will find this edition more useful than the first.

Changes in Organization

This edition separates the general discussion of standards—which includes some library-specific examples—from the specific discussion of NISO, now covered in far greater detail than before. It also eliminates two of the three chapters discussing "current standards." A note on that change may be in order.

The last (and by far the longest) chapter of this book describes *every* Z39 standard and draft standard, including not only the current version but known activity toward revision or withdrawal; that chapter is current as of early 1991. The equivalent chapter in the first edition was incomplete; although the manuscript included every Z39 standard, the publisher convinced me to remove several discussions.

Appendix A discusses some current ISO standards. Although it covers much of the same material as Chapter 12 in the first edition, it appears as an appendix because the discussions are brief and the set of standards is not entirely current.

My original outline for this edition included selected ASC X3 standards in Appendix A as well, just as Chapter 11 in the first edition covered them. After considering the activity of X3, my ability—or lack thereof—to explain the most significant X3 standards in nontechnical terms, and the length of this edition, I concluded that it would be more responsible to omit the section altogether than to include a sketchy and fairly useless section. Yes, X3 is important, but, in most cases, its standards are used far beyond the library field and operate as underpinnings to library automation efforts.

Acknowledgments

From the First Edition

Many of my friends and colleagues helped make this book possible, directly or indirectly. A few played specific roles and deserve credit for much of what's right about the book. Assertions, errors, clumsy wording and poor organization are all mine.

Two people instigated this project: Adrienne Hickey, my former editor at Knowledge Industry Publications, and Ruth C. Carter, then chair of LITA TESLA, the Technical Standards for Library Automation Committee. My wife, Linda Driver, supported the idea and provided her usual support and good advice; my boss, Glee Harrah Cady, also provided critical support.

Susan Schwartz was my editor at Knowledge Industry during the preparation of the manuscript, and provided cogent, insightful criticism that eased the route from rough draft to final submission. Joan Aliprand, Robert Beebe, Wayne Davison, and Charles Stewart of RLG all gave me helpful review comments; Kathleen Bales, also of RLG, provided critical review of the indexes. Sandra K. Paul of SKP Associates, chair of the National Information Standards Organization (Z39), went out of her way to do a careful review of the manuscript. My thanks to them all.

Two colleagues in the library field are indirectly responsible for this book and for *MARC for Library Use*. David Weisbrod was unable to prepare an article on MARC for *Library Trends* and suggested my name instead. That article started a series of events leading to *MARC for Library Use*; I would never have started this book without the experience of that one. Brian Aveney, then editor of *Information Technology and Libraries*, prodded me into active writing for publication at a time when I found such writing difficult. Neither should be held accountable for the results.

John Kountz deserves some of the blame for my interest in technical standards. When I first joined ALA in 1975, he was running TESLA with a flair that made the committee meetings fascinating. Somehow, my fascination with the early meetings resulted in long-term involvement with TESLA and, through TESLA, with technical standards.

For the Second Edition

Mary Ellen Jacob (then chair of NISO) and Paul Evan Peters (currently chair of NISO) convinced me to create *Information Standards Quarterly*; Patricia Harris, Executive Director of NISO, has provided the information, inspiration, and encouragement to keep the publication going. Without them, I doubt that this edition would have emerged; and, if it had, the information on current NISO activity would be nowhere near as current or complete.

Five colleagues at RLG, all in the Development Division, reviewed this manuscript and provided useful comments and, in some cases, information I had been lacking. My thanks to Kathleen Bales, Wayne Davison, Lennie Stovel, Joan Aliprand, and Jay Fields for their help.

1

Introduction

W e all rely on technical standards, but most of the time we don't worry about them. When you plug in a television set, add oil to your car, or use a Library of Congress record on the Online Computer Library Center (OCLC) or Research Libraries Information Network (RLIN), you're relying on one or more technical standards. Technical standards for libraries can help you as a librarian, writer, or researcher. You don't have to know every detail of every one, but you can use them better if you understand them.

People and companies use technical standards without paying attention to them; which generally is both necessary and proper. For example, purchasing a new personal computer is difficult enough already, what with selecting the general type, specific manufacturer, source of supply, and equipment to be installed in the box. You assume that the power cable will meet Underwriters Laboratories standards and that the circuit board has suitable dielectric qualities (or, more probably, you don't even think about those issues). You might ask for assurance that the computer has Federal Communications Commission (FCC) Class B certification—but you probably won't ask whether the motherboard was tested according to EIA RS-162-56, *Test Standard for Ceramic Board Printed Circuits.*[1]

On the other hand, a company that designs PC motherboards and contracts actual circuit board construction to another company

---

1 Please don't. I'm not sure that's the proper standard; I am sure it's several levels below what you should worry about as a consumer.

might very well want to request certification that appropriate tests have been performed. Asking whether a board has been tested is really asking a pointless question; asking whether a specified test procedure has been followed—as in one of thousands of technical standards for testing—should yield useful information.

As a rule, we take technical standards for granted or fail to recognize their existence even when we should be directly aware of them. Sometimes, we even assume that we're following standards when we're not. For example, consider Figure 1.1, a version of which appears on the back-of-title page in this book. One library-related magazine decided to use the figure to indicate the use of alkaline paper in books being reviewed. But the symbol, which is a trademark of NISO, doesn't simply

Figure 1.1: Z39.48 Symbol

mean that paper is alkaline; it means that paper is certified to meet the minimum requirements of *American National Standard for Information Sciences—Permanence of Paper, ANSI Z39.48-1984*. That's not the same thing, since the standard requires more than just alkalinity; the magazine stopped using the symbol.

The extended example that follows[2] may seem mundane—but the standard catalog card has had considerable impact on American libraries in the twentieth century, and millions of catalog cards are still being printed every month.

Three-by-Five Catalog Cards

The Research Libraries Group (RLG) produces large numbers of catalog cards for users of RLIN. Until early 1982 RLG produced cards using an IBM line printer. Cards were printed two at a time on special

---

2 Retained from the first edition, with the permission of my good-natured employers, who haven't made this mistake for almost a decade now.

continuous-form stock with perforations between each pair of cards. When RLG acquired the stock, we specified that it meet all applicable standards.

In 1982 RLG decided to use a Xerox 9700 laser printer to print the cards. These were prepunched sheets of stock, each of which would contain four catalog cards. The producer certified that the material itself met applicable standards, and that the holes were punched in appropriate places for standard cards. The RLG staff would cut the sheets into individual cards after they were printed.

Production began beautifully. We purchased a good character set, tested the programs, and started shipping laser-printed cards. RLG followed standards at all steps along the way, including, of course, the 3 by 5-inch standard for library catalog cards. A few weeks later, we began to get complaints: the cards wouldn't fit in some catalog drawers. The RLIN production staff was troubled by the reports. The stock was manufactured to standard, the holes were punched to standard, and the cutting machine was carefully adjusted to cut at precisely three inches by five inches. The three-by-five catalog card is well-known: those dimensions occur repeatedly in library literature, even in the specialized literature of library standards.

After some consideration and research, we found the problem: we had relied on a common but false simplification of the standard size for a catalog card. It isn't three-by-five, even though everybody calls it that. The standard dimensions are 75 mm by 125 mm. That's almost three-by-five, but not quite: it is actually 2.95 inches high and 4.92 inches wide. If a catalog drawer is precisely five inches wide, it will hold standard catalog cards nicely—and it won't hold three-by-five cards. RLG readjusted the card cutter, reran the oversize cards, and solved the problem, which could have been avoided by explicitly checking the standard.

RLG used a standard (ANSI Z85.1) without referring to it, as we all do most of the time. This time, relying on memory and oral tradition created problems, which RLG solved at some expense and with some difficulty. The standard was misused through inattention and had been steadily corrupted by years of casual reference to three-by-five library cards.

The Standard in Question

Library suppliers know how to make standard catalog card stock: the color, the thickness, where the holes should be punched, and how big the holes should be. Suppliers follow a voluntary technical standard, originally established in 1969: ANSI Z85.1-1980, *American National Standard for Permanent and Durable Library Catalog Cards*.[3] When RLG printed cards on perforated stock, the organization didn't worry about ANSI Z85.1. Suppliers have no motive to produce nonstandard cards: there are no real markets for library card stock other than libraries and library suppliers.

Z85.1-1980
Permanent and Durable Library Catalog Cards

Like most standards approved by the American National Standards Institute (ANSI), ANSI Z85.1-1980 includes a *scope and purpose* note, an *explicit standard*, and a *foreword* that is not actually part of the standard. Unlike many other standards, ANSI Z85.1-1980 does not include practice guidelines, appendixes, or an abstract. It is a short standard: explicit, unambiguous, and clearly written. The foreword provides background for the standard.

Foreword

The foreword provides background for the standard:

> A de facto standard for the dimensions of catalog cards used in American libraries was established in the nineteenth century by Melvil Dewey. For the past fifty years, at least, almost every card catalog cabinet manufactured in the United States has been designed to accommodate cards of those dimensions.[4]

---

3 Available, as are all Z39 and Z85 standards cited in this book, from Transaction Publishers, Department NISO Standards, Rutgers—The State University, New Brunswick, NJ 08903. At this writing, Z85.1 may be temporarily unavailable; a revised version, ANSI/NISO Z85.1, will be available in the early 1990s.

4 ANSI Z85.1-1980, 3.

Z85.1 was originally approved in 1969. The 1980 version specifies hole placement more precisely and adds test methods for ink feathering and erasing qualities. Committee Z85, the *American National Standards Committee on Standardization of Library Supplies and Equipment*, never issued any other standards. Z85.1 is now maintained by NISO.

Scope and Purpose

A technical standard should have a well-defined scope; many problems arise because they are used beyond their intended scope. Z85.1 states a clear, straightforward scope and rationale.

> This standard establishes performance standards for permanent and durable library catalog cards. It specifies the size, caliper, hole size and location, and other characteristics of these cards.
>
> Although requirements for permanence and durability of library catalog cards differ according to the type of library, the standard specifies the minimum factors necessary to meet the needs of the research library. Research libraries ordinarily retain the majority of their acquisitions permanently. Catalog cards for such acquisitions must be durable library cards made from stock which will not deteriorate more rapidly than the books due to either (1) the composition of the paper or (2) the relatively heavy use conditions they must endure in the card catalog.[5]

In this case, what's good for the research library is certainly good for the public library as well. Even public libraries that must discard one book for every book added will keep some volumes for decades. No library should be concerned that catalog cards will cease to be useful before the books are discarded. More to the point, no library should have to worry that the catalog card drawers purchased from Highsmith won't hold cards provided by Baker & Taylor.

---

5 Ibid., 5.

Details

The standard specifies 17 explicit dimensions and characteristics of catalog cards, including the following:

- **Size:** 75 mm x 125 mm, with a tolerance of +0 to -0.5 mm;

- **Cutting:** If cards are guillotined (knife-cut) rather than cut by a rotary blade, the knife must be sharp, the cards back-trimmed to be free of burr.

- **Hole:** The hole must be centered in terms of width, 7.9 mm in diameter, with a lower edge 4.8 mm from the bottom of the card: the bottom placement has a tolerance of -0, +0.8 mm. (These dimensions all sound more familiar in common measure: a 5/16-in. hole, 3/16-in. from the bottom of the card, with a 1/32-in. tolerance.) This section also says why the hole must be placed properly.

- **Finish, surface, color:** Smooth, lint-free, white or cream-white.

- **Weight and thickness:** Lightweight cards 0.020 cm (0.008 in.) thick, weighing 200 gm per square meter (110-pound stock); medium-weight cards 0.025 cm (0.010 in.) thick, weighing 235 gm per square meter (130-pound stock). In other words, medium-weight cards should pack 100 to the inch.

- **Writing, printing, erasing qualities:** Explicit test methods to assure that cards take ink cleanly and that pencil marks can be erased cleanly.

- **Acidity:** pH of no less than 5.5, "measured by the hot extraction method described in TAPPI T 435 os-77."

- **Endurance:** The card must stand up to 800 double folds with 1 kg tension using a standard test method.

- **Stock:** Card stock must not contain ground wood, unbleached fibers, or optical brighteners, and can contain only 2% fluorescence due to natural properties.

Technical standards build on other technical standards. Z85.1 refers explicitly to four standards established by the Technical Association of the Pulp and Paper Industry (TAPPI), including *TAPPI T 435 os-77, Hydrogen Ion Concentration (pH) of Paper Extracts—Hot Extraction Method*, and *ANSI/TAPPI T401 os-74, American National Standard for Fiber Analysis of Paper and Paperboard*.

This summary doesn't include all pertinent aspects of the standard. If you're planning to produce (or cut) catalog cards, or want to check on your suppliers, you should order a copy of ANSI/NISO Z85.1. If you're buying stock, you need only specify that it must be produced in accordance with Z85.1. Typically, you'd simply call for "Library Catalog Cards (Permanent and Durable)" or "catalog card stock meeting applicable standards."

Defining Technical Standards

In "Organizations Contributing to Development of Library Standards,"[6] the authors set forth some basic varieties of standards.

> Standards themselves take a variety of forms. They may be guidelines or models against which services, etc., are to be compared. Library service standards fall into this category. Other standards take the form of rules for activities that should be applied as consistently as possible but which, by their nature, will not necessarily produce the identical results even when followed. Cataloging rules are of this type. A third class of standards are specifications or "technical" standards for which strict observance is necessary if sharing is to take place. Format structure, character sets, and code list standards fall into this class.[7]

Technical standards are definitions, or specifications; they communicate specific agreements. They can:

- **Record** agreement on specifications;
- **Extend** the agreement beyond the original parties, as other parties obtain and follow the standards;
- **Communicate** to others that a set of specifications has been followed: reference to a technical standard is a brief way of referring to the specifications contained in that standard.

Chapter 3 discusses varieties of technical standards. For most of this book, two different definitions of technical standards are used, one very broad and one fairly narrow.

---

6 Henriette D. Avram, Sally H. McCallum, and Mary S. Price, "Organizations Contributing to Development of Library Standards," *Library Trends* 31, no. 2 (Fall 1982): 197-221.

7 Ibid., 198.

As a broad definition, a *technical standard* is an explicit definition that can be communicated, that is not subject to unilateral change without notice, and that, if properly followed, will yield predictable and consistent results.

The Need for Standards

Complex societies require agreement on standards to support cooperative relationships of many kinds. Industrial and postindustrial societies depend on technical standards for everyday life and long-term progress. Technical standards provide the common bases from which individual developments may emerge. To quote Ken Dowlin, then president of the Library and Information Technology Association, "without technical standards, systems cannot grow."[8]

We may notice a need for technical standards as follows:

- When technical standards are ignored or misused, as in the example above;
- When technological developments are stymied or made more difficult because many incompatible paths are taken in the absence of technical standards;
- When an area fails to develop quickly or economically because people working in the area have no common basis from which to proceed.

Tens of thousands of people devote hundreds of thousands of hours a year, and millions of dollars each year, developing, considering, and maintaining technical standards.

The Problems and Dangers of Standards

Standards aren't always helpful. They can hamper innovation when they are established before a field has matured or when they persist although outmoded by evolving technology. They also can lock out the most creative and efficient people in a field. Most technical standards in the United States are voluntary, but when contracts call

---

8 Ken Dowlin, caption on ALA LITA poster, 1984.

for compliance with all pertinent technical standards, nonstandard solutions may not be practical.

Technical standards can cause real damage. Efforts devoted to developing them can detract from efforts for innovation. Standards can keep old technology dominant beyond its time, costing everybody efficiency and flexibility. They may not be developed with sufficient objectivity or balance, and may favor some suppliers at the expense of others, or at the expense of users. Standards can be used to impose trade barriers or to suppress technologies.

Many standards are not American National Standards, and some things that are called standards are not formal consensus technical standards. Standards arise through various means: licensing patented innovations, de facto standards based on successful marketing, and industry standards based on poorly-understood agreements among competitors, in addition to those formally developed and approved through ANSI. Some organizations within the United States do not submit all of their standards for ANSI approval, and there are hundreds of standards organizations outside the United States, including the International Organization for Standardization (ISO), which is increasingly important to American interests.

Technical Standards for Libraries

Libraries have a set of standards developed specifically for theme and for information science and publishing industries, and also rely on complex sets of related technical standards from other fields. The first group, largely developed by NISO and its predecessor American National Standards Committee Z39, cover a range of topics from the structure of machine-readable bibliographic records (Z39.2) to a system for the romanization of Armenian (Z39.37).

Libraries use many other standards developed by a range of standards organizations. For example, library automation directly uses the ones established by Accredited Standards Committee X3 (Information Processing Systems) and, to a somewhat lesser extent, those from organizations such as IEEE (Institute of Electrical and

Electronics Engineers) and EIA (Electronic Industries Association). Library preservation efforts rely on standards developed by AIIM (Association of Information and Image Management) and, at least indirectly, those developed by ASTM (American Society for Testing and Materials) and TAPPI, as well as those developed by NISO. ISO, the most important international standards organization, develops many standards vital to library automation and operations, particularly those developed by its Technical Committee 46 (TC 46).

Organization

This book is a basic introduction to technical standards with particular focus on libraries and automation. Part 1 deals with the whole field, although many examples are specific to library operations. It should help you to understand what technical standards are (and how they differ from all those other things called standards); what life might be like without them; some motivations for developing them; the ways that standards build on and relate to one another; problems and dangers of standardization; how standards are developed and how that process is changing; who develops them; and how you can maintain a general awareness of them.

Part 2 focuses on NISO. It includes some notes on NISO's history and status, a discussion of the areas currently covered by its standards and plans for future development; how the organization operates and who belongs; and how you and your library, publisher, or other agency can be involved. Part 2 ends with a description of each standard and proposed standard issued by NISO as of January 1991. An appendix provides notes on some of the ISO standards of particular interest to libraries.

Definitions

Most special terms used in this book are defined as they first appear; many appear in the glossary. Five abbreviations used throughout the book are defined below.

ANSI (American National Standards Institute): The overall organization for voluntary standards in the United States, and the U.S. member of ISO, the International Organization for Standardization. ANSI does not develop standards; ANSI standards are created by various standards organizations following ANSI procedures. Many of these standards are published by ANSI, and all are available from ANSI.

ASC (Accredited Standards Committee): A standards development organization accredited by ANSI; many ASCs were formerly committees within ANSI, called American National Standards Committees (ANSCs).

ISO (International Organization for Standardization): The leading international body for technical standards except in electrical and electronic areas. ISO has representatives from national standards organizations.

NISO (National Information Standards Organization, formerly ANSC Z39): The ANSI-accredited standards organization preparing standards for library and information science and related publishing practices. NISO-developed standards continue to be numbered beginning Z39, as in ANSI/NISO Z39.57-1990.

Z39 (Earlier name for NISO [see above]): The organization changed names in 1984 when it incorporated as a standards development organization.

PART 1

Standards and Standardization

Without standards, contemporary civilization would be impossible. Even today, the lack or misuse of a standard may be a matter of life or death, or, more commonly, misunderstanding and consequent economic damage. Chapter 2 shows a few of the ways in which you rely on standards every day and what life might be like without them.

To use standards effectively, you must first understand what they are, how they are created, and how they relate to one another. Although this book is primarily about technical standards, with a focus on formal consensus technical standards and an emphasis on American standards for libraries, publishing, and information science, the field actually is much broader, and some aspects of it are touched on in the next two chapters.

Many things called standards don't deserve that name, at least in my judgment; many other things that can legitimately be called standards don't fit the broad definition stated in Chapter 1. Does that make them useless? No, but you should understand the differences among types of standards before relying on them. Chapter 3 discusses varieties of standards, including some noteworthy examples. Chapter 4 extends that discussion to show how standards work together and build on other standards.

Standards don't generate themselves, and they can raise legal and ethical questions. Chapters 5 and 6 discuss some reasons that people and organizations create standards and some problems and dangers of standardization. Chapters 7 and 8 go through some processes used to build formal technical standards and some major organizations involved in standardization in the United States and throughout the world.

2

Technical Standards in Action

Technical standards affect each of us every day. When you buy a set of sheets for your bed from a manufacturer other than the bed maker, you depend on them: the sheet manufacturer and the bed manufacturer both followed the same standards for sizes. Technical standards affect you before you awake and throughout the day. Depending on your interests, they may also affect you by being absent from some areas.

A Morning's Worth of Standards

Tens of thousands of technical standards have been established in the United States, including more than 10,000 established by ANSI-accredited standards agencies.[1] The following examples represent only a few of the ones that directly affect your everyday life.

Explicit Standards Before Work

Before you wake up, you're probably in bed. *ANSI Z357.1, Bedding Products and Components*, may have influenced your sleep. If you are wakened by an electric clock, that clock is probably covered by *ANSI/UL 826, Safety Standard for Household Electric Clocks*, one of the

---

1 See Chapter 3 for a discussion of this and other varieties of technical standards.

many ANSI standards developed by Underwriters Laboratories, Inc. *ANSI/UL 499, Safety Standard for Electric Heating Appliances* covers your electric space heaters; gas heaters have their own standards.

If you turn on a light, you're relying on some of the 18 ANSI standards for electric lamp bases, and 106 for electric lamps. One of these is *ANSI C78.375: Guide for Electrical Measurements of Fluorescent Lamps*. Those standards and guides mean that you can buy a lamp from one maker to put in another maker's fixture: the fixture is designed for a specified size and variety of lamp, and any current or prospective lamp manufacturer can determine the dimensions and characteristics required for a lamp to work in a standard fixture. When you get dressed, you wear fabrics that may be covered by one or more of 37 ANSI standards for fabrics and dozens more for textiles. For example, *ANSI/AATCC 124* specifies a *Test Method for Appearance of Durable Press Fabrics After Repeated Home Launderings*.

Some of you use electric shavers; some use electric hair dryers. *ANSI/UL 1028* provides a *Safety Standard for Hair Clippers and Shaving Appliances*; *ANSI/UL HD1* states a *Method for Measuring Performance of Household Electric Hair Dryers*. You plug appliances in to outlet boxes covered by *ANSI/UL 514: Safety Standards for Outlet Boxes and Fittings*; the plugs and wiring follow standards and codes such as *ANSI/NFPA 70: National Electrical Code* and *ANSI C2: National Electrical Safety Code*. Household and other wiring is based on other standards developed by various agencies, including *ANSI/IEEE C37.13: Low-Voltage AC Power Circuit Breakers Used in Enclosures* and a dozen standards for electric line construction.

As you get ready for work, you may use a drip-type coffee maker (covered by *ANSI/UL 1438: Safety Standard for Drip-Type Coffee-Makers*), an electric toaster (partly covered by *ANSI/AHAM T-1: Method of Measuring Performance of Household Electric Toasters*), or your refrigerator (covered by standards such as *ANSI/UL 250: Safety Standard for Household Refrigerators and Freezers* and *ANSI/AHAM HRF-1: Household Refrigerators, Combination Refrigerator/Freezers, and Household Freezers*). Other safety, performance, and specification standards deal with other appliances and objects you encounter each morning, including the hardware on the door you open to bring in the paper. The newspaper you read was produced thanks to the thousands of component, electrical, and systems standards that make automation possible; identity and test standards for ink and paper; and many other standards in other fields.

On your way to work, you depend on hundreds of technical standards relating to cars, fuel, roads, and traffic control. Several textile standards cover tires. *ANSI/ASTM D1120: Method of Test for Boiling Point of Engine Antifreeze* affects the well-being of your car, as do *ANSI/ASTM D2699: Test for Knock Characteristics of Motor Fuels by the Research Method* and *ANSI/ASTM D2602: Method of Test for Apparent Viscosity of Engine Oils at Low Temperature Using the Cold-Cranking Simulator*. When you buy a specific grade of oil or a specific octane of gasoline, you rely on grading standards as specified in formal consensus standards such as those above.For example, 10W-30 has the same meaning for all brands of oil in all service stations across the United States; it is an SAE weight, defined by Society of Automotive Engineers standards. Your trip to work is also probably affected by a whole group of technical standards for "CAMAC," *Computer Automated Measurement and Control* of traffic. Seven CAMAC standards are grouped together as *ANSI/IEEE Camac.*

Explicit Standards in the Library

When you arrive at work you're still surrounded by technical standards, including many of those mentioned above and several others. Some of these are standards related to public places, some are related to general business, and some are specific to libraries; many others affect nonprint materials within the library.

Chapter 12 examines the current library, publishing, and information science standards in some detail. In a typical day, you may be affected indirectly by a few of these:

- *ANSI Z39.7: Standards for Library Statistics;*
- *ANSI Z39.9: International Standard Serial Number;* (ISSN)
- *ANSI Z39.15: Title Leaves of a Book;*
- *ANSI Z39.32: Information on Microfiche Headings;*
- *ANSI Z39.45: Claims for Missing Issues of Serials.*

If you deal with computers at all, even if only to search remote databases, you depend on *ANSI X3.4, Code for Information Interchange,* which defines ASCII, the American Standard Code for Information Interchange. If you're using a recently installed terminal or computer, you may be more comfortable and more efficient if the workstation was set up using *ANSI/HFS 100: American National Standard for Human Factors Engineering of VDT Workstations. ANSI/IES RP1: Practice for Office Lighting* may have been used in specifying lighting for your offices. If your library entrance was recently modified, the architects probably used *ANSI A117.1: Specifications for Making Buildings and Facilities Accessible to, and Usable by, Physically Handicapped People.*

If you work for one of the 10,000-odd libraries that use OCLC, RLIN, the Western Library Network (WLN), or Utlas for cataloging, you're relying on a web of technical standards, some of them from Z39 or X3 and some of them from other sources. *ANSI Z39.2: Bibliographic Information Interchange* forms the basis for all MARC record interchange. If you use EasyNet, EPIC, or one of several other systems with similar syntax, you're relying on *ANSI/NISO Z39.58: Common Command Language* (still in draft form at this writing). Increasingly, information and requests will flow from library system to library system (including LC, RLIN, OCLC, and state and local networks and systems) using standards such as *ANSI/NISO Z39.50, Information Retrieval Service Definition and Protocol Specification.*

This simple listing of standards that affect your daily life could go on for many more pages; those above are only some of the more obvious ones in the ANSI catalog.

Implicit Standards

When that alarm clock went off, what was the basis for the time setting? If you opened a quart of milk, how do you know how much milk is in the container? Similarly, what does it mean to buy a pound of meat, a kilogram of caviar, or a gallon of gasoline?

If those seem to be silly questions, that shows just how basic standards really are to your daily life. There's nothing inherently natural about the second, minute, or hour as a measure of time. The year, day, and (to a lesser extent) month are based on the physical realities of the earth's orbit around the sun, and hours, minutes, and seconds represent a standard (and artificial) way of splitting a day into component parts—and, not incidentally, defining a "standard day" in the process. When you press **5, 0, 0** on your microwave to heat something for five minutes, you're relying on an implicit standard for time measurement. Units of time as used around the world represent fundamental measurement standards. On the other hand, the convention that when it's 5:30 A.M. in San Francisco it's 7:30 A.M. in Chicago is an arbitrary simplification of real differences in sunlight; that is, the rotation of the earth brings sunlight to Chicago roughly two hours earlier than to San Francisco. The time zone itself is a standard (typically a legislated standard); it reflects physical reality, but only loosely.

The length measure called a foot is presumably based on the use of the human foot as a measuring device, but, fortunately, you don't have to worry about ordering new driveway, to be paid for by the foot, and finding out that the contractor's foot is only 11 inches long. The foot, meter, quart, liter, pound, and kilogram are all (at this point) well-defined technical standards, representing widespread agreement about the way things are to be measured.

Living With Standards

Technical standards should be in the background unless you're developing something that directly depends on their application. Consider the simple act of writing a brief business letter. You take a sheet of standard letter paper, probably purchased citing standard paper weight specifications and certainly using a standard size, and an "all-purpose" envelope, which may be identified as a #10 envelope. The envelope and the paper may have come from different suppliers, but you'll confidently assume that you can fold the paper into thirds and that it will fit neatly into the envelope, as though they were made for each other.

You may think of the paper as 20-pound, 20-weight, or substance 20 paper. For regular sheet stock, the weight is that of one uncut ream, or 500 17 by 22-inch sheets. Thus, a ream (500 sheets) of 20-pound paper, cut to 8½ by 11 inches, weighs 5 pounds.[2] You probably think of the envelope as a "standard business envelope"; whereas you probably know that the sheet of paper is 8½ by 11 inches, you probably don't know or care that the envelope is 4⅛ by 9½ inches (or 106 by 241 mm). So far, you're relying on at least three American standard specifications and possibly more.

You take the paper over to a convenient electric typewriter; it may not be the one you normally use, but you're confident that you can use it. You assume that the home row of keys (middle alphabetic row) will have A, S, D, F, G, H, J, K, and L on the keycaps in that order — or, to name the standard keyboard layout, that the top alphabetic row will begin QWERTY. You also assume that the plug will fit into any convenient wall socket, and that the typewriter will run on the current available from that socket. You're relying on several additional standards: *ANSI X4.23: Keyboard Arrangement for Alphanumeric Machines*; various standards for electrical connections; national consensus on voltage and frequency for current delivered through standard connections; and others. If the paper is one of many sheets in a laser printer and you prepare the letter on a personal computer, you're relying on even more technical standards as well as many other standards and pseudo-standards.

In each case, you can carry on normal activities with ease because you can make assumptions. You assume that your paper will fit in the envelope. As a touch typist, you assume that your fingers will hit the right keys. You assume that the plug will fit in the socket and that you won't electrocute yourself or fry the typewriter.

Living Without Standards

Civilized life without technical standards would be difficult at best, and impossible on any large, organized, or industrialized scale. Consider trying to write that business letter without them. The type-

---

2   For the metrically inclined, 20-weight paper has a mass of 75 gm/m^2; that is, one sheet a meter on each side would be 75 gm.

writer (if it existed) would be quite expensive. The manufacturer would have to negotiate with each supplier of materials as to what is meant by, for example, "a large enough sheet of hard enough steel" (and define what "steel" means in this case), and do his or her own materials testing to determine that the materials are what were agreed to.

Then the manufacturer would have to hand-craft each part of each typewriter, and would certainly have to decide where keys should go and what forms of paper might be used. Should the platen be one hand wide, one and a half, or two? It could not be "10 inches wide" since inches are a technical standard for measure. The manufacturer would have to show salespeople or customers what this particular machine was and what it could be used for, possibly referring them to papermakers who would produce hand-wide paper of "enough" thickness, and probably setting up some sort of ribbon-crafting center (to make thumb-wide ribbons?). The typewriter wouldn't be electric; establishing electrical distribution systems without a complex web of measurement, safety, and specification standards would be unthinkable.

This is only one aspect of your problems in sending a business letter in a world without standards. In any case, you would rarely have to send such a letter, since most business would be carried on with people with whom you could talk directly or through associates. After all, every transaction would require negotiation about what you were buying or selling and what quantity and quality were involved in the bargain.[3]

Living with Conflicting and Delayed Standards

The above example could never happen; when people begin to act outside their immediate circle, they create standards. Larger and more complex societies must have larger and more comprehensive

3 While early civilizations certainly carried out business over long distances without electric typewriters, such civilizations did have technical standards for weights and measures.

sets of standards. Industry requires detailed and formalized technical standards; technology rests on a basis of standards. When standards aren't developed in time, or when different groups develop different (and conflicting) ones, problems arise. Two examples follow, one from consumer electronics and one from bibliography.

Quadraphonic Sound

High-fidelity specialists have long been aware that two speakers can't provide a fully accurate rendering of a "musical space" such as a concert hall. Two sound sources simply don't provide enough information for accurate reproduction, although our minds fill in much of the missing information. Quadraphonic sound provides a possible solution to the problem: four speakers, two in front of the listener and two behind, make a much more accurate musical space possible. After years of experiments with four-channel quadraphonic sound on tapes, quadraphonic records were produced in the early 1970s. Initial reports were good: the new medium opened up the acoustic space, providing a potentially much more realistic listening environment. Despite good early reports, quadraphonic sound died a slow and economically painful death in the marketplace.

Rear speakers are difficult to place in most living rooms. Quad was expensive: two speakers, another stereo amplifier, and the circuitry to decode quadraphonic information from two-channel recordings. Perhaps most important, three different standards for quadraphonic recording appeared, with no dominant early standard.

Columbia/CBS developed a matrixing system called SQ, for Stereo/Quadraphonic. Sansui developed another matrixing system called QS, for Quadraphonic/Stereo. RCA developed CD-4, a discrete four-channel stereo-compatible system. Each system was clearly and unambiguously defined, used by more than one agency, and not subject to unilateral change. Equipment manufacturers released amplifiers supporting one, two, or all three of the quadraphonic systems. Millions of long-playing records were produced in quadraphonic sound.

Three different standards competed in the consumer marketplace. Record stores weren't sure what to stock and how to stock it, and many quadraphonic versions had more noise than straight stereo versions, although all three systems were compatible with stereo. More time was spent considering *which* standard to follow than considering *whether* quadraphonic was worth the trouble. Equipment stayed expensive, partly because manufacturers had to include not one decoding circuit but three. Eventually, the whole enterprise failed.

While quadraphonic sound was sufficiently disruptive to living rooms and budgets that it might not have succeeded in any case, the three-way split may have prevented it from getting a fair trial.[4]

Bibliographic Citations

"There is no common agreement among scholars, editors, bibliographers, or publishers concerning the exact forms to be used in making either footnote citations or bibliographic references to books, articles, or other printed works."[5] Peyton Hurt's statement was true in 1968; it was still true in 1977, when ANSC Z39 developed *ANSI Z39.29, American National Standard for Bibliographic References*.[6] It remains true today.

The problem is not a lack of recommended standards, but too many different ones. *Bibliography and Footnotes*, cited above, presents 2 recommended formats (one for bibliographies, one for footnotes) and cites more than 30 manuals of style, each of which includes recommendations for citation form. The most widely known standard is probably the one in *The Chicago Manual of Style* (Chicago: University of Chicago Press, 1982 [13th edition]). Others include guides from the American Institute of Chemical Engineers, the American Psychological Association, the Modern Language Association,

---

4 Curiously, quadraphonic sound—or, rather, surround sound involving as many as seven sound sources—is making a small resurgence as part of "home theater" systems, using the licensed Dolby Surround sound used in so many recent motion picture soundtracks and present on the videocassette and videodisc releases of these motion pictures.

5 Peyton Hurt, *Bibliography and Footnotes*, 3d ed. (Berkeley, Los Angeles, London: University of California Press, 1968), 2.

6 See Chapter 12 for a description of Z39.29.

and the U.S. Government Printing Office. Most publishers have in-house standards, some of them published as style manuals.

The net effect of this multiplicity of formats is that no single standard exists or is likely to arise. *The Chicago Manual of Style* receives wide use and wider lip service, but many associations and publishers use styles that vary to lesser or greater degree. The consistent, clear rules set out in *ANSI Z39.29* provide a single style for use in footnotes and bibliographies, one that is straightforward enough to make computer support for bibliographies more practical.

Unfortunately, the normal format for Z39.29 omits the use of italics and quotation marks and is thus less immediately informative than most competing styles. Publishers have not seen it as offering economic advantages over existing usage. PC-based programs for building and maintaining bibliographies support any number of different styles, reducing the potential economic advantage of Z39.29 even further.

While some journals and publishers moved to use of Z39.29, the standard was too late to avoid the established proliferation. Indeed, any movement toward standardization may have stalled. For example, for my first two or three books (including the first edition of *Technical Standards*) I convinced the publishers to accept Z39.29 style in the bibliographies. Since then, I've become convinced that the standard serves no useful purpose, and have returned to the Chicago style that most publishers prefer. They know that copy editors and proofreaders are familiar with Chicago style; that saves them money.

For quadraphonic sound, clear damage resulted from conflicting standards. Damages resulting from conflicting citation formats are subtler, and affect writers more than readers. A reader can usually gather needed information from any citation. A writer who works in more than one field may find it difficult to prepare proper citations for each manuscript, but relatively inexpensive programs will reduce that effort for the rare author who works in many different fields.

Well-Timed Standards

Where conflicting standards may cause confusion and damage, well-timed standards can help to establish new techniques and technologies. Two brief examples follow; again, the first is from consumer electronics, the second from the library field.

Digital Audio Discs

For digital audio discs or compact discs, an industry-wide consensus standard was adopted before commercial introduction. The compact disc (CD), developed by Philips and Sony but established as a multi-company standard, has been recognized as the most successful new consumer product in history. In considerably less than a decade, CDs have surpassed vinyl discs in sales volume. Here, a single licensed standard was adopted before commercial battles were waged; as a result, ads focus on comparative advantages of a particular player—but all CD players play all CDs and consumers don't have to worry about such problems.

Bibliographic Information Interchange

ANSI Z39.2, American National Standard for Bibliographic Information Interchange, described in Chapter 12, was first approved in 1971. It established a structure, better known as MARC (machine-readable cataloging), to carry bibliographic information. Although the standard was not approved and published until 1971, it was used for MARC II as early as 1969. An international equivalent, ISO 2709, was adopted in 1973.

The single structure, adopted early in the history of machine-readable bibliographic information, helped encourage the enormous growth of shared cataloging in the United States and abroad. OCLC, RLG, Utlas, WLN, LC, Blackwell North America, AMIGOS, and other agencies that provide services based on such information may all use their own internal formats to store and process that information. All such agencies use a single structural standard to write tapes of bibliographic records, making interchange possible and relatively straightforward.

Summary

We're protected by the complex web of standards that support our civilization; sometimes, we're damaged by missing or conflicting standards. We rely on standards without knowing, or needing to know, their precise nature; we can have problems when building on a base of standards without accurate knowledge of what they are. Systems designed with insufficient or conflicting standards have difficulties and may fail. Standards developed at the right time, and with the right care, can speed technical development and improve the quality of life.

3

Varieties of Standards

Standards evolve in different ways, taking on different forms. Some evolutions lead to formal national or international standards, and others do not. Some standards are technical; others, though perfectly legitimate, are not. Technical standards exist at different levels of formality and arise through different means, yielding different final forms. Finally (and unfortunately), some things that are called "standards" fail to satisfy any reasonable definition of a technical standard.

Most of this book concerns formal consensus technical standards as developed and maintained by accredited standards organizations. It's easy enough to define such standards, although the definition is somewhat circular:

> A formal consensus technical standard is an explicitly stated, uniquely identified document developed, adopted, and maintained by an accredited standards organization following its established procedures for developing, adopting, and maintaining such standards.

That definition is accurate enough, but it is neither particularly useful nor helpful if you wish to distinguish among all the other varieties of standards, technical and otherwise. The rest of this chapter is an attempt to make those distinctions, using a combination of discussion and examples.

The discussion deals with varieties of standards in terms of how they arise and how they function. It does not deal with *levels* or *families* of standards: All formal consensus technical standards constitute a single variety of standard, although they may form many different families and work at many different levels. Chapter 4 takes up those issues as they relate to formal technical standards (not all of them consensus).

The discussions within this chapter deal with two aspects of standards that can be called *type* and *status*:

- **Types** of standards include rules and guidelines, goals and performance standards, qualitative standards, and technical standards.

- **Statuses** of standards include internal standards, pseudostandards, industry and de facto standards, first-agent and dominant-agent standards, mandated or legislated standards, licensed standards, and formal consensus standards.

Domains

The domain or scope of a standard must be well established before the standard can be effective, whether it is a technical standard or a set of rules. Technical standard Z85.1 thoroughly specifies the dimensions and, to a lesser extent, the material to be used in a catalog card, but it says nothing about the text printed on that card. A standard catalog card may contain nonstandard cataloging (that is, cataloging not done to *AACR2*), and such cataloging may be transmitted in a standard MARC record.

Technical standards tend to state their domains more precisely than do rules, guidelines, and goals. Sets of rules with well-defined domains usually are more workable than those with fuzzily defined domains: if people understand when to apply the rules, they may be more likely to do so.

Rules and Guidelines

The *Anglo-American Cataloguing Rules,* 2nd edition revised establishes a standard set of rules for descriptive cataloging. Different catalogers using those rules to catalog the same book will, however, frequently produce significantly different cataloging records. *AACR2R* provides a standard, but it is distinctly not a technical standard.

Every technical standard is, in some sense, a set of rules, but most sets of rules are not technical standards. One difference is ambiguity, as in cataloging rules: most rules do not provide totally predictable outcomes. Within its domain, a technical standard should provide predictability; if a set of rules does not, it can't be a proper technical standard.

The difference between rules and guidelines is usually a matter of formality or of the difference between "shall" and "should." Guidelines are even less likely than rules to constitute technical standards. When technical standards include guidelines, the latter are usually less formal extensions of the former, because they produce less predictable results.

Standards for specific kinds of libraries are, in the main, guidelines. They are neither rules nor technical standards. You can't say that a library at a college isn't a college library because it doesn't meet ALA's published standards for collection and staff size. You might choose to say that the library is substandard, or you could regard the standard as a goal, and say that the library has not yet achieved that goal.

On the other hand, you can absolutely say that a string of 11 numbers, or a string of 10 characters of which the fourth is an X, is not an ISBN: it fails to meet the precise definition that makes ISBN a technical standard. It can't be a substandard ISBN or a nonstandard ISBN; it simply isn't an ISBN at all, just as a machine-readable record without a suitably defined leader, directory, indicators, and subfields simply isn't a MARC communications record.

Goals and Performance Standards

Whereas technical standards may involve specific performance criteria, many so-called performance standards are quite different. When a university library establishes two trucks per hour as the standard rate for reshelving books, it is asserting a performance standard. Students who shelve more slowly may be reprimanded or may have hours reduced, and those who shelve much more rapidly may be candidates for promotion (or may be candidates to have their work checked for quality).

The distinction between a performance standard and a goal must typically be based on a reality check. When the management of an assembly-line factory states that their standard is that every operation will be carried out perfectly, they're suggesting a goal (albeit an unreachable one). When they say the standard is that no finished goods will leave the factory without meeting established, quantifiable measures of correctness, they're stating a legitimate (and reachable) performance standard. If the workers don't meet the first standard, they're human; if the factory doesn't meet the second standard, it must have better quality control.

The performance standard in this example will probably rest on a series of technical standards; the goal will not. A good performance standard must be measurable and should be realistic; a goal may not be either one. An agency for temporary employees could reasonably establish a performance standard for typists—say, an average of 80 words per minute over 15 minutes for transcribing written material, deducting 5 words from the total count for each misspelled word, with a maximum error rate of 2 words per 100. That standard (which, I suspect, is quite difficult to attain) is measurable. If the agency can demonstrate that it gives the same test to all applicants, hires all of the applicants who meet the standard, and doesn't hire any who don't meet the standard, it would be difficult to sue for discrimination. On the other hand, if the agency's standard is "perfect high-speed typing," it's in trouble: that's a goal, and not a quantifiable one.

Qualitative Standards

The agency that only hires typists who achieve high speed with virtually no errors, and fails to specify what constitutes adequately high speed or a sufficiently low error rate, is stating a qualitative standard. Qualitative standards are notoriously difficult to deal with, and are inherently unsuitable as technical standards.

A technical standard must be explicit and predictive. A qualitative standard cannot be. A labeling standard that requires that type be at least six points and be chosen from one of a specified set of typefaces is explicit and workable. The standard that does not specify typefaces, but rather specifies "highly legible," goes into the qualitative area, and raises real questions about enforceability. What constitutes illegibility? What constitutes substandard typography?

Sometimes, the distinction between qualitative and technical standards shows in the difference between nonstandard and substandard. When RLIN or OCLC establishes that a certain set of fields must be assigned (if feasible) for a record to be considered standard cataloging, they establish testable criteria. Records that don't meet those criteria are nonstandard. Substandard cataloging is quite a different matter: it's cataloging that isn't good enough. The lists of "bad guys" (that is, other libraries that produce substandard cataloging) that some libraries maintain in order to decide whether to use copy cataloging found on a network are based on qualitative standards.

What does it mean when a product is claimed to be "the standard of the industry?" Nothing, really; the advertising agency is simply asserting some level of quality. If Cadillac asserts that it sets the standard for luxury cars because it provides a certain stated amount of seat, leg, and head room for passengers, cushions road shocks of a specified magnitude, reduces exterior and self-generated noise by a certain number of decibels, and offers other measurable attributes of luxury, it is making a useful statement. It would require, say, Lexus to establish *objectively* that it "sets a new standard for luxury cars" by showing that it meets all the Cadillac measures and exceeds them in useful ways.

But of course, that isn't what Cadillac means. The company wants you to think of Cadillac as embodying the *idea* of a luxury car, regardless of actual measurements. That sense of "standard" may be the most commonly used in advertising and public relations; it has no relation at all to technical or any other meaningful standards. (That's why I regard "We build excitement" as a better slogan than "We set the standard for excitement." The first is inherently puffery and purely subjective; the second suggests an unreal objectivity.)

Technical Standards

Technical standards must be explicit and predictive, and must have well-defined, frequently narrowly defined, domains or scopes.

- They provide rules rather than guidelines, and the rules are unambiguous enough to be predictive. If two people apply a rule to the same situation, they will obtain the same or equivalent results. If rules don't meet that criterion, they don't constitute a technical standard.

- They state achievable conditions unambiguously. They provide measurements: something claimed to meet a standard can be determined to be standard or nonstandard through objective tests.

- They provide known, quantitative criteria. Qualitative standards cannot be technical standards, although technical standards may include qualitative comments. Substandard motor oil fails to meet specific quantitative criteria for its claimed SAE standard or other standards; it is not substandard because it isn't "slick enough" or "sufficiently temperature resistant," but because it fails to meet explicit measures for slickness (or viscosity) and temperature resistance (or resistance to breakdown).

The remaining varieties of standard discussed in this chapter are, or at least should be, varieties of technical standards; that is, explicit definitions that permit clear, objective judgments whether something does or does not comply. Modern weights and measures provide the most clear-cut cases of proper technical standards. You can legally and objectively prove that you've been short-weighted when you buy a pound of butter, but you can't prove that you've been "short-beautied" when you buy a painting.

Internal Standards

Internal standards are the most changeable form of technical standard. When a person produces something, that person has internal standards for the product. To maintain a consistent product over time, the person may set down production guidelines. When that person hires an assistant and tells the assistant to follow the guidelines, the guidelines become internal technical standards.

General Motors and IBM could not maintain production facilities without clear technical standards for each piece, assembly, and machine being assembled. Mass production without detailed technical standards is nearly impossible. Internal technical standards are essential if more than one person is ever expected to work on a single item.

Every organization develops internal practices, some of which are technical. Any internal practice that unambiguously defines actions to produce a desired effect may be considered a technical standard.

Limitations of Internal Technical Standards

Internal technical standards fill gaps in external standards. Standards within a single organization should be recognized as limited to that organization. Unless an organization moves to establish its internal standards widely, it may change or abandon them unilaterally and without notice. That will happen frequently in a changing field, as the organization finds better ways to do things.

Competitors and entrepreneurs wishing to build on the work of an organization may happily seize on internal technical standards as a basis for development. Such developers may build substantial systems based on standards that were never intended for external use. But these external developers are not part of the consensus required to maintain or modify an internal standard. At some point, the organization may change its internal standards to improve quality, to lower costs, or simply because they are no longer appropriate. Systems developed by external agencies no longer function properly, and the external agencies have no recourse.

An organization may make an internal document available to others without asserting that its contents are eternal and unchanging. When the document is shared, its domain and stability should be clearly understood, although this is rarely the case. If a library automation vendor provides its customers with a document specifying the internal structure of the database and indexes, that document should properly indicate the conditions under which the vendor is free to change the database. It's quite likely that a competing vendor, hoping to replace the system, will use the document as the basis for building a file conversion system. If the document is current and the first vendor has assured its users (under contractual terms) that it is correct, and if the conversion fails because the database is structured differently, the user and second vendor have legitimate reasons to fault the first vendor.

However, issuance of that document, which describes structures internal to a system, does *not* bind the first vendor to retain those data structures for all time to come. Unless the vendor and users have clear understandings, the vendor may be free to change those structures for any number of reasons. If a competing vendor has relied on out-of-date documentation in building conversion routines, and if the first vendor has complied with contract terms, the competing vendor has no reason to complain. The internal data structures were never really more than an internal standard, although they were externally documented. By providing a document with disclaimers such as "draft," "for internal use only," or the like, the vendor is asserting that the document describes internal standards that are subject to change at any time and without notice.

Pseudostandards

Systems built based on another agency's internal technical standards should be approached with the greatest caution, as these standards can easily become *pseudostandards*. Pseudostandards are constructs improperly called or treated as industry standards. Pseudostandards can be:

- **Misapplied internal standards,** definitions used outside an agency without any promise of stability;
- **Apparent standards for practice** that actually represent temporary or special situations;
- **Single names for many definitions,** where a named "standard" has many versions, some of them incompatible;
- **Anticompetitive standards,** where a proposed standard provides special advantages to the agency making the proposal.

Misapplied Internal Standards

When an internal standard moves beyond the originating agency, it may become an industry standard or a formal consensus standard, if the originating agency intends that it be used by others, and does not unilaterally change the standard. Technical standards, other than those internal to a single agency, *must not be subject to unilateral change*. If a company distributes its standards with proper assurances of stability, an industry or de facto standard may evolve properly.

There's no good reason to assume that internal standards will be stable. Indeed, given the pace of technological change, it is fair to assume that those within any organization dependent on technology will change, and will change fairly frequently. A company cannot afford to freeze its internal procedures based on informal distribution of information; to do so can be crippling or even fatal.

We've already considered an example of misapplied internal standards. The general lesson to be learned is that, whenever an agency takes action based on the internal standards of another agency, the first agency is taking a considerable risk, and one for which the other agency cannot properly be held responsible.

Apparent Practice Standards

Technical standards have limited scopes. Informal and unwritten standards may be more limited than they appear. If your experience is within a single region, or with one type of organization, you may find that certain practices are uniform and thus conclude that they are industry standards. Much of the time you'll be right, but some of the time you'll be mistaking a set of examples for a rule. When such pseudostandards fail, the usual comment is "but that's the way it's always been done." Which is another way of saying "I've never seen it done another way, and assumed that this way was standard."

The library field has suffered from a few such assumptions, including, for example, fallacious assumptions about how fields in MARC records are arranged, the format of MARC record identifiers, and the normalization that can be assumed for searching online catalogs.

In the first case—the arrangement of MARC fields—some system designers assumed that fields within a MARC record will always be in the same order as the tags in the directory, with no extraneous space, thus making it possible to ignore portions of the directory. That's not a safe assumption; an agency creating or modifying MARC records might very well choose to add a new field or modify an existing field without rebuilding the entire record, simply appending the field to the record and modifying the directory. This is a real case; because poorly written processing systems[1] could not handle "out of order" fields correctly, I was forced to add an extra step to RLIN MARC record maintenance in order to completely rebuild the records when writing tapes.

The second case—invalid assumptions about the format of USMARC record identifiers—is also real. Unlike the first, it could not be solved by changing reality to match flawed assumptions of standards. In the late 1970s and early 1980s a surprising number of agencies assumed that the format used by the Library of Congress to create record IDs was the standard format for MARC record IDs, and that the record ID was fixed length. Wrong on all counts, although the first error was spread by OCLC's decision to use a similar format for its own record IDs. When we (and other agencies) generated records with properly variable-length record IDs, we were informed by some parties that the records were "nonstandard." This time, we did not cave in. Since LC's record IDs are actually variable length (although they begin with a fixed-length portion), we could sustain our position.

The third case—normalization for online catalogs—affects library patrons who use more than one online library catalog. It is a case where some appropriate set of guidelines or, potentially, technical standard may be called for. The Technical Standards for Library Automation Committee (TESLA) of the American Library Association's Library and Information Technology Association (LITA) recently investigated current practice within online catalogs. When the report from this investigation is issued, it may form the basis for future work in this area. At the moment, it is clear that you can't necessarily assume that similarly constructed searches will

---

1 These will go unnamed, particularly since this happened almost a decade ago and they may since have been corrected.

work identically in all catalogs; there are no current technical standards on which to base such an assumption.

Single Names for Many Definitions

Calling something a standard doesn't make it so, and sometimes, several different things may be called by the same name. For example, microcomputer languages tend to run to pseudostandards. The programming language Pascal has been heavily touted as being standard and transportable. It's a nice idea but it isn't always so. There is an ANSI standard for Pascal, but most real-world Pascal versions go beyond the standard, and the extensions don't usually work the same way. Within the MS-DOS (IBM-compatible) personal computing world, the most widely used Pascal is Borland's Turbo Pascal, and that Pascal, besides including major extensions to the ANSI standard, does not conform completely to the ANSI Pascal standard.

When you say "standard blank catalog card," you're naming something that has a precise definition. If you buy standard catalog cards from OCLC or RLIN or Utlas, you can be reasonably certain that they'll fit in the card drawers you bought from Highsmith or Gaylord, and that they'll blend in with the catalog cards you used to buy from Midwest or Baker & Taylor. But if you receive source code for a Pascal program, you have no assurance that you'll be able to compile the program: unlike catalog cards, the real world of Pascal software has no single standard.

Pseudostandards frequently evolve into actual standards, but are dangerous until such evolution reaches formal recognition. If all the libraries that a vendor has dealt with do something the same way, the vendor may assume that a standard exists. When the vendor sells services based on that standard to a library that has always followed a different (and equally legitimate) practice, the result will certainly be lost time and resources, and such situations can easily develop into lawsuits. It isn't a formal consensus standard unless it's in writing and has an established formal consensus.[2]

---

2 Even then, there's no guarantee that everybody will follow the standard; still, vendors who base their services on formal consensus standards have better defenses than those who follow pseudostandards.

Anticompetitive Standards

One reasonable principle for technical standards is that they should help to level the competitive playing field; that is, they should not unreasonably favor one company against its competitors. From that perspective, I assert that industry standards that offer special treatment to a single company are, in fact, pseudostandards: anticompetitive and counter to the basic precepts of standardization.

During the late 1980s personal computer users interested in desktop publishing had to deal with one such pseudostandard, the PostScript page definition language. Adobe, a software company and digital type foundry, created the PostScript language and released specifications for most of it. They went on to license printer manufacturers to use the PostScript interpreter and Adobe's digital typeface outlines, pointing out that other type foundries also sold PostScript outlines, and that it was possible to create PostScript clones, programs that could interpret the language and produce correct printed output.

So far, so good: while Adobe charged high prices for its licenses, it appeared to be providing sufficient information to work toward a licensed standard that could become an industry standard. Except that Adobe didn't release all the information on PostScript. They retained proprietary information that made their own typefaces look better than others when printed at small sizes on laser printers. By doing so, they made PostScript an anticompetitive pseudostandard, one that deliberately placed other type foundries at a disadvantage.

The situation has changed; Adobe recently released the remaining elements of PostScript. They did so not because they suddenly saw the light, but because Apple and Microsoft grew tired of the high Adobe license fees and put together another page description language and typeface-handling system that would be truly open and feasible as an industry standard (TrueType/TrueImage). Not at all surprisingly, many users, with a fuzzy understanding of what technical standards should be, assailed the other companies for challenging the "PostScript industry standard." Adobe, meanwhile, saw a forceful challenge to its position within the industry and realized that making PostScript a legitimate industry standard was the only way to protect it.

Anticompetitive pseudostandards abound in personal computing and in other fields. They are usually fairly obvious, if you take time to think through all their aspects. If a so-called standard *inherently* offers a special advantage to one company (in addition to the license fees that are appropriate for patentable technology), it is an anticompetitive pseudostandard and should be evaluated in that light. The consensus process followed for formal technical standards includes fairness requirements that should assure that standards are not anticompetitive, but industry standards are not generally formal consensus standards.

Industry and de Facto Standards

The popular term *industry standard* is frequently used for pseudostandards and common practices that are subject to change. There are also true industry standards, many of which begin as dominant-agent standards and end as formal consensus standards. Proper industry standards are those that are explicitly defined and formally supported by several agencies, where the explicit definition is not subject to unilateral change. In other words, it is both a de facto standard (it is common industry practice) and a proper technical standard (it is explicitly defined).

The best licensed standards (those enforced through licenses, discussed later in this chapter) are also industry standards, but not all industry standards are licensed standards. An industry standard may not be a licensed standard because:

- The standard in question is in the public domain, not subject to copyright or patent;
- The developing agency is part of the federal government and as such neither copyrights nor, typically, licenses the development;
- The standard was developed by a group of agencies working in concert, and the group chooses not to require licensing.

The term industry standard is also used for many other purposes, including those mentioned below.

Empty Words

When promotion people proclaim that a new program or product is "a new industry standard," they're not saying anything at all. They may mean to say that the product should gain a significant share of the market, or that it does something new and useful, or that it is better than existing products. None of these makes a true industry standard.

You might try the following test on anything you read that uses the phrase *industry standard*. Treat the words as nonexistent, or change them to a nonsense noun or just to "thing." Does the text make just as much sense? Frequently, it will, because the most common use of the term these days is as empty hype.

OS/2 was proclaimed as a new PC industry standard in 1987, when it first emerged. Current predictions are that OS/2 might be used on as many as 5% of all personal computers by 1994; the usage in 1990 is much lower. That may be fairly typical of the significance of the term industry standard.

Preemptive Attempts

Slightly more respectable than empty words is the deliberate attempt by one firm to establish a given standard within the industry. If this is done properly, and not as an anticompetitive pseudostandard, it can help to broaden a particular market and allow competitors to innovate rather than spend their energy duplicating a set of functions.

A preemptive attempt to establish an industry standard will most commonly be a licensed standard based on patents. Licensing allows one company to ensure that all users of the standard do, indeed, use it correctly. But preemptive standards need not be licensed standards; these days, it's not unusual for a company to propose some set of options as a standard way of doing something new, fully publicizing the details in an attempt to clarify the marketplace.

Ethernet, the local area network architecture jointly introduced by the Digital Equipment Company (DEC) and Xerox in the late 1970s, had much the flavor of a preemptive standard, except that there was already a widely used proprietary local area network architecture in place (ARC/ARCnet). Fortunately for the developers of Ethernet, Datapoint (the company that owned ARCnet) didn't open its use rapidly enough to make it a widespread industry standard.

Although never the only standard, Ethernet did become the marketplace leader and the network with the most widespread vendor involvement. The originators moved to see it established as a formal consensus technical standard through the IEEE (as part of IEEE 802); Datapoint's resistance to similar status for ARCnet helped to isolate that earlier system.

One sign of a useful preemptive standard is that the company will find other users rapidly, and, as with Ethernet, will usually move to formalize the standard in some manner. As long as a preemptive standard is maintained only by its originator, it has some of the defects of an internal standard. When maintenance passes to an association or external agency, the standard gains stability.

Marketplace Realities

Frequently, industry standards arise through marketplace realities. The most commonly used internal electrical and data connection system (bus) in personal computers is based on the design that IBM introduced for its PC/AT[3] in 1983. IBM did not directly treat the AT bus as an industry standard, but the specifications were readily available and IBM did not attempt to prevent replication of the bus by other manufacturers.

Marketplace realities made the AT bus an industry standard, and an enormously successful one despite the lack of adoption as a formal standard by any agency. Tens of millions of computers were sold using the bus, and the standardized design encouraged production of thousands of circuit boards at increasingly competitive prices.

In 1987 IBM abandoned the AT bus, moving to the MicroChannel Architecture (MCA) bus, which it protected with a string of patents. Rather than paying high royalty rates for rights to the new bus—and asking users to discard all their present circuitry when moving to new computers—most other manufacturers con-

---

3 "Advanced technology"—how times change!

tinued to produce computers using the AT bus. A group of PC manufacturers, the "Gang of Nine," gathered to design a bus with the advantages of MCA but maintained by a multivendor organization, thus having the form of a formal consensus technical standard. They named the new bus the Extended Industry Standard Architecture (EISA) bus, and in the process, established a new name for the AT bus, which is now the ISA or Industry Standard Architecture bus.

Informal Consensus Standards

Informal consensus standards seem to begin along the lines of, "hey, I like that. Can I use it?" One agency introduces an innovation or a particular solution to a common problem. Another agency likes the solution, and either asks permission to duplicate it or does so without permission. The ball starts rolling, and soon an informal consensus has been achieved among a large fraction of a market, sometimes a majority.

It's generally difficult to spot such cases in retrospect, and they can frequently look like combinations of preemptive standards and cases of marketplace reality. The differences are subtle and typically not important; in either case, a key development takes place when the consensus standard becomes formalized, if it ever does.

The library field includes one case in which an informal standard has become fairly widely used and is now becoming a formal consensus technical standard, although it does not precisely replicate the informal versions. That case is the Common Command Language, ANSI/NISO Z39.58 and ISO 8770, which began at Stanford University as the BALLOTS command syntax and has grown through a variety of library systems, mostly on the West Coast.

First-Agent and Dominant-Agent Standards

Technical standards are frequently based on the first practical example of a new technique or design. If an agent does so well with that design that other agents see no advantage in developing a different one, the first design takes on the appearance of a standard. Sometimes, the complete design *becomes* a standard, either because there is no real competition, because the design is not subject to patent or copyright protection, or because the first agency attempts to create a licensed standard or industry standard. In other cases, certain fundamental aspects of the design are copied by other agents who make complementary or competitive products, and those basic aspects take on the force of an informal, first-agent standard.

If the first agent makes plans available and asserts that the definitions involved will not change arbitrarily, first-agent standards can evolve into industry standards. Such cases are quite common. Unfortunately, other cases are also common—where the standard is, and remains, a pseudostandard, subject to change by the first agent at any time. If the standard has become sufficiently well established in other agencies, it may well survive as an industry standard, even though the agent that created it no longer follows it. (ISA is a prime example of such a standard.)

First-agent standards aren't always created by the first company to create a new design. Sometimes, a large or otherwise important company creates a somewhat different design; if that company dominates the market in question, a dominant-agent standard may be created. All the remarks and cautions that apply to first-agent standards also apply to dominant-agent standards.

First-agent and dominant-agent standards are the least formal levels of community standards with good prospects for succeeding as standards. For long-term success, any community standard must have some form of explicit consensus; generally, it begins in a single agency. The second step is typically to establish a licensed standard or a consensus industry standard.

Mandated (Legislated) Standards

Technical standardization within the United States is a voluntary process, typically nongovernmental. Most technical standards are consensus standards and do not have the force of law. Some, however, do have the force of law for one of two reasons:

- Existing standards may be incorporated into legislation by reference. For example, a law may state that all new buildings must conform to explicitly stated ANSI standards for handicapped access;

- Standards may be created by government mandate, either directly through legislation or indirectly by government agency. For example, the Department of Defense creates many standards for its own needs—37,000 of them as of 1989—although it is working toward heavier reliance on already developed standards. (During the 1980s, Defense cancelled 6,000 of its own standards, created 1,800 new ones, and adopted 1,800 externally developed standards.)

Licensed Standards

Licensed standards can establish a new technology quickly and painlessly. They are created when a company (or group of companies or agencies) establishes a new design, gains patent or copyright protection for it, and explicitly sets out to persuade other companies to use the same one. When a company establishes a licensed standard, it is certifying that the standard will not be changed unilaterally. Companies may license a new technology for profit or simply to establish it in a widespread compatible fashion. In either case, the key is that the use of the technique is protected by law, and that the technique is clearly described and stable.

Some of the more astonishing successes in licensed standards have come about when companies license to spread a technique rather than for direct gain. One of these is the Compact Cassette, now simply known as the audiocassette. Philips of Holland designed the Compact Cassette two decades ago, and gained patent protection on several elements of the design. Philips licensed the cassette design (and critical design elements for cassette players) to all interested parties, at no charge.[4]

---

4 According to one history, Philips intended to license the technology at a royalty amounting to two cents per cassette, but was convinced by Sony to make the license royalty-free to establish the design as a standard. See Nick Lyons, *The Sony Vision* (New York: Crown, 1976), 105.

Philips took the view that the market for cassettes was potentially enormous, and that they were likely to make more money by gaining some portion of a large market than by controlling all of a small market. Their planning was sound, and cassettes succeeded far beyond Philips' original expectations. Part of that success came from the absolute compatibility of all cassettes and players, a compatibility ensured by Philips' strict license agreements. Monaural tape players will always play both channels of stereo cassettes; any compact cassette recorded in any recorder will fit, and should play back at least moderately well in any other player.[5]

Formal Consensus Standards

Most of this book deals with formal consensus standards, those established by standards-making bodies. One common (though imprecise) term for such standards in the United States is "ANSI standards." As noted above, formal consensus standards may begin as internal, first-agent or dominant-agent, licensed, or industry standards. They also may be developed within standards bodies to meet recognized needs, without originating in another body.

Formal consensus standards vary substantially in terms of recognition and use. The United States, with its successful voluntary, nongovernmental standards-making system, has the richest set of standards of any country. You might usefully distinguish among three varieties of formal consensus standards discussed below, but it is important to note that the distinction between the first two (association and national standards) is imprecise at best and unworkable at worst.

Association Standards

Many associations create formal consensus technical standards. Some 270 private American agencies and associations currently do so; another 150 maintain some existing standards but no longer

5 These have become formal consensus standards: ANSI/EIA RS-399-A and ANSI/EIA RS-433.

actively develop them. Not all these associations seek accreditation through ANSI; for those that do not, the significance of the standards rests solely on their own significance.

That can be more than sufficient, particularly for standards with a domain restricted almost entirely to activities of members of the association. For example, the Video Equipment Standards Association (VESA) was formed to develop appropriate PC video standards beyond IBM's Video Graphics Array (VGA) dominant-agency standard. VESA includes most of the major manufacturers of PC video adapters; as a result, its standards (when formalized) are likely to be workable even if VESA does not attempt to gain ANSI recognition.

Perhaps the largest and grayest area is made up of standards issued by accredited agencies but not submitted for ANSI approval. Thousands of such standards exist, created by agencies such as the Electronic Industries Association (EIA), American Society for Testing and Materials (ASTM), and others.

You may not wish to distinguish between association standards issued by accredited agencies and those that achieve the status of national standards. I can see no clear distinction that would make one better than the other, unless you are particularly sensitive to the certifying activities of ANSI or to the availability of standards through ANSI's distribution service.

National Standards

The simplest way to categorize American national standards is to see that they contain the identifier "ANSI" somewhere in their name, either as the only prefix to the standard itself (e.g., *ANSI Z358.1, Emergency Eyewash and Shower Equipment*) for those actually published by ANSI, or as the first portion of the identification (e.g., *ANSI/UL 1429, Pullout Switches*) for standards published by individual associations but approved by and available through ANSI.

ANSI is the primary nongovernmental standards coordinating body in the United States, and is the American member of the International Organization for Standardization (ISO) and the International Electrotechnical Commission (IEC). ANSI coordinates the work of more than 200 accredited standards organizations, such as NISO.

ANSI standards are voluntary; they do not in and of themselves have the force of law in the United States. On the other hand, evidence of compliance with an ANSI standard can be useful as a defense in a product liability suit; at the very least, lack of such evidence drastically weakens a case.

National standards in other countries may be voluntary or may inherently carry the force of law. Most national standards bodies are governmental. In 1990, some consideration was given to establishing a governmental standardization body within the United States to supplement or supplant the work of ANSI. Almost all testimony during the hearings (held by the National Institute for Standards and Technology [NIST], formerly the National Bureau of Standards [NBS]) supported the current private, voluntary system. Although at times it may be confusing and slow, it does the job and avoids a new federal bureaucracy that would inherently favor certain interests, cost more federal money, and probably work even more slowly.

International Standards

Two of the most important international standards organizations are ISO and IEC. International standards are inherently voluntary, although they may be adopted as regulations within individual nations.

International standards may be based on national standards; alternatively, national agencies may elect to adopt international standards or substitute ISO or IEC numbers and standards for previously adopted national standards. The foremost standards organization in each country can belong to ISO and IEC; for example, ANSI in the United States, the *Association française de normalisation* (AFNOR) in France, and the *Deutsches Institut für Normung* (DIN) in Germany.

ISO and IEC split the standards arena[6] but share one of the most active, the area of information technology (largely the province of Accredited Standards Committee X3 [ASC X3] in the United States). ISO/IEC Joint Technical Committee (JTC) 1 is a young and very active

---

6 Except telecommunications, handled by the International Telecommunication Union (ITU) and its committee, the International Telegraph and Telephone Consultative Committee (CCITT).

body; given the international nature of information technology, its work is crucial.

International standards represent the most widely useful variety of technical standards. Some are most definitely trivial and useless, but well-drafted ones can do much to encourage global cooperation and competition by establishing interchangeability and common definitions. Increasingly, standards developers within a country can be most effective by working to develop ISO and IEC standards that meet their needs. Good international standards discourage the development of national and regional standards that would serve to discourage free trade (such national and regional standards are one form of nontariff trade barrier). Thus, for example, NISO now works actively within ISO TC 46, its international counterpart, to ensure the best possible international standards.

One recent example of the relationship between national and international standards involves the High Sierra Group standard for volume and file structure of CD-ROM. This standard, originally developed by a group of CD-ROM producers and others meeting in the High Sierra Hotel & Casino in Stateline, Nevada, was refined by NISO to become draft standard Z39.60. It also went forward on the international front and was adopted as ISO 9660 before NISO completed publication of Z39.60. As a result, to clarify and simplify national and international compliance, NISO withdrew Z39.60 and adopted ISO 9660 in its stead.

Summary: Standards Are for Sharing

Technical standards at whatever level are established so that people and agencies can share information in a known, consistent manner. Standards evolve in various ways depending on how techniques are created, when information must be shared, and who wishes to use the information. In every case, they succeed if they allow shared use of stable definitions for desirable purposes.

The need to share techniques is so strong that apparent standards evolve or are assumed to apply even where none actually exist; such pseudostandards endanger the health of the systems built upon them. Alert observers can distinguish pseudostandards from legitimate industry standards; the best way to establish and maintain the most useful standards is to develop them into formal consensus national and international standards.

Libraries, publishers, and most information science organizations exist to share information. That sharing can be enhanced through the intelligent use and creation of standards.

4

Implementations, Levels, and Families

Every technical standard is a definition: words and figures that, if the standard is a good one, provide an unambiguous specification for the subject. While every standard is a definition, you should not assume that each one leads directly to a product or system. Just as they arise through different methods and come in different varieties, they work at different levels.

Some standards specify characteristics of a finished product. Others provide nothing more than ways to think about something. Most technical standards for library use and automation fall between these two extremes. Many standards offer choices, such that products following them may differ from each other in understandable ways. Most standards are based on other standards, and are themselves used as bases for more complex standards, building toward standard systems.

Technical standards may provide only part of the information necessary for an implementation, through oversight or through choice. There are "families" of technical standards, all designed to achieve similar goals but maintained separately. Some of these families are explicitly interrelated, whereas others are the result of changing needs. One standard may lead to additional standards, and, sometimes, several may be combined into one.

Weights and Measures

The most fundamental standards establish units to describe the physical universe. As such, they provide consistent measures for time, distance, area, and volume. We take weights and measures for granted, and rarely think of them as technical standards. Yet technical standards for weights and measures underlie most other standards. Weights and measures, or *units*, establish the basic vocabulary for specifications. Without a consistent vocabulary, consistent standards cannot be developed. It does no good to specify that the two current-carrying prongs of a standard 110-volt plug are ½-inch apart, center to center, if "½-inch" doesn't have a clear, consistent meaning.

In 1215, British barons found it necessary to stress formal standards for weights and measures. Clause 35 of the Magna Carta can be summarized as follows: "There is to be one measure of wine and ale and corn within the realm, namely the London quarter, and one breadth of cloth, and it is to be the same with weights."[1] Five centuries later the Constitution of the United States provided, in Section 8, that "The Congress shall have Power ... To coin Money, regulate the Value thereof, and of foreign Coin, and fix the Standard of Weights and Measures." Weights and measures are now commonly established and maintained by governmental bodies at the national and international levels. The National Institute for Standards and Technology (NIST), formerly the National Bureau of Standards (NBS), established in 1901, is the primary U.S. agency for physical measurement standards. The Institute for Basic Standards within NIST works to provide and improve a complete and consistent system of physical measurements, and coordinates that system with measurement systems of other nations.

Technical standards are definitions. Those for weights and measures must be far more precise than for most other units, and must be much more stable.

---

1 *Encyclopedia Brittanica*, vol. 14 (Chicago: Encyclopedia Brittanica, 1957), 651.

Standards and Implementations

Technical standards are not implementations. Some distance always exists between standard and implementation, even if a standard permits only one implementation. For weights and measures the distance is the smallest possible. The standard kilogram, a metal ingot stored in France, is an object that embodies a definition. Even here, the technical standard for mass is an abstraction. The definition of 1 kilogram is not the same as the standard kilogram, and relates only to one aspect of that ingot: its mass. Uniquely, weights and measures standards can incorporate implementations into their definitions. Others work at a higher level of abstraction.

Unambiguous Physical Implementation: Catalog Cards

One of the oldest technical standards for American libraries is also one of the least abstract; it specifies the characteristics of a physical object distinctly and unambiguously. That standard is *Z85.1, Permanent and Durable Library Catalog Cards*, described in Chapter 1. Any proper catalog card is an implementation of Z85.1, but Z85.1 does not constitute a catalog card; it specifies characteristics of a physical object. The standard provides:

- **Complete specifications** for catalog cards, such as size, hole, finish, color, weight, acidity, endurance, and stock;
- **Distinctive specifications** such that variations are explicitly noted and any good papermaker could work directly from the standard;
- **Explicit tests** to determine whether an object is, in fact, an implementation of the standard.

Even this most clear-cut standard allows for four different possible implementations. Cards may be either white or cream-white, and may be either lightweight or medium-weight. What most librarians think of as a "standard catalog card" is really cream-white, medium-weight standard, and a lightweight white card would also be standard.

Incomplete Physical Implementation: Permanent Paper

Standard Z39.48, *Permanent Paper for Printed Library Materials*[2] is *not* a complete specification for a physical object. Like most physical technical standards, it describes only a few aspects; its purpose is to certify permanence. It specifies alkalinity, lack of groundwood or unbleached pulp, and, in the 1984 version, folding endurance and tear resistance for various weights of paper. It does not specify weight, thickness, size, or color of paper. Such specifications would be unreasonably restrictive.

Z39.48 is a testable standard: a laboratory can determine whether a sheet of paper meets its specifications. It is not possible to say what an implementation of Z39.48 would look like, except that it would be paper and it would be durable. This is a narrow standard, unambiguous within its own scope, but insufficient to create wholly predictable physical implementations. It can be applied to paper making, but it will not yield a direct physical manifestation.

Unique Implementations: Standard Numbering Systems

Most standard numbering systems establish unique implementations. Given proper labeling and an assignment agency, there can be no question what such numbers should look like and whether a given number conforms to the standard. Such standards have only one implementation: there can be but one pattern for an ISBN and one for an ISSN. These standards may not specify all of the implementation (e.g., the typography to be used in printing an ISBN), but do describe how to complete the implementation (i.e., how numbers are created and the punctuation to be used in display). Any standard numbering system requires one or more maintenance agencies, but the standard need not identify the agencies.

Standards with Multiple Implementations

A standard numbering system permits only one implementation. Z85.1 permits four, but is still effectively a single-implementation standard; that is, all implementations are essentially equivalent, dif-

---

2   This and other Z39 standards are described in Chapter 12.

fering only in known areas. Other technical standards do not provide such precision; some explicitly provide for a wide range of diverse implementations, whereas others are insufficiently well-defined to narrow the range of implementation.

Z39.2 and Z39.49

Z39.2 is the *American National Standard for Bibliographic Information Interchange.*[3] It specifies a record structure to accommodate bibliographic and related information: a leader and its contents, fields, subfields, and indicators. Z39.2 was created together with MARC II, and provides the structural basis for the MARC formats. As interpreted by most librarians, Z39.2 is the MARC standard.

But Z39.2 is not equivalent to USMARC, and USMARC is not the only possible implementation of Z39.2. The original version of Z39.49, *Computerized Book Ordering,* may help to make this clear.[4]

USMARC is a specific implementation of Z39.2, an instance of the class of objects defined by Z39.2, just as a specific USMARC record is an instance of the class of objects defined by USMARC. The original Z39.49, in its variable-length version[5], is also an implementation of Z39.2, but one that differs greatly from USMARC. Z39.2 allows for an enormous variety of implementations. Because of its provisions, each implementation is (at least partially) self-defining, but different implementations can have very different characteristics.

The record leader defined by Z39.2 is always 24 characters long, and most positions in the leader are defined by Z39.2. Five of those positions contain the following variables that define any specific implementation of Z39.2.

---

3 For more information, see Chapter 12 of this book and Chapters 2 and 3 of Walt Crawford, *MARC for Library Use: Understanding Integrated USMARC* (Boston, Mass.: G.K. Hall, 1989).

4 As discussed in Chapter 11, a new version of Z39.49 will probably abandon the Z39.2-based variable format, as an X12-based record appears more suitable.

5 Sometimes known as the BISAC format, since it was originally designed by the Book Industry Standards Advisory Committee (BISAC).

- **Indicator count:** Number of indicators at the beginning of each variable-length field. USMARC: 2. Z39.49: 0. There are no indicators in Z39.49 (BISAC) fields.

- **Identifier length:** Length of the "subfield code." Both USMARC and Z39.49 use 2, as each subfield is identified by a delimiter and a character. Z39.49 uses capital letters for subfield characters, while USMARC uses lower case letters and numbers.

- **Length of the length-of-field portion:** Part of the directory entry map, defining the directory. USMARC: 4. Z39.49: 0. Z39.49 directories do not include length of field; that must be determined by scanning the fields themselves. This choice conserves space (the length-of-field in the directory is redundant information) but reduces the error-detection capability of Z39.2.

- **Length of the starting-character-position portion:** Both USMARC and Z39.49 use 5, allowing for very long records. It is possible to eliminate this element as well, but doing so requires that records be processed end-to-end, considerably reducing the flexibility inherent in Z39.2.

- **Length of the implementation-defined portion:** Both USMARC and Z39.49 use 0: neither includes an implementation-defined portion. Such a portion could be used to add meaning to directory entries (e.g., to store multiple subrecords within a record).

Programs to process MARC records may not work well with BISAC (Z39.49) records. Well-written USMARC-processing programs will detect that a Z39.49 record is a different implementation of Z39.2 and reject the record. For most uses, different implementations of Z39.2 are not fully compatible. It is possible to write programs that can break down any Z39.2 record into component parts, and it would be possible to build systems that used such generalized record parsers as tools. Most computer programs, however, are designed to work with a *specific* implementation of Z39.2. It isn't clear that a generalized record parser would be very useful, since a Z39.2-based record doesn't make sense without the data dictionary for the implementation; that is, the explicit definition of legal tags and subfields and what they mean.

The five variable elements of Z39.2 yield 100,000 different possible implementations, ranging from a minimalist format with no subfields, no indicators, and nothing in the directory but tags, up to an extremely complex format with 9s for all values. To make matters more confusing, choices used for the five elements only define the mechanical parameters of an implementation; they do not identify the implementation. Thus, for example, any number of different implementations can use the same element choices as USMARC without being identical to USMARC: the data dictionaries could be entirely different. For example, field 100, Personal Name Main Entry in USMARC, could just as easily be title or part number in some other Z39.2 implementation using the same options as USMARC.

Ambiguity doesn't make Z39.2 a bad standard, but one that is more distant from final objects than some others. The standard provides enough information so that a computer program based only on the text of Z39.2 could test records to see whether they appeared to be consistent with Z39.2 implementations. A generalized record parser would perform such tests as part of its operations, but might not be able to do much with the results.

RS-232C: Standard Connections

Electronics Industry Association standard RS-232C[6] was established many years ago to provide standard connections for data communications. It defines 25 signal paths, usually implemented as a two-row 25-pin connector (DB-25 connector). Most terminals, modems, and serial printers use RS-232C; however, cables are not always interchangeable among different devices.

RS-232C applies to "interconnection of data terminal equipment (DTE) and data communication equipment (DCE) employing serial binary data interchange." The standard is quite explicit. It defines electrical characteristics, mechanical characteristics, functional description of circuits, and a group of standard subsets for the 25 lines called for in the standard. The 13 standard subsets provide for specific applications, and require as few as 5 or as many as 20 electrical paths. The standard includes specific voltage limits and other requirements so that two pieces of equipment connected through RS-232C will not

---

6 Electronic Industries Association, *EIA Standard Interface Between Data Terminal Equipment and Data Communication Equipment Employing Serial Binary Data Interchange, EIA RS-232C* (Washington, D.C.: EIA; August 1969).

damage one another and will communicate properly. Three of the 25 lines are undefined, and 2 are used for testing. Lines 2 and 3 are the most important: transmitted data and received data. There are no ambiguities in RS-232C as written. The standard does *not* call for the DB-25 connector; it does specify that data terminal equipment should have a female connector (with holes in the flat plate) and that data communication equipment should include a cable terminating in a male connector (with pins protruding from the flat plate).

Problems with RS-232C arise for several reasons. Twenty-five-wire cables are expensive and cumbersome, and no devices require all 25 signals. Most RS-232C cables use either five or nine wires. Although devices requiring five wires will work with nine-wire cables, nine-wire devices won't work with five-wire cables. Most RS-232C cables are sold with male connectors on both ends, but some devices and computer ports (including one on the ubiquitous IBM PC) carry male connectors, requiring a female cable end. Finally, a cable that connects pin #2 to pin #2 and pin #3 to pin #3 works for DTE-to-DCE connections, but some device pairs are both DCE, requiring that the two pins be reversed at opposite ends of the cable.

In short, a standard RS-232C cable is largely mythical; the cable that connects your printer to your computer may not work between your computer and your modem, or between your computer and your terminal. "An RS-232C cable for minimal Subset D, female-to-male, DTE-to-DCE, using DB-25 connectors" is a precise specification that can only have one implementation. There are many stories of important demonstrations that couldn't be held for lack of an appropriate RS-232C cable. With the proliferation of microcomputers and video display terminals, most using RS-232C in various implementations, the problem has grown large enough to generate new products as partial solutions. One company makes an intelligent RS-232C cable with internal electronics to attempt to configure the correct connections; it costs four times as much as a standard cable, but generally provides universal interconnection if the microprocessor is able to make the correct deductions. Other companies make other devices so that cables can be reconfigured as needed and devices can be tested for presence of signals on various pins.

The case of RS-232C is complex. The standard itself is thorough and precise; problems arise with imprecise use. Some novice microcomputer users have purchased so-called standard RS-232C cables from incompetent computer store clerks, then found that their equipment wouldn't function.

Z39.29: Bibliographic References

As a final example of a standard with several implementations, consider Z39.29, the standard for bibliographic references.[7] It includes tables of mandatory, recommended, and optional elements for various types of material, and does specify order of elements and punctuation. At least four elements of ambiguity make it difficult to determine what a citation should look like, based on the text:

- The standard allows citations to be title first or author first, in cases where authorship is apparent;

- Brief and comprehensive forms of citation are described, besides the variety of optional elements within a comprehensive citation;

- Use of quotation marks to surround article or chapter titles, and boldface, italic, or underscores to indicate monograph or journal titles, is allowed but not prescribed;

- Titles may be capitalized according to "library rules" (first word and each proper noun) or according to "bibliography rules" (each significant word).

The citations that follow are all for the same chapter, and are all proper Z39.29 citations:

Online Search Strategies. White Plains, NY: Knowledge Industry Publications; 1982: 175-212.

Patents. William G. Andrus [et al]. *Online Search Strategies*. Ryan E. Hoover, ed. White Plains, NY: Knowledge Industry Publications; 1982: 175-212. 345 p. (Professional Librarian Series.)

---

7   This discussion is based on the standard in effect as of this writing; a new version is being developed, which may be more workable and less ambiguous. It is also possible that Z39.29 will be withdrawn.

Andrus, William G. [and others]. Patents. In: Hoover, Ryan E., ed. Online Search Strategies. White Plains, NY: Knowledge Industry Publications; 1982: 175-212.

Andrus, William G.; Heyd, William E.; Lustgarten, Ronald K.; Pollack, Norman M. "Patents." In: Hoover, Ryan E., ed. *Online Search Strategies*. White Plains, NY: Knowledge Industry Publications; 1982: 175-212. 345 p. (Professional Librarian Series.) ISBN 0-86729-004-8 (paper).

Such ambiguity means that an author (or editor) must make a series of decisions to create a consistent bibliography using Z39.29. The author first/title first ambiguity must generally be resolved on a case-by-case basis (as in cataloging). Bibliographies within published NISO standards tend to use the simplest options for Z39.29, including the preferred single type. Users might prefer a slightly more complex implementation. Without careful observation, it is not always clear that citations or bibliographies are done according to Z39.29.

Application Rather than Implementation

A number of NISO standards appear not to lead to implementations as such. Rather, they can be applied to improve communication. Guideline standards may be some of the most useful generated by NISO, although their direct impact is nebulous.[8] Ambiguities within them are common and reasonable. Such standards are intended to provide guidance for intelligent human application; the human mind can resolve ambiguities. Guidelines for computer application cannot reasonably permit such ambiguity: computers are not inherently able to resolve ambiguity.

For example, Z39.29, which permits ambiguous implementation, can be used well for computer-generated output but not so well for computer recognition. Computer programs exist to generate Z39.29 bibliographies given identified data elements provided in any order. Developing a program to break a machine-readable bibliography down into identifiable data elements would be far more difficult, as

---

8 It is quite likely that some or most NISO guideline standards will be withdrawn as standards and converted into guideline publications.

the options and rules in Z39.29 do not provide enough information to allow complete mechanical parsing.

Levels of Standards

Any body of technical standards can be viewed as including standards at various levels (and generally some that work at more than one level). They can be categorized by level of abstraction, application, or reliance on other standards, or in other ways. One observer may establish a different set of levels than another observer, depending on the outlook of the observer and the purpose of the categorization.

Several writers have attempted to provide theoretical frameworks for standards. Lal C. Verman devotes a large portion of *Standardization: A New Discipline*[9] to the philosophy of standards and to various frameworks in which to place standards. David Hemenway[10] also develops categories of standards, from a considerably different perspective. In both cases, the discussions should be read in their entirety; summarizing them here would serve little purpose.

James E. Rush suggested a seven-level model for NISO standards:[11]

- **Level 0: Message boundaries**, the precise limits of a message;
- **Level 1: Data structures**, such as chapters, fields, subfields, and paragraphs;
- **Level 2: Data element identifiers**, explicit and implicit methods for identifying data elements within a structure;

---

9 Lal C. Verman, *Standardization: A New Discipline* (Hamden, Conn.: Archon, 1973); 461 pp.

10 David Hemenway, *Industrywide Voluntary Product Standards* (Cambridge, Mass.: Ballinger, 1975); 141 pp.

11 James E. Rush, "A Proposed Model for the Development of an Integrated Set of Standards for Bibliographic and Related Data," *Library Trends* 31, no. 2 (Fall 1982): 237-49.

- **Level 3: Data element values**, permissible values or types of value for a given data element, such as code tables or thesauri;
- **Level 4: Display (representation) formats**, the manner in which messages are presented to users;
- **Level 5: Media**, the carrier for a message;
- **Level 6: Housing of media**, standards for storage.

This was one of the simpler models, and provided one useful way of looking at NISO standards. It assumed that everything of interest to NISO is either a message or a means of conveying or storing a message. This message-oriented model differs from process-oriented models that concentrate on activities, actor-oriented models that concentrate on users, and other possible models and frameworks.

Specific models for levels or layers of standards may arise as part of the standardization process. The most important example of this for library automation is the Open Systems Interconnection (OSI) Reference Model, which establishes seven layers of standards to build communications links between computers. Figure 4.1 shows the layers within OSI.

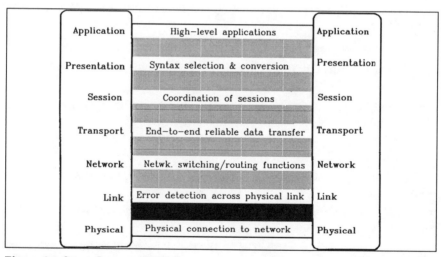

Figure 4.1: Seven Layers of OSI

This book does not present a formal model or framework for standards. Every proposal has some validity and some weakness. Informally, this chapter and others have categorized standards by level of abstraction, but these categories are vague. Most standardization efforts have proceeded without any formal framework. Most users can enjoy the advantages of technical standards without any concern for formal models. Interested readers may wish to consult sources mentioned in this chapter or other sources (some noted in the bibliography) to consider and compare various frameworks.

Layers of Standards in Complete Systems

Unquestionably, any complex system will involve standards working at many different levels or within different layers. For example, an online catalog in a library could be based on thousands of technical standards, from those used by parts suppliers, through those used to create and maintain information, to those used to maintain links within the catalog and with other systems.[12]

The lowest layer of standards in this case (other than those for weights and measures) consists of standards for basic materials and testing those materials—dimensional tolerances, specifications for materials to be used within components, tests for everything from circuit boards to water to be used in processing circuitry. ASTM is the largest single source of such standards, but many other developers also create basic material and testing standards.

The next layer covers components—resistors, capacitors, transistors, wall plugs, circuit breakers, mechanical fasteners, and power cables. Developers such as UL, EIA, IEEE and ASTM, along with many others, create standards for components.

At an intermediate level, hundreds of standards help to define the peripheral equipment and supplies required for an online catalog: terminals, keyboards, mass storage devices, communications

---

12 This discussion, together with many examples of standards at each layer, appeared as Appendix B in the first edition of *Technical Standards: An Introduction for Librarians*. If "thousands" seems like an exaggeration, an hour or two in a good standards collection—as in any good engineering library—should convince the reader that it is not.

links, bar code readers, paper, and even optical fibers in today's high-speed networks.

Finally, various standards define languages and character sets for software, software protocols for computer-to-computer linkages, codes to identify states and countries, and such library codes as ISBN and ISSN. Many online catalogs of the 1990s will support a primary or secondary access mode based on the Common Command Language. In short, it takes many standards at several layers to build a complex system.

Standards Based on Standards

Most standards are based on other standards, explicitly or implicitly. Those that provide for direct implementation may well rely on several levels of more fundamental ones. Z39.49 (discussed above) is itself an implementation of Z39.2; in turn, Z39.2 relies on ASC X3 standards for magnetic tape, character sets, and tape labels.

Some standards exist *only* for the purpose of creating other standards. Z39.33, *Development of Identification Codes for Use by the Bibliographic Community*, a "standard for standard numbers," is one example. In some standards communities, such underlying standards might precede any implementations; this was not so within NISO, as Z39.33 was established after the most successful codes (ISBN and ISSN) were already in use. Standards for standards are not necessary to develop higher-level standards, but do help to pull together families of related ones.

Families of Standards

Standards don't always fall neatly into any given level, but many do fall neatly into families. Like levels, families may exist more in the mind of the reader than the text of standards; unlike levels, families need not encompass all standards or be exclusive. A single standard can be part of more than one family. For this book, a family is any group of standards with a recognizable common aspect.

Organization into families helps to reduce the apparent complexity of NISO's work, or that of any other standards organization.

Some organizations explicitly relate closely linked families by giving them the same overall standard number, using a decimal suffix for each individual standard. Figure 4.2 shows just a few partial families out of the thousands that can be recognized or created through analysis.

Members of a family don't necessarily work equally well, or in precisely the same way. For instance, some romanization standards

---

Romanization standards

Z39.11	Japanese
Z39.12	Arabic
Z39.24	Slavic Cyrillic
Z39.25	Hebrew
Z39.35	Lao, Khmer and Pali
Z39.37	Armenian

Numbering standards

Z39.9	International Standard Serial Number (ISSN)
Z39.21	Book numbering (ISBN)
Z39.23	Standard Technical Report Number (STRN)
Z39.33	Development of identification codes
Z39.43	Identification code for the book industry (SAN)
Z39.56	Serial item identifier (draft)

Programming languages

X3.9	FORTRAN
X3.23	COBOL
X3.37	APT
X3.3	PL/I
X3.60	Minimal BASIC
X3.74	PL/I, general-purpose subset
X3.97	Pascal

Optical character recognition

X3.17	Character set for OCR-A
X3.45	Character set for handprinting
X3.49	Character set for OCR-B
X3.86	OCR inks

Figure 4.2: Families of Standards

can be applied without knowledge of the original language, whereas others require that a user know the original language to use the standards effectively. Families of current and potential standards form much of the basis for NISO's future work plan. These families are discussed, as is NISO's plan, in Chapter 10.

Summary

All technical standards are abstractions; some are more abstract than others. A single standard may yield a single implementation or allow for a variety of implementations. Standards are based on other standards, and may involve several levels of nested standards. Some allow ambiguity in implementation, and others allow a deliberate but precisely specified range of choices. Explicit standards with several options may be cited improperly (i.e., cited as though they only had one option), giving the impression that they are flawed. Standards may be arranged into various frameworks or models, and may be grouped into families. Such groupings and arrangements can help make sense of standards, but they can be arbitrary.

5

Motives for Formal Technical Standards

Formal consensus standards cost more and take longer to develop than other technical standards.[1] Companies, associations and other organizations pay membership fees to support standards development organizations and to have a voice and vote on standards. Those same companies and associations pay time and travel expenses, and other forms of support, so that people can serve on committees to develop new standards and maintain existing ones. Indeed, without such support, most development organizations could not survive.

Even the simplest technical standards require thousands of dollars in time and effort to write, distribute, review, and establish. Complex ones can require years of effort and hundreds of thousands of dollars. International standardization efforts can be extremely expensive when travel costs are factored in; an organization can expect to spend thousands or even tens of thousands of dollars each year to maintain effective representation in an active area of international standardization. Such effort and expense require economic justification.

Reasons for supporting standards differ from standard to standard, from company to company, and from field to field. This chapter considers some reasons that agencies develop and support formal consensus standards.[2]

---

1   This statement is true *for a given standard in a given company*. On the other hand, it may cost less for half a dozen companies to cooperate in developing a single consensus standard than for each of them to develop a separate one.

The Benefits of Standards

Naming and Symbol Standards

Two people must speak a common language in order to agree on something. Common names and meanings permit successful shared specifications. Some standards establish consistent naming conventions to improve communications and to make more complex standards possible. Many standards agencies develop standards for standards. Standard symbols provide an agreed shorthand to improve communication. Good symbols compress verbal information in unambiguous, immediately recognizable form.

Specification Standards

Precise specifications are basic to industrialization. Internal standards are created because of needs for precise specifications, and consensus standards can come about when such needs are generalized across an industry. All standards for simplification and interchangeability are specification standards.

Test, Analysis, and Safety Standards

Buyers and sellers alike want assurance that products are safe. Underwriters Laboratories, Inc. (UL) and the American Society for Testing and Materials (ASTM), two of the most important standards-making groups in the United States, develop standards for testing, analysis, and safety, as do many other standards agencies.

Producers and consumers both have reason to support the efforts of these organizations. Standards for testing and analysis allow producers and consumers to verify claims. Given a proper testing standard, any agency testing a given product should achieve comparable results to any other agency.

The NISO standards for permanent paper (Z39.48) and catalog card stock (Z85.1) both use testing standards developed by other

---

2 An extended study of motivations for consensus standards can be found in David Hemenway, *Industrywide Voluntary Product Standards* (Cambridge, Mass.: Ballinger, 1975).

agencies for bending strength, alkalinity, and other aspects of paper and cards. Many specification standards rely on testing and analysis standards, as do most safety standards.

Safety standards range from the UL standard 753B (safety standard for electric hair dryers) stamped on most hair dryers sold in the United States, to ANSI/IEEE standard C2, the National Electrical Safety Code, which specifies hundreds of rules for transmission and handling of electricity. Producers benefit from safety, testing, and analysis standards because they can determine that their products meet recognized standards for safety. Consumers benefit because they can choose safe products through standard labeling, rather than relying strictly on known brands. The marketplace is open to new producers that follow standards (and whose products pass standard tests), and all legitimate elements of the marketplace benefit.

Grading and Classification Standards

Grading and classification standards usually concern natural products or refined natural products: wood, oil, and the like. Buyers support them because they permit rational tradeoffs between price and quality. Suppliers support grading standards because they provide a common vocabulary and basis for negotiation. These standards rarely extend past material standards; none of the Z39 or X3 standards are primarily grading standards.

Simplification: Competition, Efficiency, and Stability

Many standards simplify by reducing pointless diversity where it raises costs or reduces stability. Simplification standards should meet both criteria: only *pointless* diversity should be reduced, and diversity should be reduced only if it causes economic harm or impedes some useful endeavor. Much of the push for standardization in the early twentieth century was for simplification.

Suppose that neither the American Library Association nor the Library of Congress was involved when libraries became fascinated with card catalogs in the late nineteenth century. Each library would buy card stock and catalog drawers. The New York Public Library might contract with the Library Company to produce card drawers to hold 4-inch by 6-inch cards with two rods for greater stability; the Library Company would probably also supply the card stock. Harvard might contract with a local furniture builder and paper company to make cards and single-rod drawers, the cards being 5 inches by 8 inches to hold Harvard's elaborate entries. The Chicago Public Library might set out to acquire 2-inch by 4-inch cards, saving considerable space and leaving enough room for nominal entries.

That may seem far-fetched, but that's how automobile companies worked until 1910. Parts—washers, tubing, bolts, sheet steel—were custom manufactured to each car maker's own specifications: there were 300 different lockwasher designs and 1,100 varieties of steel tubing. If a supplier went out of business, the car maker might be left without a vital part, and would have to wait for another supplier to alter production lines to produce it. This needless and injurious diversity was remedied when the Society of Automotive Engineers (SAE) began to develop standards—224 of them by 1921. The results: 35 different lock washers, 150 varieties of steel tubing, and similar reductions elsewhere. A 1916 estimate was that the SAE had effected a 30% reduction in the cost of ball bearings, 20% in steel costs, in all, savings equivalent to 15% of the retail value of automobiles.[3]

Libraries had little time to establish diverse sizes and styles for library cards. The Library of Congress began selling printed cards at about the same time that card catalogs became popular. Melvil Dewey also started various library supply companies (including the Library Company), and he believed in standards. A dominant-agent standard of catalog card stock about 5 inches wide and about 3 inches high, taking a single rod about ⅓-inch from the bottom, became commonplace in the United States long before ANSI Z85.1 was written.

The 75-mm by 125-mm card standard had the same effect on libraries that SAE standards had on the automotive industry. Customers could put contracts out for competitive bids in the expectation that more than one supplier would make a particular part. New suppliers could enter the market, since the standards were published

---

3 Ibid, 14-15

and readily available; by offering better prices, better delivery, or other special features, they could hope to take business away from old suppliers. Without simplification, new suppliers would find it very difficult to break into a field. Customers and suppliers would be so tightly involved that the thought of changing suppliers would rarely arise.

Simplification eases entry for new suppliers by specifying what a market will accept. It also makes existing suppliers more competitive by allowing them to improve production efficiency. Assembly lines have startup costs and retooling costs. A factory that produces a million lock washers in each of five sizes will produce them more cheaply than one that produces 50,000 lock washers in each of 100 sizes. Increased plant efficiency was certainly the prime motive for any existing automotive supplier to support SAE standards, and has continued to be a primary motive for simplification standards.

Another feature of simplification standards is that they promote stability. If one supplier goes out of business, a buyer can go to another one that will probably have identical parts available. The need for stability has become such a driving force in some industries that a new product won't be accepted until more than one supplier exists. In the microprocessor field, for example, a new (and protected) CPU design may be licensed by its creator to at least one second source company in order to make the CPU more competitive in the market. Until recently, computer manufacturers were reluctant to buy a CPU that would become unavailable if its only supplier was backlogged or went bankrupt; the second source provides important stability. Supply disruptions in the most popular single-source microprocessors have confirmed the wisdom of this now-abandoned insistence on second sources.

Simplification was the earliest major success of formal consensus standards in the United States. Simplification standards can be damaging if they reduce diversity; if such diversity is valuable enough that customers are willing to pay for it, the standards will be ignored. Where customers and producers have reasonably equal power, simplification standards are self-regulating: those that work will be followed, those that are too restrictive will fade away.

Interchangeability

Because simplification works on a product-by-product basis, the variety within a single product category is reduced so that producers can produce more cheaply and buyers can encourage competition among sellers. The catalog card example also involves interchangeability: catalog card drawers must accept standard catalog card stock.

Interchangeability implies cooperation as well as competition. If the Library of Congress had not been on the scene, producers of library furniture could have met with paper makers to develop standards that would ensure that any catalog drawer would work with any catalog card. The primary light bulb makers in the United States are not very important in the field of light fixtures, but can compete among themselves in the knowledge that all standard normal-size light bulbs (whether 20-watt, 60-watt, 75-watt, 100-watt, or higher wattage) will fit in standard Edison sockets.

Consensus standards require cooperative work among agencies that may be competitors. Work on them is generally not considered anticompetitive and has rarely been attacked by the Justice Department.[4] Most consensus standards enhance competition by lowering the barriers to new companies. Furthermore, interchangeability permits new companies to build on the work of old companies, using their products and making new ones based on them.

Long-playing records have involved a series of standards, some of them first-agent, some the result of voluntary consensus effort. Freely available standards for speed and size of long-playing records made it easy for new manufacturers to introduce turntables. They also allowed Windham Hill to compete with CBS, which promulgated the 33⅓-rpm speed standard. Because the size, speed, and primary groove dimensions of records are standard, companies can focus on developments to enhance the medium. Record manufacturers can work with new materials and new pressing methods; turntable makers can work on lower rumble and more sophisticated features for ease of use; cartridge makers can concentrate on lowering distortion and generally making cartridges do a better job of reproducing sound.

---

4 Some additional comments on standards and antitrust appear in Chapter 6.

The 12-inch and 33⅓-rpm standards of the late 1940s began the process; voluntary consensus standards for encoding stereophonic sound, adopted in the late 1950s, allowed stereo to take over within a few years.[5] More recently, one company (Technics) promulgated a new first-agent standard for cartridge mounting, making it possible for consumers to mount cartridges without studying tracking force, overhang, and other high fidelity arcana. The P-Mount was made freely available to other turntable companies and cartridge companies. This is another case in which a standard improves interchangeability and makes competition easier and more efficient. It's probably fair to say that licensed standards helped CDs to overtake LPs so rapidly, since total interchangeability was fully guaranteed from the start, leading to rapid and effective competition.

Z39.2, the underlying standard for USMARC, is a standard for interchangeability. As stated in the standard itself, it is intended for interchange rather than for use within a single system. USMARC records have the same characteristics whether produced by RLG, LC, OCLC, WLN, or Blackwell North America. A new company wishing to develop an online catalog can rely on the USMARC structure and can compete with older companies on an equal footing. If there was no standard for bibliographic interchange, libraries using OCLC would have to specify what sort of system tape they wanted: Innovative, CLSI, or Science Press.[6] If Carlyle or Dynix wanted to bid to replace a Data Research system, they'd be out of luck: the data would be in a format proprietary to Data Research. Such a situation would serve neither the new companies nor the old ones. Among other consequences, it would prevent a library from building a bibliographic base before selecting a system.[7]

---

5   The stereo standard was a reactive rather than an active standard, as discussed below; several other methods of stereo were tried, but none became commercially successful until several companies agreed on the standard geometry now used.

6   This example is totally hypothetical: it isn't at all clear that OCLC would ever have developed or grown without USMARC.

7   In practice, each system may well have its own data extensions, but the form of the data is common to all MARC-compatible systems.

Interchangeability and Innovation

Interchangeability standards foster innovation because they establish a baseline; they can also hamper innovation because they restrict variety within the baseline. Optimists would say that this channels innovation to more useful areas. Standardized battery sizes allow toy makers and radio companies to build products with battery cavities and terminals of known sizes and placement, assuming that several highly competitive producers make batteries to fit those cavities. The battery companies don't spend much time on new sizes or shapes; instead, they develop new and better varieties of batteries within the old sizes and shapes. Today's rechargeable nickel-cadmium cells and long-lasting alkaline cells show the effects of channeled innovation. Those who use portable computers may be well aware of the negative consequences of abandoning existing standards; the distinctive shapes and sizes of batteries for such computers have helped to keep replacement prices high and replacement units difficult to obtain.

Mass Production and Standards

Simplification and interchangeability standards help make mass production possible. When there are fewer varieties of a product to make, a full-line producer can expect to make more of each one. When one product is so well defined that other products can be based on that definition, producers of the one product can anticipate larger markets and produce in larger quantities.

Mass production is the economic success story of the industrial revolution. Some futurists have said that mass production doesn't matter in the postindustrial society toward which we appear headed, but this overlooks the fundamentals. An information-based society may well favor diversity over uniformity, but can only maintain that diversity because the underlying tools of society are mass-produced. Microcomputers have become cheap and powerful thanks to mass production and competition; although research and development have helped to increase the density of circuits, only mass markets and standard circuit packaging have brought prices down to the point that some microprocessors cost $5 or less. Furthermore, a postindustrial society will depend on information standards.

The economics of production favor comprehensive standards. More standardized products offer opportunities for longer production runs. On the other hand, the economics of innovation favor less comprehensive standards, so that new designs and new products can be based on standardized individual parts.

International Competition

Every industrialized nation has a body of technical standards, some voluntary and some reflected in laws and regulations. Any manufacturer expecting to operate within a country or to sell products in that country must be familiar with those standards to compete effectively. Often, failure to meet the standards of a country will prevent a manufacturer from even offering products for sale. That's particularly true when the products are components to be used within other products: even if it is legal to place them on sale, there will be no market for them.

Increasingly, these concerns lead to international and multinational standards. To the extent that American firms ignore such standards, they will find their future markets shrinking. Already, some may find themselves locked out of some markets because national standards make it difficult or impossible for them to compete. In such situations, a move toward international efforts may be the best solution.

Guidelines

Most technical standards are explicit specifications. Many library-related standards, and some in other organizations, are guidelines that will produce better results if applied, but that are not designed to produce mechanical uniformity or interchangeability.

Guidelines are difficult to quantify in economic terms. Motives for them tend to be purer in that they do not involve direct economic gain for the parent organization. A consistent standard for proofreading makes authors and editors more efficient, but has little direct economic impact. A standard for index preparation should improve scholarly access, but the economic benefits of standard back-of-the-book indexes have not been demonstrated.

Many standards organizations would argue that guidelines should not be adopted as formal technical standards but should have another designation. The point is valid, although (for example) the Open Systems Interconnection (OSI) model adopted by the International Organization for Standardization (ISO) is both a *reference model* and a formal standard (ISO 7498). It is a model for developing other standards and a way of thinking about links between systems, but, unlike typical technical standards, it does not provide explicit definitions that will, when correctly applied, always produce the same results.

Active and Reactive Standards

Technical standards can be grouped broadly into active and reactive categories. Reactive standards are formed after a technique or product is in use, when agencies see a need to regularize it. All early SAE standards, and most American consensus standards in the first half of the century, were reactive standards, that is, created to improve an existing situation.

Active Standards

Active standards tend to begin with licensed standards (discussed in Chapter 3) and dominant-agent standards, but can be developed through cooperative effort. Libraries stand to benefit in years to come from the active efforts to develop standards based on the OSI model. If successful, the US and international efforts for OSI will result in flexible, effective methods of communicating between computers of different types, from different manufacturers.

Z39.2, the standard for interchange of bibliographic information, is also an active standard. The Library of Congress designed the MARC format, and prepared text for Z39.2. In that sense, Z39.2 is a dominant-agency standard blessed by ANSI. Like many other federal agencies, LC is committed to consensus standards. It proposed Z39.2 in such a way that it was not a direct reflection of LC MARC but a generalized standard applicable to any interchange of bibliographic information.

Reactive Standards

Technologies emerge faster than standards organizations can form or meet, and premature standards can have a stifling effect on a new technology. Reactive standards begin when agents within a field find the field mired in confusion. The standards stories of the early twentieth century provide clear examples; current examples are subtler. David Hemenway begins his book on standards with the Baltimore fire of 1904:

> So serious did the fire become that help was solicited from surrounding communities. Washington, D.C. fire engines reached the scene within three hours, and additional units arrived from as far afield as Annapolis, Wilmington, Chester, York, Altoona, Harrisburg, Philadelphia, and New York. Unfortunately, most of these units proved of little assistance, for their hoses would not fit Baltimore hydrants. Though there was never a shortage of water many fire fighting units had to stand by, virtually helpless . . .[8]

When lives are lost due to different methods of attaching fire hoses, the need for reactive standards seems obvious, and cries for government intervention will be heard. Most reactive standards arise from less obvious losses that are no less real. Safety standards have saved thousands of lives by giving manufacturers and consumers alike a basis for building safe appliances. Interchangeability standards have saved billions of dollars in industries where confusion would otherwise reign. If simplification standards for electric lamp sizes, threads, and socket styles had not been established, you might need to stock separate bulbs for each light fixture in your home or office, and might be required to buy your bulbs from the socket manufacturer. Quite apart from the much higher prices you could expect to pay for bulbs and the cost of storing more complex inventories, you would have real problems if the sole producer of your bulbs went out of business.

---

8 David Hemenway, *Industrywide Voluntary Product Standards* (Cambridge, Mass.: Ballinger, 1975), 3.

Standards for the Sake of Standards

Not all motives for standards are legitimate. Some people write standards because they like to write standards. Such motives aren't unique to standards work. Most of us are aware of the explosion of scholarly and specialist journals, and of the mixed quality of articles in some of them. Some suspect that this profusion of articles relates more to tenure and reputation than to advances in knowledge.

Such problems arise infrequently and are not likely to last long. The policies of most standards development organizations discourage superfluous standardization activities. Typically, activities must be approved before they can begin, sometimes by a vote of the membership. Standards are expensive to write and to see through to adoption. Each organization with a standards committee member can expect to spend travel funds two to four (or more) times a year to work with the committee. People who write standards for their own sake tend to run out of corporate support.

Summary

The basic motive for most consensus standards is economic. Standards are adopted to save money or make money. Economics is not a simple field, and standards flourish for a variety of subtle motives, most of which are justified and reasonable.

Library standards have less obvious economic impact. Most are guidelines rather than precise specifications. They enhance the literature and improve scholarship, an indirect economic benefit.

6

Problems and Dangers of Standards

Regardless of how fundamental they are to organized society, not all standards are good, and not all are positive achievements. Like most other instruments of civilization, they can be good or bad.

Standards and Competition

Standards may lower or raise barriers to new competitors by making it easier or more difficult to enter an industry. In both ways, they influence competition. Although the historical record is generally good, there can be cause for concern.

Antitrust

When the major competing companies in an industry meet to decide pricing or territories, it's called collusion. When employees of those companies meet to determine common specifications for parts used by the industry, it's called standards making. The government has been known to object to the first type of meeting, but rarely to the second.

In 1964, antitrust questions were raised about an American Society for Testing and Materials (ASTM) standard on asbestos cement; it was suggested that the standard constituted a form of price fixing. The District Court of Pennsylvania said that "because of the heavy reliance of federal, state and municipal governments upon

79

ASTM for specifications, the Society may be regarded as an essential arm, or branch, of the government, and its acts may be entitled to the immunity from antitrust laws accorded governmental acts."[1]

Standardization organizations have generally been considered immune to antitrust laws. Such immunity is not inevitable, and does not mean that technical standards development never functions in a collusive manner. The processes used by major organizations should work to prevent standards that promote monopoly and oligopoly, but collusive standards are possible. Any standard that limits variety can potentially limit competition.

Competition

Uniformity standards can indirectly encourage illegal price fixing simply by their existence: when products are known to be uniform, it's easier to fix prices. Technical standards that set minimum quality specifications may also be anticompetitive by raising barriers to new competitors. There are two ways to write minimum quality standards. One concentrates on performance: to meet the standard, something must pass specified tests under specified conditions. Unfortunately, performance-based standards are not always feasible: technology to make proper measurements may be lacking, or the nature of performance may be such that any tests would be prohibitively expensive.Standards;uniformity.

Minimum quality standards can avoid such problems by specifying materials and methods. They are prevalent in building codes and similar regulations. This form of standard can be directly anticompetitive and usually impedes technological development by barring innovation. It directly bars one form of competition. If the specified techniques or materials are proprietary, the technical standard is directly anticompetitive.

Totally unfettered competitive methods can include product adulteration, cutting prices by reducing the size or quality of the product. Standards for weights and measures specifically eliminate

---

1   U.S. *vs.* Johns-Manville, et al, Finding Fact on Application of ASTM, District Court for Eastern Pennsylvania, July 20, 1964. Cited in Hemenway, *Industrywide Voluntary Product Standards*, 10–11.

the competitive thrust to charge less by selling less (and calling it more). Thousands of technical standards, including most of those developed by ASTM, are anticompetitive in that they prevent the sale of inferior materials. Such forms of competition endanger life and health; proper technical standards shift competition to more acceptable areas.

Nontariff Trade Barriers

National standards can be barriers against free trade, either by establishing sufficiently specific and unusual criteria for products that most external producers will be unwilling to meet them, or by including directly anticompetitive criteria, such as requirements that extended testing be carried out by agencies within the country, where internal producers have priority access to limited test facilities.

Countries have many ways of limiting free trade. Anticompetitive formal standards should be one of the less common, if only because formal standards are, of necessity, written documents, making them easier to identify and challenge in trade negotiations. Other less formal barriers can be far more effective. Still, it is certainly the case that when a less-developed country adopts a set of standards recommended by a more-developed country, that second country is likely to have some competitive trade advantage over other countries for some period.

The United States has been lax in working with developing nations to develop their national technical standards; some European countries have been diligent in this regard. Sometimes the US appears to have lost trade because of its laxity.

Competing Economic Motives

Companies and other agencies develop standards within the real world. That inevitably means that the internal needs of agencies influence their attitudes, and that some technical standards will favor certain companies over others. Competing economic motives can cripple the standardization process or result in less-than-ideal standards.

That can particularly be the case when, as is frequently true, a formal consensus technical standard arises after implementations are already in place. Which implementation will form the basis for the technical standard, or will they all be forced to change?

In the case of local area networks, the IEEE committees adopted several standards to handle different fundamental networking schemes. The standards did not incorporate all existing local area network schemes, but the most significant exception (ARC/ARCnet, the original local area network) was excluded because Datapoint was unwilling to submit the protocols for consideration as a standard.

There have been cases where no agreement could be reached, where each originator of a technique insisted that his or hers was the only sound basis for a technical standard. In such a case, unless a neutral standard can be developed, the standardization effort will eventually be abandoned (unless, as in the case of LANs, the potential market is large enough to justify several standards).

The worst case is probably that in which one agency or group of agencies manages to maneuver the process such that a particular solution is adopted as a formal standard without the knowledge or participation of those using or preferring a different solution. Cases definitely exist in which agencies attempt to use standards developers for their own gain; it is the responsibility of the developers and coordinating agencies such as ANSI to prevent such perversion of the process. ANSI maintains procedural safeguards that provide good protection against this; although no safeguards can be universally effective, it can generally be assumed that any ANSI standard has been developed in a legitimate manner.

Standards and Innovation

Well-written standards can encourage innovation, allowing creators to focus on new tools, techniques, and products while taking for granted established tools, techniques, and materials. Timely standards for new techniques and products can also encourage widespread adoption, moving innovation into practice. Although they have aided innovation, they can also work against it.

Premature Standards

When a new technology is emerging, different developers may move along similar but distinct paths. At some point, one or more of them may initiate technical standards. If standardization begins too soon, however, it can damage innovation in two ways:

- **Draining energy:** Technical standards require significant amounts of time and energy spent on standards committees, which may be diverted from innovation and development. Sometimes, standardization may be a deliberate attempt to slow development by draining the energy of competitors.

- **Establishing uniformity:** If a standard is written and adopted, it will establish some level of uniformity. Innovation in those aspects will cease or at least be slowed for some time. The more successful the standard, the more innovation will be slowed.

Consumer videocassette recorders (VCRs) lack a single standard. This lack may have slowed early acceptance of VCRs, but increased the rate of innovation. Beta, almost always the minority format, typically led VHS in new ideas and techniques. Beta recorders were the first with special effects; they introduced high fidelity sound recording and extended picture quality to VCRs. In each case, VHS engineers followed the innovative lead of Sony (the developer of Beta). More recently, the battle has shifted to camcorders; the new players are VHS (and VHS-C) and 8 mm. Here again, it is fair to assert that the heated competition improves quality within all formats. Whereas consumers and prerecorded tape producers may suffer from the conflicting formats, consumers have benefited from competitive innovation and sharply competitive pricing.

Within the library field, it is fairly clear that any attempt to standardize user interfaces for online catalogs in 1985 would have been grossly premature, by freezing development at a relatively crude stage. A strong case can be made that such standards would still be premature; indeed, user interfaces for online catalogs may be one of those areas in which formal standards are inappropriate. For that matter, while the time is probably ripe for establishment of Z39.58, *Common Command Language*, the lack of such a standard in the middle and late 1980s probably resulted in the development of several innovative alternatives. Common Command Language will appear as an alternative (rather than primary) user interface in many online systems; that may be its most appropriate implementation.

Established Standards

Well-established standards pose barriers to innovation. Sometimes, the barrier may be impossible to overcome. The QWERTY typewriter keyboard[2] was created in the late nineteenth century. QWERTY was used on the first popular typewriters, and became familiar to the thousands, then tens of millions of trained typists, and faced no serious competition in the early twentieth century.

Some decades ago the Dvorak keyboard promised to improve typing speeds and reduce typing fatigue. Typewriters with that keyboard have been available by special order for many years, but the system has never made any dent in QWERTY. Most students still learn QWERTY in typing class, and the system continues to maintain near-universal domination. Many microcomputers permit reassignment of keys; the Apple IIc has a switch to convert the keyboard to Dvorak arrangement. A few pioneers use the switch or reassignment programs and tout Dvorak's advantages, but no significant move away from QWERTY has been made, or seems likely to be.

Innovation is the largest single factor in abandoning standards, but standards can make innovation difficult. In the library field, some commentators assert that Z39.2 and the MARC formats are outmoded standards and should be replaced by more innovative standards. Although MARC is less than three decades old, the speed and extent of its success raise a major barrier against any replacement.[3]

---

2 ANSI X4.23, *Keyboard Arrangement for Alphanumeric Machines*, though the ANSI . standard came much later than near-universal adoption of the industry standard.

3 In this case, no replacement with any suggestion of improvement actually exists; unlike supporters of the Dvorak keyboard, opponents of MARC have to date proposed no desirable replacement.

Overstandardization

Overstandardization damages the cause of standardization and can damage standards users. It can occur for many reasons and can take on several guises.

Excessively Rigid Standards

Interchangeability standards enhance competition and reduce costs. Good ones specify tolerances sufficient to ensure real interchangeability; bad ones specify tolerances in excess of such assurance. A dimensional standard with no specified tolerances is incomplete; a standard with extremely narrow tolerances is anticompetitive or useless.

Such a standard is anticompetitive when the tolerances are such that they can only be met using equipment too expensive for a newcomer to obtain, or ones that can only be met using patented or licensed techniques. Suppose that Z85.1, *Permanent and Durable Library Cards*, specified tolerances of +0 to -0.005 mm for all dimensions. To meet such narrow tolerances under a variety of measurement conditions, the card stock might have to be specially treated, requiring patented equipment available only to one paper maker. A tolerance of 0.005 mm (0.0002 in.) has no possible bearing on interchangeability of cards with an overall size of 75 mm x 125 mm; such a standard would be a deliberate attempt to prevent new paper makers from entering the market.

A standard is useless when the tolerances are so narrow that it costs more to ensure compliance than any realistic value for the item. At worst, tolerances could be beyond the resolution of existing test instruments: the standard would be meaningless, since nobody could ensure compliance. At best, it would simply be ignored. If paper makers were required to spend $1.00 per card to make sure that each card met Z85.1 standards, they would not attempt to meet the standards as the resulting products would not be saleable.

Standards of this sort tend to be self-limiting. First, any standards developer maintaining a proper consensus approach will almost certainly avoid such useless precision. Second, when a standard appears to have been overstated to limit competition, courts may be inclined to ignore the traditional antitrust exemption of standards agencies. Finally, when a standard is uneconomically precise, it will be modified or ignored.

Excessively Detailed Standards

The standard for ISBNs specifies how the numbers are formed, how they should be displayed, and how they are assigned. It does not specify how they are to be stored in MARC records, the typeface that must be used to display them, or precisely where on a publication they must be displayed. Such specifications would be too detailed, reducing the use of the standard by overstating the requirements.

The library and publishing fields seem prone to excessively detailed standards. The standard for single-title orders, Z39.30, begins with a useful set of information to be included on an order. It then goes on to specify how many characters to allow for each item and exactly where on the form each item should appear. What could be a generally applicable standard, ensuring that a certain amount of information is included in orders, becomes a rigid standard that some sensible agencies refuse to implement. (At least one NISO standard, Z39.52, *Order Form for Multiple Titles*, goes so far as to specify the typeface to be used on forms!)

The tendency to excessive detail is quite natural and one that requires care to avoid. Quite probably, standards committees build in too much detail because they fail to focus on the intent of the standard. For each detail, the committee should ask whether it is necessary to carry out the intent, and whether it is justified to carry it out. Requiring that a publisher's name and address appear on the title leaf is necessary to provide catalogers with sufficient information; requiring that the publisher's name appear on the recto, no less than 3 and no more than 4 inches from the foot of the page, does little to serve the cataloger but much to restrict the book designer. The first is a necessary detail; the second, excessive detail.[4]

When is a standard too detailed? The answer is subjective, but one clue might be that agencies generally favoring standardization find the standard impossible to implement. For example, some ver-

---

4　This example is hypothetical, but Z39.30 is not: to the author's eye, Z39.30 fails due to excessive detail.

sions of Z39.1, *Periodicals: Format and Arrangement,* include detailed and restrictive requirements that make the standard nearly impossible to follow for any newsletter published on a limited budget. Those requirements (some of which may disappear in newer versions, or be changed from requirements to desiderata) don't necessarily make Z39.1 a bad standard; they do, however, restrict its usefulness. The requirements can leave publishers in a quandary: since they can't or won't meet all the requirements for Z39.1, should they ignore it altogether or establish some form of partial compliance—and what does partial compliance mean?

Standards at the Wrong Level or at Mixed Levels

ANSI Z39.30 is an example not only of excessive detail, but also of mixed levels. The list of data elements is a valuable checklist. The standard form with its detailed placement of elements may well be valuable for typewritten orders. If these were separate standards, agencies producing computer-printed or machine-readable orders could follow the first while ignoring the second. Examination of standards will reveal many with mixed levels. Inappropriate levels represent another issue, one more difficult to judge. A national standard for the size and threads of lightbulb bases seems appropriate; one specifying all physical characteristics of a lightbulb seems inappropriate.

Standards arise at too high a level through the assumption that if some standardization is good, then more is better. Take, for example, the personal computer used to prepare this book. That computer uses many standards: ASCII, RS-232C, the QWERTY keyboard, a standard three-prong plug, and any number of materials, testing, and component standards. All those lower-level standards, and several de facto ones such as Industry Standard Architecture, helped a relatively new company (H.I.M.S. Technologies) to compete with much larger PC makers. So far, standards encourage competition. On the other hand, a high-level standard might specify *all* characteristics of a personal computer, creating an ANSI standard PC. If such a standard had existed in 1981, this computer would probably be considerably more expensive and considerably less powerful. The VGA color monitor, tower cabinet, 32-bit memory bus and 16-bit data bus, high-speed

16-bit run length limited hard disk controller, and 8-mHz bus speed would all violate the 1981 standard. An inappropriately high-level standard would slow innovation and discourage competition.

Standards with No Clear Scope of Application

Just as standards work best at a single level of specification, they should always have a defined scope and meet a defined need. Those for the title page of a technical report would be inappropriate for the title page of a novel. Z39.2 is appropriate for bibliographic records, but would be inappropriate for full-text storage or transmission.

Occasionally, standards lack clear scope definitions. A larger problem is their misuse beyond intended or appropriate scope. Well-drawn standards will frequently see use beyond original scope, and such extended use may be appropriate. The line between appropriate extension and inappropriate use is fuzzy. Use of a standard outside of scope represents overstandardization in a post facto sense: although the standard may have been drawn correctly, it is being used incorrectly.

Verification Expense and Difficulty

Standards that are too expensive to *verify* are poor. Users should be able to ascertain that producers have followed appropriate standards. If such verification is unreasonably difficult or costly, adherence won't be verified. In such a situation, no certainty exists that any particular producer is actually following a standard. An unscrupulous producer who recognizes that the standard won't be verified may gain an unfair economic advantage by taking shortcuts and falsely claiming adherence to standards while producing substandard goods.

Subjective Standards

Standards that involve subjective criteria are inherently flawed. If verification is only possible in the mind of the beholder, it should be called a guideline rather than a standard. Z39.6, *Trade Catalogs*, calls for body type 8 points or larger: an objective, easily verifiable standard. If it went on to state *as a requirement* that the type should be "attractive," it would be flawed. (If it specified Baskerville type, it would be far too specific, including a specification that has no relation to its function.)

Solutions to Trivial or Nonexistent Problems

Standards makers can err on the side of overly ambitious standards. Similarly, they may err in the other direction. A standard should solve some problem; if the problem is trivial, or does not exist, the standard is a waste of time and energy. Most developers provide safeguards to ensure that a proposed standard will meet a specific need sufficient to justify the cost of developing it. That need may prove to be less significant when the standard is being reviewed or revised, however.

Several Z39 and ISO standards seem to address trivial problems, or at least to address problems in ways that may not be useful. Z39.6 supposes that trade catalogs were being produced that didn't include sufficient information. Presumably, it also supposes that publishers would be aware of and follow the standard specification once it was created. Z39.13 must be based on the assumption that publishers don't know what information is necessary in advertisements, and that, lacking such knowledge, they are likely to order and follow an American National Standard.[5] Elements of ISO 8 (see Appendix A) appear to consider use of different typefaces for different articles in a periodical to be a problem; the nature of the problem is unclear. Most writers developing structured documents (with numbered divisions and subdivisions) probably don't consider it difficult to establish a scheme for such numbering, although maintaining the numbers may be difficult. But ISO TC 46 developers apparently found it worthwhile to develop a standard, ISO 2145.

The first question to ask when any new standards activity is proposed would appear to be, "What is the problem?" Standards should always be solutions, and should always be solutions to problems that deserve expenditures of time and energy. If one writer uses

---

5 Admittedly, the problem with both Z39.6 and Z39.13 may be awareness and acquisition, addressed later in this chapter, more than triviality. Smaller publishers might indeed be helped by both standards, but they are unlikely to be aware of the standards.

"1.A.iii.b" for a subdivision, where another writer uses "1.1.3.2" for the same level, that "problem" seems so minor as to be wholly innocuous; at worst, it scarcely justifies a multi-year, multinational effort to solve.

Defective Standards

Defective standards come about for several reasons, including some of those mentioned above. Some are poorly written and invite misinterpretation. Committees that create them may lack appropriate expertise. Some standards may be approved despite legitimate objections, and others fail to retain compatibility with earlier versions. They may be outdated. Finally, they may fail to consider privacy issues or other issues affecting individual rights.

Poorly Written and Ambiguous Standards

As a rule, standards are drawn up by interested parties with specialized experience. When no one on a committee has good English writing skills, the resulting standard may be poorly written. In extreme cases, poor writing may result in a defective standard, one that does not yield the intended results. Defective material, testing and safety standards can kill people. Preparing a clear standard requires a combination of skills: an editor without specialized skills may damage the standard while clarifying its text.

Those who work on consensus standards or guidelines may know the difficulty of achieving good finished text. Many feel that committee time should not be spent on matters they regard as simple editorial questions, which appear less important than "substantive matters." When people have spent weeks of time spread out over years of meetings, their reluctance to give attention to editorial questions is natural enough. This viewpoint, while common, is unfortunate and shortsighted. Clear text allows standards users to make the most of good substance. Standards makers understand the details of their standard better than a later reader will. If those details aren't set down in clear, effective language, the standards makers are weakening their efforts.

Language problems may also arise when standards are made less explicit in order to achieve consensus. If a standard becomes sufficiently ambiguous that each user can interpret it differently without apparently violating it, it will be useless and will not in fact standardize anything.

Insufficient Knowledge

Most standards develop from perceived needs, and they tend to be developed by the community that perceives a need. That community may not contain sufficient expertise to prepare a highly effective standard. ANSI standards boards attempt to coordinate the efforts of different accredited developers partly to address this concern. Good standards developers make special efforts to reach out for appropriate knowledge. Thus, Z39.48, *Permanent Paper for Printed Library Materials*, took advantage of standards developed by ASTM and the Technical Association of the Pulp and Paper Industry, and representatives of paper companies served on the developing committee.

Standards developed without sufficient expertise may not be bad, but they are unlikely to take advantage of the most current and complete information in special fields. Predictably, many are developed without help from the best experts in some fields, either because the specialists are not well known or because the developing group is unable to enlist their cooperation.

Consensus Problems

NISO makes a special effort to resolve every negative vote on a standard. ANSI rules do not require unanimous approval; standards developers can and do approve standards despite strong objections from members. Consensus implies more than simple majority, but falls short of unanimity. That distinction is necessary for any standardization effort to take place; otherwise, one determined agency could unfairly block all efforts to approve standards.

Consumer agencies claim that some standards organizations give little weight to consumer votes; whereas a negative vote from a single large manufacturer would doom a proposed standard, a negative vote from a consumer agency may be overridden. ANSI instituted the Consumer Interest Council to deal with this problem, but the question is still valid.

NISO includes many consumer members and has stiffer requirements for consensus than some other developers. Such requirements do not assure that legitimate objections will succeed, however. Politics plays a major role in NISO, as in all organizations; negative votes can be resolved by political means rather than by resolving the technical problems. When standards are approved through political consensus rather than technical consensus, they begin weakly, have less chance of success, and are less useful.

Compatibility

New versions should encompass prior versions, but such is not always the case. When a new standard deviates sharply from a previous version, good-faith agencies are left in the lurch. However, it is not always feasible or desirable to maintain full compatibility; if it were mandatory, standards could never take advantage of additional knowledge and new technology.

The best that can be hoped is that new versions will include some indication of the ways in which products prepared according to the previous version may now be nonstandard. To my knowledge, this has not always (or even usually) been done; rather, the user is expected to compare two standards and determine the differences.

Awareness and Acquisition

Technical standards don't do any good if people who need them don't know about them or can't afford to acquire them. More than four hundred agencies within the United States develop or have developed formal consensus technical standards; the most prolific private standards developer, ASTM, includes more than 9,400 in its 1991 publications.

The sheer number of standards, with many agencies using different numbering systems, serves as a barrier to awareness: you can't use a standard if you don't know it exists. Even if you do know that it exists, acquisition may pose a barrier. For example, the complete set of 1991 ASTM standards costs $3,900 if you're not a member of ASTM; at less than $0.45 per standard, that's not a bad price. Individual NISO standards cost anywhere from $10 to $49[6]; recently published ones typically cost $25 or more. That's not particularly unusual in the standards arena; many ANSI standards cost that much, or much more.

It costs money—a lot of it—to develop and publish standards, and it costs more to publicize them. Some developers rely on publication sales to help fund their other activities; in other cases, the standards may serve sufficiently small audiences that no large revenue flow can be anticipated. Smaller developers working in smaller areas have more trouble publicizing standards, which causes difficulty in making the standards more effective.

Summary

Most standards reflect explicit solutions to real problems, developed by people with sufficient knowledge and adopted through reaching legitimate consensus. They generally benefit society directly or indirectly, encourage competition and innovation, and maintain a reasonable balance between timeliness and stability.

This chapter covers some problems, and problems do occur in standardization as in all areas of human endeavor. ANSI, ISO, and other standardization agencies have established thoughtful procedures to defend against defective standards. Although those procedures help to make standardization slow and expensive, they are necessary. But they can never be perfect: there will always be defective standards, and they will always hurt the cause of standardization.

---

6   As of early 1991. Prices are likely to change without much notice, going either up or down.

7

The Standards Process

As we have seen, a standard can be anything from the practice of one person to the legally mandated practice of a nation or nations. When knowledgeable people in the United States refer to technical standards, they usually mean formal voluntary consensus standards established by an ANSI-accredited standards developer, ISO or IEC. An inaccurate shorthand for that phrase is "ANSI standards." This chapter reviews some of the history of formal consensus standards in the United States, and discusses the processes required by ANSI and those normally followed by other developers.

Historical Notes on Standards Organizations

Standards have been with us for thousands of years. The oldest standards organizations are but a few decades old. In the United States, the oldest one is the U.S. Pharmacopeial Convention, which established standard definitions for 219 drugs in 1820. One of the oldest organizations specifically devoted to testing and safety standards is Underwriters Laboratories, Inc. (UL), organized in 1894. The National Bureau of Standards (now the National Institute of Standards and Technology, NIST) began in 1901, marking the start of significant, continuing government interest in standards. The International Electrotechnical Commission (IEC) started in 1906, and substantive interest in technical standards for industry appears to date from that decade. In 1910 the newly formed Society of Automobile

95

Engineers (SAE) began vigorous development of standards, an effort that has continued to this day.

Key national and international organizations began to form later in the first quarter of this century. The American Society for Testing Materials (ASTM) and four engineering societies organized the American Engineering Standards Committee in 1918.[1] That committee became the American Standards Association (ASA) in 1928. In the mid-1960s, the ASA became the United States of America Standards Institute (USASI), and later the American National Standards Institute (ANSI).

The national standards body for the United Kingdom (BSI, the British Standards Institute) also began in 1918. Germany's national standards body (DIN, *Deutsches Institute für Normung*) began a year before ANSI, in 1917. In 1919 Belgium, Canada, Switzerland, and the Netherlands formed national standards bodies; by 1924 eight more countries had followed suit.[2]

Apart from the IEC, international standards organizations did not begin until the second quarter of the twentieth century. Fourteen countries worked together to create the first one outside a particular discipline: the International Federation of the National Standardizing Associations (ISA), founded in 1926 and largely abandoned because of World War II. The United Nations Standards Coordinating Committee (UNSCC) worked from 1943 to 1947, and led to creation of the International Organization for Standardization (ISO), which continues as the primary international standards organization. The IEC continued to work on electrical and electronics standards, and remains as an independent body; it is also considered the Electrical Division of ISO.[3] Recently, ISO and IEC formed Joint Technical Committee 1 (ISO/IEC JTC 1) to develop information technology standards. Although young, JTC 1 is an extremely active and important body.

---

1 David Hemenway, *Industrywide Voluntary Product Standards* (Cambridge, Mass: Ballinger, 1975), 81.

2 Lal C. Verman, *Standardization, A New Discipline* (Hamden, Conn.: Archon, 1973), 110.

3 Ibid, 151-152.

Standards bodies of greatest interest to libraries and automation are relative newcomers. American National Standards Committee Z39 originated in 1940, and became the National Information Standards Organization (NISO) in 1984; Part 2 of this book discusses NISO and its history in more detail. American National Standards Committee X3 (now Accredited Standards Committee X3) was not formed until 1961. ISO/TC 97, the ISO technical committee related to automation, was also formed in 1961.[4]

The developers and coordinating organizations listed above, as well as others in the field, carry out different functions in a variety of ways. All, however, work to build, recognize, or process *formal consensus standards*. Two key words make that phrase important: formal and consensus:

- **Formal:** The standard must take the form of a document, prepared according to the forms and rules of the standards body. These forms and rules help to ensure that the standard does not conflict with other standards, that it was properly developed, and that it can be properly identified for use

- **Consensus:** The standard must represent general agreement among interested parties. *General agreement* and *interested parties* are the two key terms; both are vague, with definitions varying from developer to developer.

Principles and Processes

Common principles for technical standards usually include the following:

- Standards should meet a recognized need.
- Standards should protect producer and consumer interests.
- Standards should reflect consensus of concerned parties.
- Standards should make economic sense now and for the immediate future.

---

4   R.D. Prigge et al, *The World of EDP Standards* (Blue Bell, Pa.: Sperry-Univac, 1978), 165 pp.

- Standards should reflect current technology but should also be practical.

- Standards should be studied periodically and revised or abandoned as required by changing times.

The best and most successful standards meet all these principles. Not all of them meet the full set, and organizations develop procedures to help ensure at least partial conformance.

Two Basic Procedures

ANSI recognizes two basic ways to establish consensus standards, the canvass and the project procedures:

- **Canvass procedure:** When an organization has existing or new standards that it wants to turn into American National Standards, it may elect a canvass (mail poll) of all organizations known to be concerned in the field. The proposing organization becomes the sponsor of the standard; the canvass list is reviewed by an ANSI Standards Management Board concerned with the field, and a six-month time limit is established for responses. When a canvass is taken, the sponsoring organization submits all the results to ANSI, including the list, comments received, and responses to negative comments. Approval is based on firm evidence of sound practice and of a clear consensus. ASTM and UL, among others, use the canvass method to establish many of their standards. It is potentially the fastest and least expensive, *if* the proposed standard achieves a clear consensus.

- **Project procedure:** This method is used by many developers to build a standard "from scratch." NISO and ASC X3 normally use it, and it typically requires at least three to five years (and sometimes much longer). The project procedure is described below more fully.

Project Proposal

Some person or agency asserts that a new standard is required in a particular area, or that an existing standard should be revised, amended, or withdrawn. Anyone can submit a project proposal to any standards developer, if they know where to send it. Companies, associations, governmental bodies, special conferences, and existing committees may all generate new project proposals. Sometimes, the most difficult part of proposing a project is determining what body should deal with it; some proposals result in the formation of entirely new standards developers or committees.

A proposal may be a single sentence, a study demonstrating need, or a fully developed draft standard being proposed for ratification.[5] It may even be a licensed standard that is now being proposed for adoption by an agency. A proposal may also arise because other work done within a standards agency demonstrates the need for a particular standard.

Initial Review

When a standards body receives a proposal it must determine what to do with it. Some possible results of that review are as follows:

- Existing standards cover the need; they are noted, and the proposal is returned.
- Work on the same area, or a closely related one, is currently taking place. The proposal may be forwarded to those doing the work.
- The proposal is inherently unsuitable for standardization; reasons for this finding are noted.
- The proposal has insufficient impact to justify the cost of standards development.
- Development in the area is not yet at a point calling for standards activity; the proposal is rejected as premature.
- The proposal is out of scope for the particular standards body; it may be returned with a suggested alternative destination or, sometimes, the standards body may forward it directly to another group.
- The proposal merits development.

In any case but the last, the process ends at this point, although any one of the last four outcomes may require a vote of the members of the standards organization. Initial review is a critical and difficult part of the work of a standards body. Some bodies are reluctant to decide that a proposed standard is simply not economically sound; as a result, working groups may be formed and spend considerable time and money without achieving any useful result.

---

5 In this case, as in the next, the canvass method could also be used.

Note that the outcomes above are all somewhat idealized. In practice, proposals may well fall through the cracks; the agency making the proposal may not learn its disposition for months or years, or may never hear what happened.

Approval

If initial review shows that the proposal merits development, the standards body should determine whether and when development should take place. Even meritorious proposals must sometimes be postponed for lack of resources; certain proposals have more immediate impact than others. Here again, a vote of the organization's members may be required.

Assignment

The proposal is sent to an existing subcommittee or working group, or a new subcommittee or working group is formed to deal with it. Some developers maintain standing committees to work on standards within a certain area; others, like NISO, typically establish new committees, by membership vote, for each new standard. Standards bodies generally rely on voluntary labor, and a good working group must include representatives with the proper skills and from the proper interest groups to handle the project well. Identifying these representatives and assembling a functioning group can be difficult. Attempts to establish working groups can demonstrate that a particular project is not economically justified, as interested parties are unwilling to participate in the development.

Development

A working group meets to consider the need, assess the state of affairs, determine the proper form of one or more standards, and prepare the draft standard(s). This process involves meetings, mail, telephone, and other methods of working singly and together to formulate sound standards. The process also involves review and feedback from a larger group of interested parties.

- Questionnaires may be used to gather information on current practice and felt need in the area

- Research may be required, occasionally involving grant proposals or other sources of special funding

- Comment drafts may be distributed at several points during development

- Minutes may be distributed or published

- Standards work in related areas, within the particular organization and (ideally) within other bodies, should be studied for areas of potential conflict, support, or overlap. In many cases, this requires that the standards committee contact and work with other agencies

- International developments in the particular area must be studied to determine whether the proposed standard will conflict with an existing or other proposed standard, whether it could reasonably be forwarded to international standards agencies after adoption, or whether it should be aligned with an international standard (or have an international standard adopted in its stead)

- Draft standards may go out for draft voting and comments, with specific deadlines and with a specific commitment to consider and respond to any comments. Several rounds of draft standard voting and comments may be required.

The development process will typically lead to one of three results.

- Abandoning the proposal and disbanding the working group. This can come about because further study shows standardization to be unwarranted, because the interested parties are unwilling to come to any sort of consensus, because the length of deliberations has exceeded the useful life of the standard, or because the working group is unable or unwilling to build workable standards for voting. (If the working group can't agree, it's fair to assume that voting members won't reach consensus.)

- Referring the proposal to one or more other working groups, after detailed study has determined that the proposal conflicts or overlaps with the work of such groups.

- Proposing one or more standards for final adoption.

Most of the time and money spent on technical standards goes to development; the process as described may involve years of meetings and several rounds of review by interested parties. Ideally, the resulting standards should represent clear thinking, careful economic and technical analysis, and a high degree of consensus before balloting.

Writing and Editing

Writing and editing, the process of achieving a proper document, can be one of the longest and most difficult parts of developing a standard. A well-written standard must meet several criteria:

- It must be clearly organized so that readers understand the overall significance of the standard, its intended scope of application, the specific requirements, and whether any material is background or advice rather than requirements.

- The language must be both precise and readable; precise, since a standard must be unambiguous to succeed, and readable so that it will be understood and used.

- Terms must be clearly defined, preferably when first used (defined in context) and in a glossary or data dictionary for easy reference.

- Supporting standards must be explicitly identified.

- The standard must satisfy voting members of the body to achieve adoption.

Voting and Public Review

At some point, a proposed standard should be satisfactory to the members of the working group. The group should also have solicited and received at least one round of feedback from interested parties in the larger standards body. The next two steps may coincide. One step is publicity on the widest feasible scale, so that any interested parties not represented on the immediate standards body may be heard from. For example, the ANSI publication *Standards Action* announces the balloting period for all standards intended for ANSI approval. The second step is formal voting within the standards body. Such voting involves specific deadlines and typically requires that comments accompany negative votes.

Consensus doesn't necessarily mean unanimity. ANSI states that "substantial agreement is more than a simple majority but not necessarily unanimity."[6] Any specific group will have its own standards for consensus, which may vary with the issue at hand. In some bodies, certain single agencies can prevent adoption of a standard with a single negative vote; in other cases, a standard may be adopted despite negative votes from parties with substantive concerns.

Good practice requires that the working group deal with all negative votes and with all comments received during public review. In many cases, negative votes and positive votes with comments lead to revision and reballoting. Sometimes (typically in cases where development work was faulty or rushed) votes and comments result in failure and the effort is abandoned.

Adoption

If the developer determines that a proposed standard has achieved consensus, it reports the standard as approved. In some cases and for some developers, this establishes the standard, which can then be published and promoted. For other cases and agencies, the developer must certify that approval to a coordinating agency, which goes through an additional review process and then certifies the standard as approved. ANSI works in this manner, although some ANSI-accredited agencies choose not to forward all of their standards to ANSI for review and approval: some EIA standards are not ANSI/EIA standards, for example.

The adopted standard must be published if it is to be of any use. Many developers publish their own standards; in some cases, income from such publications underwrites the activities of the organization. Other developers use third-party publishers or publish their standards through ANSI.

Publicity and Implementation

An approved standard is nothing more than words and figures on paper. Once it has been published, publicity encourages its implementation and raises the expectation that it is in use. Such expectation serves to mandate further implementation. An unused standard is a waste of time and money; useful standards should save enough time and money to justify the cost of development.

---

6 *Guide to Submitting Standards to ANSI for Approval* (New York: ANSI, 1984), 5 pp.

Periodic Review

Technical standards are not eternal. Standards bodies or national coordinating agencies establish time limits for most of them. After a certain period, they must be reconsidered, after which they may be abandoned, revised, or reaffirmed. Periodic review helps to keep them contemporary and useful, and to avoid a clutter of outmoded, pointless standards.

Periodic review often requires no more than a simple reaffirming vote: an initial review will show that the standard is widely used, contemporary, and should be retained in its existing form. A well-designed review process minimizes the costs of reaffirming such standards, leaving time and energy for those that require substantial revision. Standards may be eliminated or combined, although a working technical standard should never be abandoned prematurely. New technologies typically supplement and complement older ones; it may be many years or decades before an outmoded technology becomes wholly useless.

The ANSI Standards Process

ANSI is the primary national standards coordinating agency in the United States. With other standards developing and coordinating agencies, it follows processes like those above, with a few specific details noted below. ANSI does not itself develop standards, but reviews and approves those developed by other bodies. It will review and approve the ones that reach consensus through the canvass as well as those adopted by two kinds of developers: accredited organizations and standards committees.

Accredited Organizations

Any organization that develops standards may seek ANSI accreditation. ANSI will grant accreditation to organizations that use a procedure with safeguards equivalent to the procedures of Accredited Standards Committees; ANSI may conduct audits to ensure compliance. Once an organization is accredited, it develops and approves standards and transmits them to ANSI for approval as American National Standards. The transmittal form requires a summary of the final vote and certification of the following criteria:

- Due process requirements were met;
- The standard is within the fields registered (with ANSI) by the organization;
- Other known standards were examined for duplication of content;
- Significant conflicts with other standards were resolved;
- All appeals within the development process were completed;
- All known objections are documented as part of the transmittal;
- No substantive changes have been made since the standard was listed in the ANSI publication *Standards Action*.

NISO is an accredited standards organization, as are the IEEE, UL, ASTM, and more than a hundred other organizations. Such organizations may assign their own numbers, which will be retained by ANSI. Any given organization may have some standards that are not ANSI standards, as well as others that are. EIA is an accredited standards organization, and most of its standards are also ANSI standards; however, EIA RS-232C is not.

Standards Committees

Organizations that were formerly ANSCs have become independent, either as accredited standards organizations or Accredited Standards Committees (ASCs). ANSC Z39 became NISO, an accredited standards organization. ANSC X3 became ASC X3. Although for some (but not all) accredited standards organizations standardization is a secondary function (e.g., IEEE), ASCs almost always exist solely to develop standards.

An accredited standards committee includes a secretariat, with a set of duties defined by ANSI. The duties of a secretariat are to:

- Organize the standards committee in cooperation with and under the operating procedures of the authorizing organization;
- Submit the list of committee members to the authorizing organization for approval;

- Determine that the representatives on the committee participate actively, and that all those having a substantial concern with and competence in standards within the committee's scope have the opportunity to participate;

- Submit proposed revisions of the scope of the committee for standards management board approval, when recommended by the committee;

- Appoint the officers of the committee or arrange for their election by the committee;

- Propose programs of work, with proposed completion dates, and give direction and guidance to the committee;

- Assume responsibility for the administrative work, including secretarial services, arrangements for meetings, preparation and distribution of draft standards, letter ballots, minutes of meetings, etc.;

- Assume responsibility for processing letter ballots following the procedures of the organization;

- Report results of voting according to the procedures of the organization;

- Maintain standards within the scope of the standards committee in an up-to-date condition, and arrange for the publication and distribution of approved standards;

- Keep the appropriate standards management board informed of committee activities by sending copies of all material distributed to the committee;

- Submit status reports of the work in progress to the appropriate ANSI Standards Management Board, as required by established policy.[7]

Any standard must be submitted for written ballot with a six-week balloting period; typically, notice of the proposed standard appears in *Standards Action* simultaneously. All comments, whether from members of the committee or from other interested parties, must be responded to, and the subcommittee or working group must attempt to resolve objections.

---

7 Prigge, *The World of EDP Standards*, 10-11.

ANSI Review

ANSI reviews standards to see that the proper steps have been taken, and that consensus does appear to be present. It does not review standards for technical correctness or quality, and specifically does not interpret them. The organization does audit accredited standards organizations from time to time, but its own role is that of publisher, clearing house, and member of ISO for the United States; ANSI itself is not a standards-developing organization.

Mandatory Review Period

ANSI requires that every standard approved through its processes be reviewed after five years. That does not mean that no standard is more than five years old; it does, however, mean that after five years (following publication), a standards agency must consider the status of the standard and take one of three actions:

- Withdraw the standard;
- Reaffirm the standard;
- Revise the standard and go through the review and approval process again.

Reaffirmation and withdrawal typically require cycles for public review and voting; standards don't simply disappear any more than they instantaneously appear. Most issues of *Standards Action* include a mixture of reaffirmation, revision and new-standard comment periods; withdrawals are somewhat less common, but certainly not rare.

While the process of considering the standard continues, the existing version stays in force, but only for another five years. If, after 10 years, ANSI does not have clear evidence that action is being taken, it will unilaterally withdraw the standard (i.e., will list it in *Standards Action* as withdrawn).

Summary

Consensus standards require time and effort to ensure that they are properly prepared and that consensus has been achieved. Most standards organizations here and abroad have similar principles and similar processes. These organizations date from the beginning of the twentieth century; during that brief history, tens of thousands of standards have been drafted and adopted. The process, although apparently cumbersome, serves as a means of maintaining the quality of consensus technical standards.

ANSI standards are voluntary; they do not carry the force of law (although some are made part of other laws and regulations). Voluntary standards are preferable to mandatory ones, in that they can be ignored when they become obsolete or burdensome. Voluntary standards must be developed carefully and must serve economic needs and achieve consensus; otherwise, the years and dollars spent on them will result in useless paper.

8

A Few Standards Organizations

More than 270 private organizations in the United States actively create voluntary technical standards. Some, such as the Electronic Industries Association (EIA) and the Institute of Electrical and Electronic Engineers (IEEE), are trade or professional associations that develop standards as one of several programs. Others such as the National Information Standards Organization (NISO) exist solely to create and promote standards.

This chapter mentions a few of the many standards developers and coordinating organizations at the national and international level. NISO, the standards developer devoted to libraries, publishing and information science, is the focus of Part 2 of this book. Other standards developers, such as the Technical Association for the Pulp and Paper Industries (TAPPI) and the Association for Information and Image Management (AIIM), also indirectly affect library and publishing interests.

American National Standards Institute

ANSI has grown rapidly in the last two decades as the general clearinghouse for standards activity in the United States. It coordinates the development of national standards, provides an independent mechanism to approve and promulgate voluntary national standards, and represents the United States in nongovernmental international standardization organizations.

ANSI brings together 93% of the private standards developers within the United States. More than a thousand companies, governmental agencies, nonprofit organizations, and others belong to the institute, supporting its work. ANSI is the US member of the International Organization for Standardization (ISO) and the International Electrotechnical Commission (IEC), and is the secretariat for more than 240 ISO technical committees and subcommittees.

Two major aspects to ANSI's organization are the staff, and the officers and committees. The staff numbers more than a hundred, headed by a president, two vice presidents, and seven directors handling publications, government liaison, development, planning, operations, administrative services, and sales and services. The officers include a chair, three vice-chairs, and a board of directors with over 30 members, representing a variety of interests.

Five councils, four committees, and several boards carry out the work of ANSI:

- **Appeals Board:** Hears complaints of those who feel they have been injured by the actions of ANSI boards or councils.

- **Board of Standards Review (BSR):** Approves ANSI standards, verifying that an organization has followed due process and achieved consensus. BSR does not consider the technical content of any standard, only the process used to approve it. ANSI states, "Approval by ANSI informs the user that the standard may be applied with confidence because those directly affected have reached agreement on its provisions."[1] This presumes that "those directly affected" are actually members of the organization that developed the standard, a shaky presumption but the best available in a nation of voluntary standards.

- **Certification Committee:** Works on certification; that is, the process of establishing that an organization is qualified to develop American National Standards. Also advises the Board of Directors, which must make the final decision on certification.

---

1 American National Standards Institute, *Guide to Submitting Standards to ANSI for Approval* (New York: ANSI, 1983), 1.

- **Company Member Council:** Each company member of ANSI has one member. Large companies provide the bulk of ANSI's funding and naturally have substantial influence over ANSI's work.

- **Consumer Interest Council:** For many years, consumerists have complained that technical standards activities are dominated by corporations, which alone have the resources to support such activities. The Consumer Interest Council represents some effort by ANSI to address this complaint. Five persons considered to be experienced in the consumer field are joined by representatives from those ANSI members who choose to join the council.

- **Executive Committee:** As in most organizations with large boards of directors, ANSI's executive committee acts for the board between meetings.

- **Executive Standards Council:** Six representatives from associations, six company representatives, four government representatives, two consumer representatives, and three others constitute the Executive Standards Council, which assists and encourages organizations to develop needed standards.

- **Finance Committee:** Reviews ANSI finances and makes recommendations to the board.

- **International Standards Council:** Advises the board of directors on relations with ISO, IEC, and other international standards organizations.

- **Organizational Member Council:** Includes one member from each organizational member of ANSI (e.g., the American Library Association), and works with the Executive Standards Council to consider the need for new standards activity.

- **Standards Management Boards:** Take responsibility for a discipline or area, assisting the Executive Standards Council in coordinating standards development. For example, the Information Systems Standards Board is responsible for NISO and ASC X3 work.

- **U.S. National Committee of IEC:** With many subcommittees, oversees U.S. participation in the IEC.

Keeping Track of ANSI

ANSI publishes *Standards Action*, which appears every other week and lists every standard being proposed for adoption as an American

National Standard. Annual subscriptions are $100.00 for nonmembers. The subscription price includes the monthly newsletter, *ANSI Reporter*. Subscriptions may be requested from the American National Standards Institute at 1430 Broadway, New York, NY 10018; telephone (212) 642-4915.

The *Catalog of American National Standards*, issued once each year, lists all current American National Standards by category, giving the price for each; an index lists standards by number. The catalog is available from ANSI at the address above.

ANSI can supply not only the 8,500 American National Standards (as of mid-1990), 7,100 standards issued by ISO, and 2,800 issued by IEC, but also a rather staggering 245,000 standards issued by the 75 national standards organizations that currently belong to ISO.

Selected ANSI-Accredited Standards Developers

No point would be served in listing or describing all 200-odd ANSI-accredited standards developers. The brief notes that follow include some organizations responsible for the most standards and one (ASC X3) of particular importance to the future of automation, including library and publishing automation.[2]

Accredited Standards Committee X3
Information Processing Systems

Representatives of the Business Equipment Manufacturers Association (BEMA) and heads of some manufacturing companies met in 1960 and recommended formation of an organization to develop standards in the computing field. In September 1960 ANSC X3 was announced; its organizational meetings began in February 1961. BEMA, now the Computer Business Equipment Manufacturers Association (CBEMA) has been the secretariat throughout X3's existence.

---

2 Much of the information in this section is derived from Robert B. Toth, ed., *Standards Management: A Handbook for Profits* (New York: ANSI, 1990); and Carl F. Cargill, *Information Technology Standardization: Theory, Process, and Organization* (Bedford, Mass.: Digital Press, 1989).

X3 became an ASC in 1985. The committee is headed by a chair and vice chair, and includes four standing committees, five subcommittees and study groups, and more than 75 technical committees and task groups. The *International Advisory Committee* (IAC) coordinates the work of X3 with activities in ISO, IEC, ISO/IEC JTC 1 (for which X3 is the American Technical Advisory Group) and other bodies. The *Secretariat Management Committee* (SMC) provides general management for X3, and the *Strategic Planning Committee* (SPC, established in 1988) plans X3's future. The *Standards Planning and Requirements Committee* (SPARC) evaluates the need for new standards, audits standards development on functional and economic grounds, and checks standards for conformity to objectives. Individual technical committees and task groups develop and review specific technical standards.

As of 1989, X3 included 41 voting members, from producer, consumer, and general-interest organizations, with no segment allowed to dominate the membership. Each member pays a service fee of $3,000 to $5,000 per year. More than 2,500 volunteers participate in the more than 500 projects and responsibilities within X3.

X3 typically forms a new technical committee or subcommittee by issuing a press release inviting interested parties to participate, after the decision has been made to begin a new task. New groups form fairly frequently as needs arise.

As of this writing, X3 technical committees and working groups cluster into seven areas: X3A, recognition (e.g., optical or magnetic character recognition); X3B, media (e.g., disks, tapes, cards); X3H&J, languages; X3K, documentation; X3L, data representation; X3S, communications; X3T&V, systems technology.

American Society for Testing and Materials (ASTM)

ASTM, largely responsible for material specifications and testing procedures, publishes more standards than any other accredited voluntary standards developer within the United States, apparently, more than all ANSI-approved standards combined. ASTM maintains constant development and revision activity and acts as a major standards publisher; its free *Standards Catalog*

provides information on not only the master set of ASTM standards but many smaller publications.

The 1991 *Annual Book of ASTM Standards* consists of 68 volumes, available in hard copy or microfiche. The total set, $3,900 prepaid for a nonmember, includes 9,489 standards in a staggering 52,988 pages (including a 1,030-page index). Of that number, 1,500 to 2,000 standards will have been added or revised within the last year. The *Annual Book of ASTM Standards* is logically divided into sixteen sections and 65 subsections; for example, Section 11 (3,572 pages; 584 standards; $297) covers water and environmental technology. The smallest volume within that section, Volume 11.01, *Water (I)*, includes 84 standards in 594 pages and sells for $61 list. Standards in Section 11 include D 3558, *Tests for Cobalt in Water (by atomic absorption spectrophotometry)*, D4599, *Practice for Measuring the Concentration of Toxic Gases or Vapors Using Length-of-Stain Dosimeter*, and E849, *Practice for Safety and Health Requirements Relating to Occupational Exposure to Asbestos*. Other examples include Volume 01.07, *Shipbuilding* (within Section 1, Iron and Steel Products), which includes 109 standards in 854 pages; Volume 04.02, *Concrete and Aggregates*, which includes 186 standards in 842 pages (including 51 standards relating to aggregates!); and one of the smallest volumes, Volume 05.04, *Test Methods for Rating Motor, Diesel, and Aviation Fuels*, with 7 standards and 23 "annexes" in a 322-page volume.

The ASTM publishing program includes quite a few worthwhile volumes in addition to the *Book of Standards*. It also produces a relatively inexpensive four-volume set of *ASTM Standards in Building Codes* ($345, 1,300 standards); single-volume sets of industry-specific standards pulled from various volumes; some volumes that include not only ASTM standards but other specifications and classifications (e.g., *ASTM and Other Specifications and Classifications for Petroleum Products and Lubricants*); various measurement tables, reference photographs and other adjuncts to make standards more useful; special technical publications presenting original research, applications, and review papers related to ASTM's technical and scientific interests; several journals; and the *Compilation of ASTM Standard Definitions*, a dictionary of technical terms used in ASTM standards.

The only American organization that issues more standards than ASTM is the Department of Defense (with more than 37,000 standards); no other private organization comes close to ASTM in sheer production.

ASTM offers individual memberships at $50 per year, which includes their monthly publication, *Standardization News*; that publication is also available by subscription for $18 per year. ASTM can be reached at 1916 Race Street, Philadelphia, PA 19103-1187; (215) 299-5585; fax (215) 977-9697.

Society of Automotive Engineers (SAE)

SAE provided early leadership in developing effective standards within private industry in the United States. It is also prolific, with more than 5,000 standards to its credit; besides the many automotive-related ones (including the familiar automotive oil specifications), SAE is a major source of aerospace standards.

As an example of its activity, the two July 1990 issues of *ANSI Standards Action* include calls for comments on 65 different proposed SAE standards, including SAE AIR 1529A, *Flexure Testing of Hydraulic Tubing Joints and Fittings by Planar Resonant Vibration (Free-Free Beam)*; SAE J1194-MAY89, *Rollover Protective Structures (ROPS) for Wheeled Agricultural Tractors*; and SAE J1028-AUG89, *Mobile Crane Working Area Definitions*. The same issues note that 142 SAE standards were approved or reaffirmed in June 1990, including SAE J1916-MAY89, *Engine Water Pump Remanufacture Procedures and Acceptance Criteria*, and SAE J300-JUN89, *Engine Oil Viscosity Classification*.

SAE can be reached at 400 Commonwealth Drive, Warrendale, PA 15096.

Underwriters Laboratories (UL)

Like some other standards developers, UL not only develops standards (primarily safety standards), it evaluates and certifies products as meeting them. The UL seal is perhaps the most widely recognized certification seal in the United States; some people instinctively check for it on any electrical product as one way of ensuring that the item meets basic safety standards. UL has issued more than 740 standards.

UL develops standards in many categories. For example, listings in July 1990 issues of *American Standards Action* include calls for comments on ten different UL safety standards, including UL 891, *Standard for Safety for Dead-Front Switchboards*; UL 563, *Standard for Safety for Ice Makers*; UL 1441, *Safety Standard for Coated Electrical Sleeving*; UL 250, *Safety Standard for Household Refrigerators and Freezers*; and UL 1023, *Safety Standard for Household Burglar-Alarm System Units*. The same month included an announcement of final approval of one ANSI/UL standard and publication of five others, ranging from specialty transformers (ANSI/UL 506) to TV receivers and high-voltage video products (UL 1410).

Underwriters Laboratories, Inc. can be reached at 333 Pfingsten Road, Northbrook, IL 60062-2096.

International Organization for Standardization

The International Organization for Standardization (ISO) is the primary international agency for standardization in all fields except electrical and electronic engineering (the province of IEC), telephony and telegraphy (handled by CCITT), and information technology (ISO/IEC JTC 1). ISO is an active, complex organization involving agencies from 87 countries, working through more than 2,500 organizational units. Its units circulate some 10,000 working documents each year. More than 20,000 participants take part in ISO activities, and at least nine technical meetings will be in progress on a typical working day.

ISO's structure and requirements are much different from those of ANSI or most American standards organizations. ISO has two classes of membership: member bodies and correspondent members. A *member body* is "the national body most representative of standardization in its country."[3] No country may have more than one body

---

3 International Organization for Standardization, *ISO Memento 1990* (Geneva: ISO,

as a member of ISO, and no international organizations belong to ISO; as of January 1990, ISO had 73 member bodies. A *correspondent member* is an organization in a developing country that has yet to develop a national standards body. Correspondent members observe, but neither vote on nor participate in technical development; typically, such members change to member bodies after a few years. In January 1990, ISO had 14 correspondent members, from Bahrain, Barbados, Brunei Darussalam, Guinea, Hong Kong, Iceland, Jordan, Kuwait, Malawi, Mauritius, Oman, Senegal, United Arab Emirates, and Uruguay.

ANSI is a voluntary nongovernmental organization, and is an exception within ISO: 70% of ISO's member bodies are governmental or established by law. ANSI is one of the 25 founding members of ISO, which began to operate on February 23, 1947. The glossary includes entries for each ISO member body, including either the notation *charter member* or the year in which the member joined.

Administration

ISO has a president, vice president, treasurer, and secretary-general (chief executive officer). A council consisting of the president, vice president, treasurer and 18 elected member bodies maintains the technical structure of ISO and appoints members of administrative committees and chairs of technical committees. The administrative committees include:

- **Executive committee**, chaired by ISO's vice president, which acts for the Council between meetings;
- **Technical board**, which recommends forming new technical committees and dissolving old ones, monitors the technical work of ISO, and approves titles, scopes, and projects for technical committees;
- **Committee on Conformity Assessment** (CASCO), which studies ways to improve international acceptance of standards and possible use of ISO marks to certify standards conformance;

1990). ISBN 92-67-01059-X. Most information in this section not explicitly cited is taken from this publication.

- **Committee on Consumer Policy** (COPOLCO), which promotes consumer interests in standards;
- **Development Committee** (DEVCO), concerned with standardization needs in developing countries;
- **Committee on Information** (INFCO), which promotes information exchange and runs ISONET, the ISO Information Network;
- **Committee on Reference Materials** (REMCO), which establishes suitability of references for citation in standards;
- **Committee on Standardization Principles** (STACO), which provides a forum for discussion on fundamental aspects of standardization;
- **ISO/IEC Joint Technical Programming Committee**, which has the task of avoiding or eliminating possible or actual overlap in the technical work of ISO and IEC. Note that the most likely area of potential overlap, information technology, is now the province of ISO/IEC JTC 1, established in 1987.

Technical Committees

ISO establishes technical committees in areas as needed. Each one has a member body as secretariat, and establishes its own subcommittees and working groups to carry out its own work. Technical committees are numbered chronologically as created, beginning with TC 1 (screw threads), established in 1947. Recently established TCs, besides JTC 1, include the following (established between 1985 and 1989):

- TC 189, ceramic tile
- TC 190, soil quality
- TC 191, humane animal (mammal) traps
- TC 192, gas turbines
- TC 193, natural gas
- TC 194, biological evaluation of medical and dental materials and devices
- TC 195, building construction machinery and equipment (provisional)
- TC 196, ornamental rocks (provisional)

As of January 1990, 28 technical committees had been dissolved, leaving 168 committees, of which 8 have no new work items; thus, 160 committees have continuing standards development programs.

Technical committees vary widely in size, complexity, and activity. The simplest are the eight with no current program and no subcommittees, which exist only to review existing standards in their field: zinc and zinc alloys; lac; mica; oil burners; glass plant, pipeline and fittings; cleaning equipment for air and other gases; air distribution and diffusion; and gypsum, gypsum plasters and gypsum products. The most complex, such as TC 17 (steel), TC 20 (aircraft and space vehicles), and TC 61 (plastics), have 50 or more subcommittees and working groups. The most extensive set of subgroups is in TC 22 (road vehicles), with a total of over 100 subgroups. ISO/IEC JTC 1, with 94 subcommittees, is only slightly less complex.

ANSI is one of the four bodies, together with AFNOR (France), BSI (UK), and DIN (Germany), that provide the bulk of the secretariats for ISO technical committees, subcommittees, and working groups. Including ISO/IEC JTC 1 in the totals, these four hold 91 of the 169 TC secretariats and 1,602 of the 2,563 total leadership roles within technical committees (TCs), subcommittees (SCs), and working groups (WGs).

ANSI is the only source for ISO standards within the United States, and offers catalogs listing several thousand current ones.

ISO TC 46: Information and Documentation

ISO's TC 46 is the international counterpart to NISO, just as ASC X3 is the American counterpart to the recently formed ISO/IEC JTC 1. Some NISO standards (e.g., ISSN and ISBN) are based on earlier ISO standards, just as some ISO standards are based on earlier Z39 work.

DIN is the secretariat for TC 46; the scope of the TC is "standardization of practices relating to libraries, documentation and information centres, indexing and abstracting services, archives, information science and publishing." TC 46 was established in 1947; 57 countries either participate in its activities or observe. Subcommittees and working groups, with their secretariats, include the following as of January 1990:

• WG 2, Coding of country names and related entities (DIN)

- SC 2, Conversion of written languages (AFNOR)
  - SC 2/WG 1, Transliteration of Slavic-Cyrillic (AFNOR)
  - SC 2/WG 2, Transliteration of Arabic (AFNOR)
  - SC 2/WG 3, Transliteration of Hebrew (AFNOR)
  - SC 2/WG 4, Transliteration of Korean (AFNOR)
  - SC 2/WG 5, Transliteration of Greek (AFNOR)
  - SC 2/WG 6, Romanization of Chinese (AFNOR)
  - SC 2/WG 7, Romanization of Japanese (AFNOR)
  - SC 2/WG 8 (joint SC 2/SC 4 working group), Relations between transliteration and machine representations of characters
- SC 3, Terminology of information and documentation (DIN)
- SC 4, Computer applications in information and documentation (NISO, through ANSI)
  - SC 4/WG 1, Character sets (BSI)
  - SC 4/WG 4, Format structure for bibliographic information interchange in machine readable form (ANSI)
  - SC 4/WG 5, Commands for interactive search systems
  - SC 4/WG 6, Electronic publishing (DIN)
  - SC 4/WG 7, Data elements (SCC)
- SC 8, Statistics (BSI)
  - SC 8/WG 1, Criteria for price indexes for library materials (DS)
  - SC 8/WG 2, International library statistics (DIN)
  - SC 8/WG 3, Statistics on the production and distribution of books, newspapers, periodicals, and electronic publications (SABS)
- SC 9, Presentation, identification, and description of documents (SCC)
- SC 10, Physical keeping of documents (DS)
  - SC 10/WG 1 (joint TC 46/SC 10 TC 6/SC2 WG), Permanence of paper for documents (SIS)

NISO is the American Technical Advisory Group (TAG) for TC 46, and recognizes the increasingly international nature of standards in this area. One good way to keep up with TC 46 activities is through NISO and its *Information Standards Quarterly*, as noted in Chapter 11.

International Electrotechnical Commission

 The International Electrotechnical Commission (IEC) is much older than ISO, having been founded in 1906. It deals with electrical and electrotechnical matters, including measurement, testing, use, and safety. Many IEC standards are specification standards, listing the minimum acceptable features for conformance and ways to test for conformance.

Forty-two national standards bodies belong to IEC, which includes 80 separate technical committees and more than 200 standards groups. Each member nation belongs to every TC, unlike ISO, which has selective membership within TCs. IEC has issued more than 2,800 standards.

As examples of IEC's scope, consider the same July issues of *ANSI Standards Action* mentioned earlier in this chapter. Newly published IEC standards in July 1990 included IEC 603-7:1990, *Connectors for frequencies below 3 MHz for use with printed boards, Part 7: Detail specification for connectors, 8-way, including fixed and free connectors with common mating features*; IEC 34-9:1990, *Rotating electrical machines, Part 9: Noise limits*; and IEC 983:1990, *Road vehicle lamps for supplementary purposes*.

ISO/IEC JTC 1

This joint activity, which began in 1987, subsumed the work of ISO TC 97 (Information Processing Systems) and the related IEC groups IEC TC 47B and IEC TC 83, thus unifying international efforts in the field of information technology. ANSI serves as the secretariat; as of January 1990, 27 countries participated in JTC 1's work, and 20 more observed.

JTC 1 is extremely active at this point and will be for years to come. It includes the following subcommittees (SCs), with working group topics listed for each SC:

- **SC 1, vocabulary (AFNOR):** Fundamental terms and office systems; software; hardware, services, and operations; communication.

- **SC 2, character sets and information coding (AFNOR):** Code extension techniques; multiple-octet coded character set; 7- and 8-bit codes; control functions; coded representation of picture and audio information.

- **SC 6, telecommunications and information exchange between systems (ANSI):** OSI data link layer; OSI network layer; OSI physical layer; OSI transport layer; private integrated services networking.

- **SC 7, software development and system documentation (SCC):** Symbols, charts, and diagrams; software system documentation; software engineering and quality management; reference model for software development.

- **SC 11, flexible magnetic media for digital data interchange (ANSI):** Lower-level interface functional requirements and lower-level interfaces.

- **SC 14, representations of data elements (SIS):** Standardization guidelines for the representation of data elements; terminology; coordination of data element standardization.

- **SC 18, text and office systems (ANSI):** Document architecture; procedures for text interchange; content architectures; text description and processing languages; user/systems interfaces and symbols.

- **SC 21, information retrieval, transfer, and management for open systems interconnection (OSI) (ANSI):** OSI architecture; database; OSI management; specific application services; OSI session, presentation, and common application services; basic reference model of open distributed processing.

- **SC 22, languages (SCC):** Pascal; APL; Cobol; Fortran; Basic; Ada; binding techniques; Modula 2; C; POSIX; LISP; Prolog; Forms interface management system (FIMS).

- **SC 23, optical disk cartridges for information interchange (JISC):** Permanent editing committee; 90- and 130-mm rewritable ODCs; 300-mm WORM ODCs; 130-mm WORM ODCs.

- **SC 24, computer graphics (DIN):** Architecture; application programming interface; metafiles and device interface; language bindings; validation, testing, and registration.

- **SC 25, interconnection of information technology equipment (provisional) (DIN):** Home electronic systems; fiber optic connections for information technology equipment; customer premises cabling; inter-connection of computer systems and attached equipment.

- **SC 26, microprocessor systems (JISC):** Definitions of microprocessor instructions and their mnemonic representation, architecture, revision of publication 821, microprocessor systems quality assessment.
- **SC 27, security techniques (DIN):** Secret key algorithms and applications; public key cryptosystem and mode of use.
- **SC 28, office equipment (SNV).**

Other International and Multinational Organizations

Several other groups develop and coordinate standards internationally and among groups of nations. One of the best known is the International Telegraph and Telephone Consultative Committee (CCITT), a committee of the International Telecommunication Union (ITU). ITU is a formal treaty organization under United Nations auspices; CCITT creates recommendations that frequently have the weight of standards. Major multinational groups include CEN (European Committee for Standardization) and CENELEC (European Committee for Electrotechnical Standardization), which are developing standards to harmonize European interests as part of the European Economic Community (Common Market) and European Free Trade Association (EFTA).

Summary

Every library should be aware of technical standards. Most larger ones should maintain current awareness of ANSI and ISO standards and make sure that patrons can find needed standards and acquire them if needed. That doesn't mean purchasing every extant technical standard; except for libraries specializing in engineering and related disciplines, few can justify the expense or space needed for tens of thousands of standards.

ANSI's periodicals and catalogs, noted earlier in this chapter, provide a good starting point for ANSI standards; ASTM's $39 index to its more than 9,000 standards should be in many libraries. Information Handling Services maintains an online database of citations to more than 200,000 technical standards, available as File 92 on Dialog and STDS on BRS as well as directly; they can also provide copies of most standards. File 113 on Dialog provides another online index to U.S. government and industry standards, maintained by the National Standards Association, Inc.

These catalogs and indexes, and other published indexes, can provide good access to standards citations even in smaller libraries. A growing number of standards developers and publishers will accept telephone orders and charge cards, and even send copies of standards by telefacsimile if people have immediate need of actual standards.

One 1990 estimate is that more than 5,000 companies have active standardization programs. Corporate libraries should be directly involved in these, as a normal part of maintaining their role as information centers.

Very few libraries have the resources or need to be directly involved in standards development, except for such activities directly related to them and to publishing. Every library should be directly aware of the work of NISO, and some should be members; some librarians should be actively involved. Chapters 9 through 12 discuss NISO in detail; Chapter 11 discusses the ways that you and your library can be involved in its work.

PART 2

Standards for Libraries, Publishing, and Information Science: The National Information Standards Organization

So far, this book has treated technical standards in general, although some of the examples have been specific to libraries. The next four chapters deal with the ANSI-accredited developer that

develops standards specifically for libraries, publishing, and information science: the National Information Standards Organization (NISO).

NISO is not an association of huge corporations. Most of its members have relatively small budgets, and consumer (library) interests are far more strongly represented in this than in most other standards development organizations.

The organization has a long history under two names, although most of that history was relatively quiet. It has become much more energetic in the past few years, and its plans should ensure a healthy future. Chapter 9 discusses the history of the organization and, briefly, how it functions; Chapter 10 discusses current and future directions.

You should keep track of NISO's activities and consider the possibility of membership or other active involvement. Chapter 11 discusses possible levels of awareness and activity, including easy ways to stay informed.

Finally, Chapter 12 describes each current NISO standard and draft standard. The descriptions include the status of all new developments and all revision activity as of late February 1991, with some projections about likely future activity. Appendix A includes less detailed descriptions of some library-related standards from ISO.

9

NISO History and Operation

N ISO has grown from a small, barely active committee within the American Standards Association into an active, vital organization over the past half century. To understand where it is and where it is going, it helps to understand something of where it has been.[1]

The Early Decades: 1939–1969

In June 1939 the American Association of Law Libraries, Medical Library Association, and Special Library Association petitioned the American Standards Association to form a committee on library standards. ASA (a precursor to ANSI) was receiving papers from ISO's TC 46, the international committee on documentation standards; reviewers were needed. American Standards Association Sectional Committee Z39 began in March 1940 under the sponsorship of the American Library Association. Originally, the charge of Z39 included only "library work and documentation"; publishing was added later.

The first Z39 standard, Z39.1, *American Recommended Practice, Reference Data for Periodicals*, first appeared in 1935, before the committee began full operation. Z39 started slowly and remained relatively inactive for some years. The first organizational meeting took

---

1   Material in this section is taken from the Z39 and NISO publications noted in the text.

place in 1940; in 1943, Z39.1 appeared in revised form. The committee's activities were suspended from 1943 through 1948.

In 1951 the Council of National Library Associations took over the secretariat from ALA. Z39 continued on a small scale, with inadequate funding, producing only two standards over two decades (the second, Z39.4, *Basic Criteria for Indexes*, appeared in 1959).[2]

First Newsletter: 1957

The first Z39 news publication, *Z39 Newssheet*, appeared in Spring 1957. That four-page issue included reports from three subcommittees: one each on abbreviations for scientific periodicals titles, proof correction signs, and bibliographic citations and references. While there may have been other issues of *Z39 Newssheet* (which was prepared entirely in typescript), none seems to have survived.

News about Z39

The second Z39 publication, *News about Z39*, began in 1958 and lasted 20 years; it acquired an ISSN in 1972, but never had such trappings of a periodical as stated frequency, volume or issue numbers, or regular statement of availability. The first issue, two pages long, gave no indication whatsoever of any Z39 activity but did show the economics and standards activity of the time: a complete set of the 1,737 American Standards, a subscription to the *Magazine of Standards*, and a copy of ASA's book *National Standards in a Modern Economy* could be acquired by libraries for a total of $560.

The National Science Foundation began to provide funding for Z39's operations in 1959; further operational funding was received from the Council on Library Resources (CLR) beginning in 1961. In that year, the New York Public Library became the committee's host institution. The committee became a more vigorous proponent of national and international standards during the 1960s, taking a more active role both as the United States Technical Advisory Group (TAG)

---

2 Z39.2 did not appear until years later; there seems to be no historical record of Z39.3.

for ISO TC 46 (and helping to reinvigorate that organization) and in its own right.

For example, in 1962, four Z39 representatives attended the TC 46 meeting in Paris—a contrast to 1957-58, when Z39 was unable to send a representative to the Working Group on Bibliographic References in The Hague and could only hope that some Z39 member might be planning a trip abroad in 1958 at which time he or she could attend the TC 46 meeting in India, since Z39 could not provide funding. Four Z39 representatives also attended the Moscow TC46 meeting in 1967.

Thirteen Z39 subcommittees, including 10 working on standards, were active in 1963, with particular attention to abbreviations for periodical titles, abstracts, transliteration, and trade catalogs. The membership consisted of 31 groups. The third Z39 standard, Z39.5, *Periodical Title Abbreviations*, was approved that year.

In 1965 Jerrold Orne (University of North Carolina) became chair of Z39, a post he held until 1978, giving Z39 a stable home in Chapel Hill, still supported by grants from NSF and CLR. In April 1966 Z39 had 12 standards subcommittees (up from 10 in 1963) and was seeking funds for 2 more; however, much of its work was still review and comment on ISO TC 46 standards (and, in some cases, those of TC 37, terminology). Six standards were being revised or prepared during 1966; on the horizon was the work of SC/2 on machine input records (Henriette D. Avram, chair), which would later lead to what is probably Z39's most important standard of the first half-century, Z39.2. Only one new standard actually appeared that year: Z39.6, *Specifications for Trade Catalogs*.

The scope of Z39 was expanded to include "related publishing practices" in 1967. At the end of that year Z39 included 15 standards subcommittees, with 8 new or revised American standards being worked on, 4 of them carried over from 1966. During 1967 a subcommittee was made inactive when its work was complete, marking one instance of a shift toward task-oriented subcommittees within Z39, although the committees continued to exist (in name only) at that point. The only published standard for 1967 was a further revision of Z39.1.

While the quarterly subcommittee reports that made up nearly all of *News about Z39* seemed little changed in 1968, the pace was clearly quickening. At the end of the year, 18 standards subcommittees appeared (15 active). Their work included seven new draft standards, almost a doubling of direct standards development activity. New areas at the draft stage included proof correction symbols, machine input records, transliterations, library directories, book binding, book publishing statistics, and book advertising. Two standards appeared in 1968: a revision of Z39.4 and the new Z39.7, *Library Statistics.*

As the 1960s neared an end, Z39 activity continued to grow, albeit slowly, just as development of specific standards progressed slowly. Z39.2, *Bibliographic Information Interchange* (the MARC standard) was formally adopted in 1969 (but not published until 1970). The draft ISBN standard was being circulated, with SBN being promoted as a de facto standard; a draft ISSN also appeared that year. Near the end of the year, eight new subcommittees were organized—a strong indication of the growing activity of Z39 as it entered the 1970s. It was represented by six at the TC 46 meeting in Stockholm.

Still, the path toward published standards continued to be slow. Only one new standard was published in 1969 (Z39.8, *Compiling Book Publishing Statistics*), together with a revised Z39.5. At the end of the year, the total list of published standards consisted of six: Z39.1, Z39.4, Z39.5, Z39.6, Z39.7 and Z39.8, with two more (Z39.2 and a revised Z39.5) at the final approval stage.

Z39 in the 1970s

The groundwork laid in the late 1960s resulted in substantially greater results during the 1970s, including most of the standards most readily identified as major successes. Z39 membership grew to more than 50 agencies during the decade, and 19 new standards were created and approved.

Six new or revised standards were approved in 1971:

- Z39.2, *Bibliographic Information Interchange on Magnetic Tape*
- Z39.7, *Identification Number for Serial Publications* (ISSN)

- Z39.10, *Directories of Libraries and Information Centers*
- Z39.13, *Advertising of Books*
- Z39.14, *Writing Abstracts*
- Z39.15, *Title Leaves of a Book*

Three new standards were approved in 1972:

- Z39.11, *Romanization of Japanese*
- Z39.12, *Romanization of Arabic*
- Z39.16, *Preparation of Scientific Papers for Written or Oral Presentation*

One of 1971's standards involved some cross-agency controversy. ASTM, which had been assigning CODEN abbreviations to scientific and technical periodicals for some years, felt that the CODEN would be an appropriate standard identifier for all serial publications. When Z39 rejected that idea and approved the SSN (which became the ISSN), ASTM appealed to the ANSI Board of Standards Review. The appeal was rejected. Since then, and particularly with the 1978 requirement of the U.S. Postal Service that all periodical publishers in the country include the ISSN if they wished to use second-class postage, the ISSN has been an enormous success, covering a far broader range of publications than CODEN ever did.

Events of the early 1970s also show that creation of a Z39 standards committee by no means guaranteed that a standard would emerge. One of the new subcommittees created in late 1969 was SC/28, *Guides for Referees of Journal Articles*. The committee chair resigned in mid-1970; the committee, which apparently had never met, was never heard from again. Similarly, a proposed *USA Standard for Minimum Performance for Binding Used in Libraries* reached draft stage in 1968, but the effort was suspended before the end of that decade; a new, preservation-related, binding standard may emerge in the 1990s. At one point in the mid-1960s the subcommittee on terminology (which had been reviewing ISO TC 39 proposals) considered a possible "American standard for dictionaries"; this too sank without a trace, as did the subcommittee on classification.

Work on a proposed music industry code began in 1971 with a committee including a number of recording companies and related agencies. The committee was never able to resolve the differing claims of its members, and the recording industry lost interest in the proposal. As with the proposed Standard Computer Software Number (SCSN) of the 1980s (although for different reasons), the effort did not result in a standard. Work has continued off and on at the ISO level, and may yet result in an International Standard Music Number (ISMN?) similar to an ISBN.

Although only one new Z39 standard appeared in 1973, it was enormously important: the Standard Book Number (SBN), which formed the basis for the International Standard Book Number (ISBN). Not that Z39 wasn't busy; quarterly reports showed activity within at least 19 standards subcommittees each quarter, with 22 active in one quarter.

In addition to three revised Z39 standards, two new standards appeared in 1974: Z39.22, *Proof Corrections* and Z39.23, *Standard Technical Report Number*.

The July 1974 *News about Z39* sheds light on one of the mysterious "missing numbers" in the Z39 list. Z39 had agreed to forward the IEEE *Recommended Practice for Units in Published Scientific and Technical Work* as Z39.17. The ANSI Board of Standards Review noted that IEEE and ASTM were working to develop an *American National Standard Metric Practice Guide* that would incorporate the material in Z39.17; as a result, they did not accept the standard.

Halfway through the decade, Z39 reached a policy decision that has served it well: standards committees should be task oriented and should be "discharged with sincere thanks" when their work was complete. Z39 has always been a small operation; maintaining a large number of standing topical subcommittees does not appear to be good practice for this sort of organization. With the decision to discharge on completion, 14 subcommittees disappeared. ANSI listed 20 Z39 standards available for purchase in 1975—more than three times the number available five years previously.

The long road toward serial holdings standards began in 1975, when Z39 SC/40 began its work. An even decade was required to complete the effort (although a summary holdings standard did appear in 1980). That is perhaps twice as long as the average course of standards development, but it is certainly not a record; work toward a standard identification code for articles within a serial began in the early 1970s and has continued off and on to this date.

Work toward the Common Command Language began no later than 1980, thus requiring more than a decade to reach completion.

Two new standards did appear in 1975: Z39.25, *Romanization of Hebrew* and Z39.26, *Advertising of Micropublications*. Three more appeared in 1976: Z39.24, *System for the Romanization of Slavic Cyrillic Characters*; Z39.27, *Structure for the Identification of Countries of the World for Information Interchange*; and Z39.31, *Format for Scientific and Technical Translations*.

What happened to the intervening numbers? They took longer. Z39.29, *Bibliographic References*—one of the most exhaustively developed and least widely used Z39 standards—finally appeared in 1977. Z39.30, *Order Form for Single Titles of Library Materials*, required another six years, appearing in 1982. Z39.28 (possibly the original American National Standard for the Code Identification of Serial Articles?) never appeared; since *News about Z39* did not identify draft standards by number, its fate is mysterious.

In late 1976, *News about Z39* added "The Chairman's Page," providing a human touch to leaven the quarterly committee reports that, together with ISO reports, made up nearly all of its contents to that date. The first letter from Jerrold Orne clarified just how lean Z39 really was: in the mid-1970s the total operating budget came to less than $30,000 per year. Almost two-thirds of that paid for travel and subsistence during standards development committees; the rest paid for a half-time assistant at the University of North Carolina and some overhead costs.

Renewing the Organization

Existing grant funds were running out in the late 1970s. The National Commission on Libraries and Information Science (NCLIS) appointed a task force in 1977 to review Z39 activities and recommend future directions. In 1978 Z39 gained an executive council, elected officers and its first executive director, Robert Frase. Z39 was invited to relocate to the National Bureau of Standards (NBS) in Gaithersburg, Maryland, where it has stayed to this day (NBS has since become the National Institute for Standards and Technology, NIST).

Meanwhile, 1977 saw three new standards in addition to one revision (Z39.8) and two reaffirmations (Z39.6 and Z39.10): Z39.29,

Bibliographic References; Z39.33, *Development of Identification Codes for Use by the Bibliographic Community*; and Z39.34, *Synoptics*. No new standards appeared in 1978; the three that appeared in 1977 have been either useless or (largely) unused, representing a weak period in Z39's history.

The Z39 membership ratified a new set of bylaws in 1979, and *News about Z39* was replaced with the *Voice of Z39* that same year. A realistic budget was prepared, showing that $128,300 (including $25,000 contribution-in-kind from NBS) would be necessary to run Z39. CLR and NSF came through for one year of transitional funding, but as the new decade began, Z39 finally had to obtain funding from its membership.

Five new standards appeared in 1979: Z39.35, *System for the Romanization of Lao, Khmer and Pali*; Z39.37, *System for the Romanization of Armenian*; *Compiling Newspaper and Periodical Publishing Statistics*; Z39.40, *Compiling U.S. Microform Publishing Statistics*; and Z39.41, *Book Spine Formats*. At the end of the decade, 34 Z39 standards could be purchased; 28 of them had been developed within the decade.

The Final Years of Z39: 1980-1983

With its new home, new elective structure and somewhat uncertain funding, Z39 began the 1980s with strong committee activity. Two new standards appeared that year, in addition to the revised Z39.21 (now ISBN, formerly SBN): Z39.42, *Serial Holdings Statements at the Summary Level* (later subsumed into Z39.44) and Z39.43, *Identification Code for the Book Industry* (SAN).

Twenty-two standards committees reported activity during the year, which ended with approval of mandatory service fees for Z39 members to provide continuing funding. Not that all of the committees yielded approved standards. For example, Subcommittee F, serial publication patterns, never yielded a standard; Subcommittee G, terms and symbols used in form functional areas of interactive retrieval systems, apparently worked toward what has since become Z39.58, Common Command Language; Subcommittee M, serial publication page margins (an unusually narrow charge), was folded into

Subcommittee Q, formed to revise Z39.1 (a process that appears to have taken an entire decade).

The first conservation-related standards committees began work in 1981: subcommittee R, environmental conditions for storage of paper based library holdings, and Subcommittee S, paper quality for library books. The latter produced Z39.48, *Permanence of Paper for Printed Library Materials*, published in 1984. Only one new standard appeared in 1981: Z39.32, *Information on Microfiche Headings*; two standards were revised. Z39 standards gained an ISSN (0276-0762) in that year, as a recognized monographic series.

Publications and conference programs relating to Z39's work increased during the early 1980s. TESLA, the Technical Standards for Library Automation Committee of ALA's Library and Information Technology Association (LITA), gave successful programs on technical standards at least once every two years during ALA's annual conferences; the Fall 1982 issue of *Library Trends* was entirely devoted to technical standards within Z39's scope; the *LITA Newsletter*, which began publication at the beginning of the decade, included a column "Standard Fare" (devoted to TESLA and technical standards topics) in every issue. Articles on Z39 and related activities also appeared in the *ALA Annual* and *Bowker Annual*, and in some issues of the *RTSD Newsletter*; other divisions of ALA also gave or cosponsored Z39-related programs during the early 1980s.

During 1982, Z39 became a nonprofit corporation and issued one new standard, Z39.30, *Order Form for Single Titles of Library Materials*. (Two standards were reaffirmed.)

Patricia Harris began work as the second Z39 executive director; she continues to the present as NISO's executive director. She brought a strong library background to the position; her personality, energy, talents, and organizational skills have provided continuity for Z39 and NISO and play a major role in NISO's growing success and importance.

The last year of Z39 was an active one. Four standards were revised and approved in 1983; three were reaffirmed; and two new ones appeared: Z39.45, *Claims for Missing Issues of Serials* and Z39.46, *Identification of Bibliographic Data on and Relating to Patent Documents*. Forty-five voting members contributed to the work and funding of

Z39 in 1983; while this was slightly fewer than in the days when membership was free, it was a good sign that the organization could succeed. At the end of the year 40 Z39 standards were available.

NISO

NISO began in 1984, the year in which Subcommittee G formally started work on the Common Command Language and the work of Z85 (which had only produced one standard, Z85.1) was formally incorporated into NISO's charge. Twenty-four standards subcommittees worked during that year; in addition to three revised standards, two significant new standards appeared: Z39.47, *Extended Latin Alphabet Coded Character Set for Bibliographic Use* and Z39.48, *Permanence of Paper for Printed Library Materials*.

The latter represents NISO's first use of a certification symbol as shown here, a trademark to be used with the statement, "The paper used in this publication meets the minimum requirements of American National Standard for Information Sciences—Permanence of Paper for Printed Library Materials, ANSI Z39.48-1984." That information appears on the verso of the title page in a growing number of books each year; it is now quite common among publishers that respect library business. The problem of disintegrating library resources requires many solutions; NISO took the lead to establish a recognizable, verifiable identification for materials that can be expected to last.

By April 1985 NISO had 55 voting members, more than had been in Z39 before fees were charged; that number has continued to grow.

NISO began work on CDROM standards in 1985; it also held a national futures conference to consider future directions and approved two new standards: Z39.44, *Serial Holdings Statements* and Z39.49, *Computerized Book Ordering*.

Several years of work toward a Standard Computer Software Number (SCSN) ended in 1985. According to the *Voice of Z39*, "After evaluating [comments from over one hundred organizations], SC-BB concluded that there was no consensus in support of the draft standard or its approach or indeed, any single approach to software identification." According to other accounts, strong personal and political actions were taken by agencies supporting the use of ISBN for computer software, to ensure that no competing standard would be adopted. The standard was abandoned; some computer software does carry ISBNs, although certainly not all major packages.[3]

The NISO archives were founded in 1986 in the library of the University of Maryland at College Park, making a half-century of Z39 and NISO records available for researchers. The first edition of this book also appeared in 1986, and the *Voice of Z39* moved to desktop publication, resulting in a more legible and attractive (if infrequently published) newsletter.

Three new standards were approved in 1987: Z39.52, *Standard Order Form for Multiple Titles of Library Materials*; Z39.53, *Codes for the Representation of Languages for Information Interchange for Library Applications*; and Z39.61, *Recording, Use, and Display of Patent Application Data in Printed and Computer-Readable Publications and Services.*.

The effort to define a standard bibliographic data source file identifier was abandoned, as was the attempt to define generalized principles for developing romanization schemes. In the latter case, the committee agreed after much effort that it was impossible to develop a general scheme for machine-executable reversible romanization.

NISO began to publish its own standards in 1988 through Transaction Publishers. The first ones to appear under the new imprint were Z39.61 (approved in 1987) and Z39.50, *Information Retrieval Protocol*; both were published in 1989. Z39.50 is the first NISO standard within the ISO Open Systems Interconnection (OSI) model, and is a key for the future of linked systems within the library field.

Two other significant standards were approved in 1988: Z39.64, *Character Set for Chinese, Japanese and Korean* and Z39.59, *Electronic Manuscript Preparation and Markup*. ANSI/NISO Z39.64 represents the NISO version of the character set developed by The Research Librar-

---

3 A quick check of my own PC environment shows three programs with ISBNs on the box or documentation, out of 15 or 20 programs.

ies Group, Inc., and formerly known as REACC (RLIN East Asian Character Code); it will be published in 1991, with the thousands of characters provided on microfiche. ANSI Z39.59 is an implementation of the Standard Generalized Markup Language, a system for encoding elements of manuscripts in electronic form. As of this writing, it is not available from NISO; its use is encouraged by EPSIG, the Electronic Publishing Special Interest Group, operated by OCLC on behalf of the American Association of Publishers.

Information Standards Quarterly

The end of 1988 was also the end of *Voice of Z39*, a free publication that had changed from appearing quarterly, to three times a year, to infrequently. Beginning in January 1989, a new publication appeared: *Information Standards Quarterly* (*ISQ*), which has an assured publication schedule and a relatively open scope. Unlike the *Voice*, it is available on paid subscription; also unlike the *Voice*, it carries a variety of articles and opinion pieces in addition to standards activity and information.

It's difficult for me to offer an objective opinion of *ISQ*. A number of long-time colleagues, including the NISO chair Mary Ellen Jacob and the vice chair/chair-elect Paul Evan Peters, convinced me to volunteer to edit "a new publication." Personally, as the founding editor, I think it's well worth the $40 subscription price and with considerable potential to become part journal, part newsletter, all in the area of library-related technical standards.

Patricia Harris has as much to do with making *ISQ* work as I do, if not more. She provides a great deal of the information; goads other contributors when necessary; oversees the actual production; and makes sure that I don't become too complacent. She also made sure that, by the end of the first year, the publication looked as good as the original pages—not always an easy task for desktop-published material.

The combination—Pat Harris's work in Washington, contributors from throughout the NISO community, and my editing and production in Mountain View—works. The first issue was 12 pages, fairly typical for *Voice of Z39*, but with quite a bit more copy (since only the last few issues of the *Voice* used proportional type). No issue since the first has had fewer than 16 pages, ranging up to 32 pages.

Beginning the Sixth Decade: 1989-1990

NISO began Z39's fiftieth year in style, by hosting the twenty-third plenary meeting of ISO's Technical Committee (TC) 46 in May 1989, the first time that TC 46 had ever met in the United States. Standard Z39.63, *Interlibrary Loan Data Elements*, was approved, as was Z39.57, *Non-Serials Holdings Statements*. The NISO standard for CDROM volume and file structure was approved. Since an equivalent (and essentially identical) ISO standard 9660 was also approved, however, NISO moved to adopt the ISO standard rather than adding a second number. The process added an interorganizational quirk: because of the way that the ISO standard was adopted, United States responsibility for it appeared to fall to ASC X3 rather than NISO. Paul Peters, then vice chair of NISO and LITA representative to X3, convinced X3 that NISO was better equipped to deal with CDROM standards; for one thing, more of NISO's members were and are producing the discs.

In September 1989 NISO held a celebratory annual meeting during which many of the key figures in Z39 discussed its history. The event was candid, interesting, and surprisingly revealing.

At the end of 1989, 17 standards were being revised; 14 committees were working on new ones. Fifty standards were either published or ready to be published, with 2 more approved but not yet available from NISO: an increase of 16 from a decade before, and more than eight times as many as two decades before.

NISO enters the 1990s with a large and growing membership, extensive standards activity and involvement in the international scene, and a clear set of directions for future activity. Chapter 10 deals with NISO's plans for the future; with the continued support of library and publishing organizations, it will continue to grow. Such growth is not assured, however; if the organization is taken for granted, it will be in serious trouble.

The Organization of NISO

NISO is headed by a chair, vice chair, and a board of directors including three directors each from the library, publishing, and information science communities. Officers serve two-year terms; directors serve three-year terms. The operations are headed by an executive director, currently Patricia Harris, and are based at NIST. Within ANSI, NISO reports to the Information Systems Standards Board (ISSB).

Standing committees of NISO work on finance, future planning, international relations, membership, standards development, and publicity. Standards committees, which develop and review NISO standards, are organized as needed based on membership votes. Typically, some 24 such committees will be active at any time; they are dissolved by the NISO president on completion of their task or if they are unable to move forward. These committees cover a range of topics, and have chairs from a range of agencies; Chapter 10 includes some notes on current NISO activity.

The standards committees depend entirely on voluntary effort. Chairpersons usually recruit members to reflect the necessary set of skills. Members must be willing to devote substantive effort over several years, including some travel. Active members of NISO contribute far more than the $1,000 to $4,500 required for voting membership; an agency may well devote over $10,000 per year to travel expenses and employee time required for standards committee work. (In some cases, NISO provides travel expenses.)

Voting NISO members contribute money and time to the standards effort. Committee members come primarily from organizations with voting membership, and each voting member should be committed to serious review of every proposal, although the extent to which members have taken this responsibility varies from member to member and year to year. A list of current voting members appears as part of Chapter 11.

NISO Procedures

NISO follows the normal process for an accredited standards organization. The elected board of directors coordinates its activities. Any voting member or other interested party may recommend a needed standard, and NISO provides a form to encourage such recommendations.

The Standards Development Committee (SDC) evaluates recommendations and forwards appropriate ones to the board of directors. If the board finds a recommendation worthwhile, it recommends formation of a new standards committee; the voting membership must approve any such formation. The chair of NISO appoints committee chairs; the committee chair recommends members for the committee, who are then appointed by the NISO chair. A standards committee generally has from 6 to 15 members, and takes about six months to form.

As a rule, a standards committee prepares a draft standard within roughly two years after its formation. The executive director sends the draft to NISO voting members for comment, a three-month process. A proposed standard will follow for formal written ballot, typically 12 to 18 months after the first comment round. The executive director mails the draft standard and sends out reminders to voting members who fail to return ballots within three months. When a draft goes out for vote, it is also registered with ANSI (and notice of the ballot period appears in *ANSI Standards Action*). Comments and negative votes are returned to the committee chair, who attempts to resolve them, usually another six-month process. If necessary, a revised draft is reballoted; standards with unresolved negative votes are always reballoted at least once.

ANSI policies require that any proposed standard receiving at least two-thirds affirmation from all voting members be submitted to the ANSI Board of Standards Review. NISO has always attempted to resolve all negative votes, although some standards have been sent forward with outstanding negative votes. The BSR review step takes three months. Thus, if all goes well, it will take four to eight years to develop and approve a new standard after the initial vote to form a standards committee. If there are problems, it can take far longer. As noted in Chapter 10, NISO's SDC is investigating a "fast track" process in order to reduce this delay when possible.

The same process is followed for revisions of existing standards. Some existing standards appear sound as written; the board of directors may recommend a direct reaffirmation balloting in such cases, avoiding the time and expense of organizing a standards committee.

Summary

Z39 followed three decades of intermittent activity with 15 years of substantial activity, transforming itself into NISO in 1975. NISO has grown in activity and membership but is still a small organization facing large demands. Several publications have informed Z39 and NISO members and friends of its progress through the years; *Information Standards Quarterly* now provides a regular forum for progress, ideas, and opinions in the field of information standards.

The NISO procedures help to ensure thorough review and consensus, but make standards development a slow process. NISO is planning its future; the next chapter considers those plans.

10

The Future of NISO

Strategic planning for NISO's future began formally with a conference in 1988 specifically addressing the topic. One portion of the resulting document recommended that NISO should "Strengthen the standards-making process:

- "Tighten program with closer monitoring of program and committee objectives and plan to ensure committees are productive.

- "Consider within three years hiring a full time staff person to coordinate/solicit/submit and work more closely with committee chairs.

- "Continue to seek, as appropriate, grants or other funds to support participation on standards committees."[1]

These strategies would support the first two objectives: to create and maintain standards as defined in the mission statement and to improve the standards making process. It all comes back to the mission statement:

NISO creates and maintains all needed standards for library and information science, publishing, printing and book selling practices, and for library related equipment. NISO participates in the development and review of relevant international standards.[2]

---

1 NISO Strategies document as cited in *NISO Technical Plan*, 26 November 26 1990, 1.

2 Ibid.

During 1990 the Standards Development Committee prepared a *NISO Technical Plan* to carry out these strategies and objectives. The plan outlines the direction NISO should take in its technical program during 1991-1993. As with any such document, it will be refined, and it is fair to assume that it will not cover all standardization activities. Nonetheless, it provides a carefully reasoned, well-organized perspective on NISO's future activities.

Most of this chapter comes from the *NISO Technical Plan* plan in its November 26, 1990, version, and is included with NISO's permission. All quoted material and all material in smaller type comes from the *Technical Plan* (except for [bracketed inclusions]). My comments and paraphrases appear in *italics*. Most of the plan is included here, since it draws such an explicit picture of how NISO can become more effective.

My particular thanks to the members of that committee: Kathleen Bales (chair), the Research Libraries Group, Inc.; Lorrin Garson, American Chemical Society; Clifford Lynch, University of California; Sally McCallum, Library of Congress; James Michael, Data Research, Inc.; Jessica Milstead, the JELEM Co.; Carolyn Clark Morrow, Harvard University Library; Howard White, American Library Association; Paul Evan Peters, Coalition for Networked Information (ex officio); Patricia Harris, NISO (ex officio).

As stated in the *Technical Plan*:

This Technical Plan addresses the objectives by laying out the specific standards activities that reflect the interests of NISO constituencies and by planning actions that will improve the standards process. These actions will enable NISO to better: determine standards needs; promote an interest in standards; develop standards; promote their use. The section for each area of standards activity contains a discussion of current status, the relationship of NISO activities to standards activities of other groups, and additional needed activities. Both short- and long-term objectives are included.

NISO Constituencies

NISO serves three general constituencies: libraries, publishers, and information services. These constituencies reflect not only institutions, but also individuals within the constituency.

Library Constituency

The library constituency of NISO is a diverse group of organizations serving information needs. At the core of this group are libraries holding collections of materials that they either lend or allow access to. These libraries serve very different clienteles: children; the general public; specialized researchers such as engineers, lawyers, or medical personnel; the academic community; general researchers. The materials they collect may be one of the many formats by which information is communicated: books, serials, other language material, maps, sheet music, computer files, recordings, moving images, two-dimensional graphic images, etc.

The library constituency needs standards that will control the media for the material they acquire (order, reply, invoicing, advertising), the processing of items into an accessible collection (format, communications protocols), and storage and preservation of items. Libraries need standards for citing items, standards that assist in the reference function (retrieval language, references), and standards for lending items to information users. Libraries especially need standards to assist the process of automating all of the above functions. As libraries make the transition to networks and the electronic world, standards become increasingly vital. NISO must take a more aggressive role in providing information to these consumers of information about standards and how the standards relate to the products and services that libraries buy.

Other types of organizations in the library constituency provide primary support services to libraries. These include automated system vendors, bibliographic and information networks, book binding firms, and shelving and library furniture manufacturers. The standards for the library functions listed above are also used by these organizations in serving libraries.

Libraries are also supported by a number of organizations, such as computer manufacturers, for which libraries are not a primary customer but rather one of many customer groups. Some library-specific standards are needed when those organizations serve the library community, although more general standards may apply in most cases and should be a compatible superset of library standards.

Publishing Constituency

The publishing constituency is also a diverse group of organizations. Publishers span the spectrum from traditional print-on-paper and audio tape publishing to a wide variety of online and other electronic publishing services. Publishers generally specialize in a certain market (such as children, elementary or high school, college, general, professional) and provide one or two kind of products (books, newspapers, magazines, journals, newsletters, online databases, etc.). However, some publishers, especially large publishing conglomerates, publish many different products for several or even all markets.

The information revolution makes it imperative to broaden representation within NISO beyond traditional commercial, nonprofit, and in-house publishers to include services and suppliers. These related areas of service must include such diverse groups as typographers, printers, book binders, and publishing software manufacturers. It must include users of information not necessarily considered part of the library constituency, such as researchers, booksellers, wholesalers, and subscription agents. And it must include the originators of information, because increasingly they are creating electronically. "Desktop publishing," with its powerful yet relatively inexpensive hardware and software, along with vast computer networks which link the entire globe in new and complex ways, has an important effect and must be included in the NISO constituencies.

Many publishers use standards effectively across all phases of their operations. Standards have been almost universally incorporated in the order fulfillment, indexing and cataloging areas where the NISO constituencies overlap. Even in such internal tasks as author-editor interaction, or production interactions between typesetters, designers, and illustrators, standards are used to aid the efficient flow of information. As publishers become even more involved in creating and/or using electronic media and very large databases, standards will play an additional role in their day-to-day activities.

Information Services Constituency

Information services constituents are institutions, agencies, and vendors involved in various aspects of library automation. These groups include organizations (often referred to as "library vendors") providing hardware or software for library systems as well as those involved in supplying other products or services to libraries. Examples of the latter organizations are: bibliographic utilities, book jobbers, abstracting and indexing services, subscription agencies, database providers, authority control utilities, networks, and the Library of Congress. NISO needs to increase the involvement of information systems vendors and other support suppliers in NISO activities.

All of these organizations have a common interest in standards used for exchanging information. The information that is communicated between the kinds of organizations listed above and the library community is just as diverse as the groups themselves, but all of the information needs to be communicated in a standard way. In addition, the data itself should follow semantic rules and have a standard abstract syntax. One challenge for the future is to enable these organizations to use the data provided by others and therefore eliminate duplicate effort. As network use by libraries increases, those supplying their services must also use the networks. All three of the NISO constituencies share concerns for creating and maintaining multi-constituent standards.

Key Study Areas for Standards Development

The interests of NISO's three constituencies overlap in many ways [as illustrated in Figure 10.1]. To concentrate on standards needs for the future and to take into account this overlap of interests, NISO officers have defined six "Key Study Areas": Information Systems and Services Providers, Telecommunications and Networking, Electronic Publishing, Indexing and Abstracting, Preservation of Library and Archival Materials, and Library Equipment and Supplies. Although not all NISO standards work is included in these areas, they reflect either heavy current standards activities or are areas where the SDC believes NISO must be involved in the near future. Individual members of the

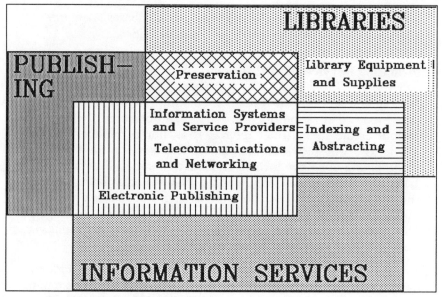

Figure 10.1: NISO Constituencies

Standards Development Committee are charged with the responsibility for a study area or with work relevant to a constituency. The Technical Plan, however, is focused on activity for the study areas. Each study area has an action agenda divided between tasks to be done in one to three years (tactical), and goals for longer term action (strategic).

Information Systems and Services Providers
Key Study Area

The supply of raw data increases at a growing, even alarming, rate, doubling every 15 years. Useful information increases at a much slower rate than raw data, and knowledge grows more slowly still, but still it is beyond any person's ability to keep up with advancing technology and the body of knowledge.

Growing demand for access to information accompanies the growing supply; NISO must provide methods for interchange of information in a standard format. NISO has roots in this area, with Z39.2, but must go much further.

In this study area, NISO's responsibility is to provide a method for interchange of information and data in a standard format, i.e., for both data and its communication. This desire for information interchange began in the 1960s with the work to develop a standard for the interchange of bibliographic records in magnetic format. This work resulted in Z39.2, the *Bibliographic Information Interchange Standard*. However, now there are innumerable interface and interchange problems in library automation. Because of the competitive nature of manufacturers, vendors, and system integrators, there can be no assurance that multi-vendor connectivity, easy access, and interchange of information will come from those communities. The only way to be certain that information will be readily accessible is for NISO to accept the challenge of providing information interchange standards.

The information exchanged includes bibliographic, holdings, acquisitions and ordering and circulation, including bar codes. The communications issues are also central to the Telecommunications and Networking Study Area.

Coordination with Other Standards Developers

This study area covers many aspects of modern technology, in areas where several other standards organizations such as IEEE, ANSI ASC X3, X12, and ISO are active. X3 controls the basic technology standards such as character sets, programming languages, and operating systems that the system providers rely on. X12 is concerned with electronic information exchange. These standards groups have many subgroups and committees which develop formal technical standards affecting this study area. Monitoring this activity is a challenge.

In addition, NISO must be aware of and evaluate the importance and effect of de facto and industry standards on library automation systems. Hundreds of manufacturers and resellers provide hardware, operating systems, networks, database management systems, and peripherals that are usually proprietary, even though they have become de facto or industry standards. The difference between technical/formal standards and industry/de facto standards is not always properly understood or appreciated and the implications for the consumer are not clear.

Other very important partners in this process of providing standards for information systems are organizations such as BISAC and SISAC (Book and Serials Industry Systems Advisory Committees) and the Automation Vendor Interface Advisory Committee (AVIAC). Not only are these groups interested and involved in the development of standards that affect their business interests, but their participation in the broader aspects of library automation is essential. NISO should make a greater effort to coordinate activities with these groups.

Areas for Review and Development

Review Existing Standards

Standards relating to information systems and service providers need review to ensure their usefulness. Some standards were developed to solve problems that existed prior to the emergence of library automation systems, but the marketplace has changed dramatically, as has technology.

For example, Z39.2 was developed to solve the problem of sharing bibliographic information by using a standard interchange format on magnetic tape. This extremely important standard has made the development of bibliographic utilities, shared cataloging, and library automation systems possible, as well as the creation of a whole new industry.

Z39.2 is used for both print and non-print materials and is currently being considered for an information and referral format and for the patron database in library automation systems. In light of demands for more non-bibliographic information, the scope of this standard should expand to include interchange for this type of data (e.g., song indices or art and museum holdings). Already vendors are using the Z39.2 format for applications unheard of even four years ago. This activity can be channelled by making needed changes to the standard.

In addition, data elements used for communicating acquisitions and fulfillment information and present in existing NISO standards are beginning to be used with a different method of interchange

(Electronic Data Interchange) than that specified by NISO standards, e.g., Z39.49. NISO will need to revise the data elements as needed and eliminate the communications sections when they have been superseded by EDI or X12 in constituent implementations, in addition to reviewing the EDI data elements proposed by BISAC and SISAC.

New Development

Work is in progress in Standards Committee LL on defining data elements needed for circulation; this effort should move along quickly. In addition, other data element sets will be needed as Z39.50 is implemented for communications.

Since users in the constituencies obtain information from more than one source, NISO should begin to explore the need for standards for the user interface. The proposed Common Command Language standard, Z39.58, addresses the search query and the results and how these are to be presented to the user; this presentation is oriented toward command-driven systems. However, libraries and system providers are beginning to experiment with graphic interfaces. NISO needs to support investigation of library-specific guidelines or standards based on a graphic common user interface.

Action Agenda

Short-Term

NISO should increase vendor participation and financial support, develop a plan for consumer education about standards, review existing standards relevant to this study area, publicize standards more actively, and investigate the need for standards in two specific areas:

- *Elements of a graphic user interface,* such as a mouse or other command surrogate for entering search commands and standardizing icons for library functions;
- *Bar codes for library identifiers,* to extend current work on circulation information.

Long-Term

- *Appoint* an education task force or committee to define and implement educational programs;

- *Encourage and sponsor* meetings that would bring together those implementing standards relevant to this study area; this will bring to light necessary revisions and will publicize and encourage implementation.

Telecommunications and Networking Key Study Area

NISO should focus on applications layer protocols that specifically serve NISO's constituencies. There is a long-term need for a family of protocols (built on existing work on Z39.50 where appropriate) allowing the interconnection of systems performing various library automation functions within a single institution, permitting the library automation systems at multiple institutions to interconnect effectively, and facilitating electronic publishing and end-user document delivery.

Currently, NISO has one adopted standard in telecommunications and networking: Z39.50, the protocol for computer to computer information retrieval. Z39.50 is one of NISO's successes and is important to the NISO constituencies, but its current status illustrates some of the challenges facing NISO in the networking arena. After a very lengthy process and early implementation by some institutions, Z39.50 was finally standardized in 1988. Since then, work on computer to computer information retrieval has moved to the International Standards Organization Technical Committee 46 Subcommittee 4. The work of the ISO group (DIS 10162/10163) is a subset of the US Z39.50 standard, roughly speaking, but includes some incompatibilities. In addition, work is being pursued within TC 46 SC 4 to extend the protocol to encompass what is called Search and Retrieve (SR). Organizations within the United States are working on implementations of the standard and need rapid agreements on the standard's options for interoperability. They have formed an ad hoc implementors group to meet their immediate requirements and to possibly contribute to the standards process as well. NISO should encourage this group and support the publicizing of the standard.

Coordination with Other Developers

Many organizations develop standards in the networking area, including ISO, ANSI ASC X3, and IEEE. In general, NISO should avoid duplicating the work of these other groups, even if it is of interest to the NISO community. NISO should be represented in these groups and should share results from these groups with the NISO community where appropriate. In a very real sense, however, NISO should have a pro-active and informational role in the development of these standards. Considerations that are of particular relevance to NISO's constituency may only be a small part of a much larger standard; NISO needs to make sure that its members' needs are accommodated.

In addition, NISO should maintain contact with the recently created Coalition for Networked Information (ARL/CAUSE/ EDUCOM), as this group will undoubtedly identify other standards in NISO's area of responsibility that are needed. NISO should also coordinate with groups such as the Internet Activities Board and its constituent organizations such as the Internet Engineering Task Force (IETF) and the IRTF. The Z39.50 Implementors Group should also be monitored.

Action Agenda

Short-Term

- **Z39.50 enhancement:** The Library of Congress is the maintenance agency for Z39.50. These maintenance and enhancement issues must be addressed:
    - **Harmonization with ISO standards:** Harmonize the NISO Z39.50-1988 standard with the international ISO DIS 10162/10163 work, add the extensions from Z39.50 into the new ASN.1 encodings derived from the ISO work, and produce a new NISO standard that is an upwardly compatible superset of ISO 10162/10163.
    - **Registry:** Continuing development will require the registry of attribute sets, transfer syntaxes, and error message sets. Begin work on registry of expanded attribute sets for text and image databases.
    - **Extensions:** Begin work on needed extensions to Z39.50, coordinating with the Z39.50 Implementors Group. The result of the

discussions may lead to modifications to the standard, as well as registry of additional attribute sets.

- **Use of Z39.50 by the TCP/IP community:** Prepare a document in cooperation with the Internet community through the IETF, defining how to use Z39.50 over TCP/IP.

Z39.50 specifies a transfer mechanism; it does not describe the format of the data being transferred, which is assumed to be provided by other standards. Implementation will generate demands from several study areas (e.g., abstracting and indexing, information systems, electronic publication) for developing transfer syntaxes to allow Z39.50 to be used in a wide variety of contexts. Z39.2 or its successors may provide such a syntax; in addition, it will be necessary to define data element sets. This work crosses the boundaries of several NISO study areas.

- **Monitoring standards activities of other groups:** NISO interest may extend over a small portion of a given standard, but this interest must be protected. Identify the groups responsible, establish working relationships with them, and find volunteers to monitor these activities. These standards activities require attention:
    - Upper-layer architecture structure, to define how multiple applications can be used together, e.g., Z39.50, the ILL protocol, FTAM (X3T5).
    - Fax and electronic document transfer.
    - Authentication, which will be important to libraries and information providers in a network environment. The work of X3T5 should be followed, as well as kerberos in the IETF.
    - Electronic data interchange (X12). The concern of NISO will be to review BISAC and SISAC data element sets for the EDI transactions of its constituency, monitoring the X12 activities to inform that development. (This is also of concern for the Information Systems and Services Providers Study Area.)
    - Compound document architecture and format, work of ISO/IEC JTC 1 SC 18. (This is also of concern for the Electronic Publishing Study Area.)
    - SQL development and remote database access (ANSI X3H2) and the work on Full Text SQL (currently not under the auspices of any standards body).
    - X Windows (ANSI X3H6).

- **Other projects**: Examine the need for standardizing downloading records across terminal emulation interfaces from online catalogs and other information utilities into programs that run on workstations or personal computers. This is a continuing source of problems whose solution would be valuable to several NISO constituencies.

Long-Term

Two general reference models need to be developed to provide a context for the development of protocol families:

- **Model for links among library automation system components**: This effort should examine standards issues concerning:
  - Links from online catalogs to circulation systems.
  - Links among circulation systems.
  - Links among acquisitions, serials control, circulation, automated binding, and online catalog functions.
  - Interlibrary loan links to the systems listed above.

To complement Standard Committee LL specification of patron data elements, protocol issues should be the subject of a separate standardization effort, and should be dealt with in the context of the reference model and follow-on work. A first priority for an actual standards effort, which might proceed in parallel with work on the reference model, should be to develop protocols and information transfer syntaxes so that online catalogs can extract circulation system data.

- **Model for document delivery**: Include document requesting and document delivery functions in this model. It should cover the entire process of selecting material for delivery, requesting it from remote machines or document delivery services, and getting it to the end-user workstation. In parallel with work on this model, begin work on a document requesting protocol. This component is the best defined in the required protocol suite, and could perhaps be developed quickly. Such a document will have a large impact on the NISO community.

Electronic Publishing Key Study Area

The foundations of electronic publishing have been established. While some of us believe that print publication offers unique advantages that will continue to make it dominant both for casual reading and for the longest-lasting material, there is no question that digital publication will have a role.

The advantages of digital publication seem obvious. Production time and cost should decrease substantially. There will be no printer or typesetter, no inventory or warehouse. Neither will there be paper to yellow or bindings to break. Texts, copied as needed, will never go out of print. They will be electronically searchable and otherwise manipulable by the reader...Yet the promised land of computer publication remains surprisingly and frustratingly distant.[3]

This statement covers more issues than can be dealt with by standards, but some of the problems are those that standards can alleviate. NISO has begun work in this area, but the combination of new media and new methods of access provide a tremendous opportunity to contribute. NISO should look beyond CD-ROM to videodisk, lasercards, and RAMcards, not forgetting diskettes and magnetic tape. In addition, the interface between CD-ROM and database systems should be explored as a possibility for needed standards work.

A good deal of additional work needs to be done in the CD-ROM area, including exploring possible standards in the following areas:

- Relationship of UNIX file system to ISO 9660, and possible extensions needed for a UNIX environment.
- Standard index formats and file formats for CD-ROM.
- The CD-RX proposal from the Intelligence Data Handling community.
- File structures for WORM disks (being pursued in X3).

One aspect of organizing NISO efforts will be to see how existing standards, developed by NISO and others, apply to electronic publishing in areas such as bibliographic citations, statistics, document search and retrieval, and handling and preservation of media.

---

3 Daniel Eisenberg, "Problems of the paperless book," *Scholarly Publishing* (October 1989), 11.

All of NISO's constituencies have interest in this study area. For instance, if CD-ROM systems could record detailed usage of materials, publishers and authors would have information available about copyright and citations, and libraries would know which information sources were important to their patrons.

Coordination with Other Standards Developers

The most influential standard community active in electronic publishing is X3 and its ISO analog [ISO/IEC] JTC 1, with a current program of work that includes efforts on compound document architectures, hypermedia, page description languages, and graphics.

A wide variety of other organizations with material interests in one or another aspect of electronic publishing have come into being over the last three to five years; many of these organizations have formulated a standards agenda or undertaken a standards program of some description. Examples include:

- The Special Interest Group on CD-ROM Applications and Technology (SIGCAT).
- The CD-ROM Standards and Practices Action Group.
- Coalition for Networked Information, Electronic Publishing Projects
- The Text Encoding Initiative (TEI).
- The Foundation for Electronic Publishing.
- CD-ROM Consistent Interface Committee (CD-CINC).
- Information Handling Committee.
- Numerous government agencies (such as the National Institutes for Standards and Technology and the Department of Defense) and industry associations (such as the Aerospace Industry Association, Air Transport Association and Association of Information and Image Management) that are working on electronic product definition and technical documentation dissemination.

Action Agenda

Short-Term

- Appoint an expert to the SDC to manage this study area.

- Implement Z39.59 within the NISO publishing activities. Produce a Z39.59 style sheet for NISO standards by building on existing style sheets within the constituency. Treat one or more new or revised standards according to this standard.

- Complete SC TT *[Additional Standards for CD-ROM]* work in a timely fashion.

- Appoint a committee to review the standards draft from the Intelligence Handling Committee, move the draft along and examine networking implications with experts from the Telecommunications and Networking Study Area.

- Appoint individuals or a committee to work with the Optical Publishing Association on the CD-ROM premastering process.

- Establish a U.S. maintenance agency for ISO 9660 to promote "full promise" implementation, while tracking interpretations, corrections and extensions.

- Clarify the status of Z39.59 and its maintenance agency so that the pace of its implementation can be increased and interpretations, corrections, and extensions, particularly in the area of indexes and indexers, can be processed.

Long-Term

- Sponsor a one- or two-day meeting of leaders from the electronic publishing constituency and related standards communities, brainstorming on needs for standards and devising a consensus strategy for coordinating the scopes and work programs of various standards development efforts.

- Appoint an expert to track and advocate multimedia extensions to existing standards in NISO, X3 and ISO (e.g., advertising and packaging).

- Monitor, contribute to, and participate in, as appropriate, the activities of X3V1 with particular attention to its efforts in the areas of standard page layouts, hypermedia, and the standard generalized markup language.

- Appoint an expert to track and advocate compound document architecture, page description language, and graphics efforts in X3 and ISO.

- Promote full implementation of the standard issued by Standards Committee TT, by publicizing it within the appropriate constituency and organizing tutorials or seminars on implementation issues.

- Write a white paper formulating the NISO role, if any, in developing applications for generic X3 and ISO standards (such as those above) for specific types of publications.

- Develop a set of reference models to clarify vertical relations in typical production chains and to focus on interfaces between various agencies in the life of a publication (e.g., CD mastering).

- Appoint an expert to track and become involved in the NIST-sponsored activities on hypertext transfer formats, coordinating with experts in the Telecommunication and Networking Study Area.

- Track the program of work in progress by TEI; when the standards are issued in 1992, review them for possible adoption, in whole or in part, by NISO.

Z39.59 will only work for writers as well as publishers when its techniques are embodied in or understood by popular computer applications such as Ventura Publisher, WordPerfect, and Microsoft Word. Until then, its provisions appear to one-sidedly favor the interests of certain publishers. Its imposition within NISO would, at the very least, cause some upheaval within the current publication program.

Indexing and Abstracting Key Study Area

Indexing and abstracting are carried out by a very diverse set of individuals and organizations. One person may index a book and submit handwritten index cards so that a publisher can create a back-of-book index. An organization providing a database for public access may employ many people who use computer terminals to key in journal abstracts or citations so that computer programs written by other employees will automatically create the entries and references in the database. These categories of indexing involve both the intellectual process of assigning terms and clerical process for making the terms available to the user of the index.

For many of us in this era of desktop publishing, indexing involves inserting index entries into the text of a manuscript (for example, the chapters of this book); Ventura Publisher or a similar program then prepares the back-of-book index, ready for a final check. The clerical process disappears; the intellectual process remains.

The type of material dictates the approach to providing an index; back-of-book indexing is not the same as indexing for an encyclopedia or bibliographic guide. These are both different from indexing or abstracting a journal article. Computer indexing offers its own set of opportunities and constraints.

Although indexing and cataloging can involve similar processes, there are far fewer standards available for indexing and abstracting than for cataloging. However, in the absence of standards for communicating indexing and abstracting information, various software suppliers, library systems, and system vendors are improvising and creating transfer formats and data elements. Individual database providers have created sets of codes in various areas (e.g., company names or geographic areas), but have left the problems of mapping between databases to the access providers. If standards were adopted for such situations, then creating data elements and a transfer format to handle them would become less of a problem.

NISO might investigate the need for a standard for product codes, which could be used to search for product information across databases.

Coordination with Other Standards Developers

The Standards Committee of NFAIS is a likely candidate for cooperative standards work, since some NISO members are members of this committee. The American Society of Indexers is eager to help revise Z39.4. In addition, there are a number of relevant ISO TC 46 standards.

Action Agenda

Short-Term

- Appoint an expert from the abstracting and indexing constituency to join the SDC and manage this area.

- Establish a mechanism for reviewing existing NISO standards; this should include surveying the constituency for opinions on relevance and general usefulness.

- Research the issue of communicating indexing information from database producers to access providers. Commission a white paper on the issues that recommends the next steps.

Long-Term

- Establish better communications lines with NISO members of this constituency to promote greater involvement and better assessment of needs. Provide speakers for appropriate meetings and conferences.

- Develop and implement a plan for tracking international standards activity, which includes appointing an individual to track the ISO activity for NISO and report to the SDC.

Preservation of Library and Archival Materials Key Study Area

The impetus for increased preservation activity in libraries and archives, and the initial reason for NISO's entry into preservation standards, was the realization that large portions of our cultural heritage are deteriorating beyond use due to unstable recording media. The most obvious example is the enormous and omnipotent problem of deteriorating paper; however, all of the recording media have problems of inherent instability due to their composition and the way that they are manufactured. These inherent characteristics are in turn affected by storage, handling, and physical treatment practices in libraries and archives, or by their proxies in the commercial sector.

The history of recording media has been one of change and technical innovation; physical media include stone tablets, papyrus, vellum, paper, film, magnetic tape, and optical disk. Libraries and archives must collect, describe, service, and preserve all of these various media, or provide for their timely transfer to another recording medium. Documentation of condition, methods to stabilize materials or prevent further deterioration, and the transfer of unstable formats to stable (preservation) formats offer opportunities for standards work. These concerns reach across constituencies. Publishers contribute to preservation by printing on acid-free paper. They will also follow the binding standards as they are published. Information providers are involved with electronic reproduction.

Coordination with Other Standards Developers

NISO preservation standards work focuses on two major issues: the longevity of recording media found in libraries and archives, and the subsequent storage and physical treatment of library and archival materials. Whereas NISO is primarily concerned with recording medium performance (its longevity), performance is always partially dependent on composition and manufacture of particular media; thus there is a potential for overlap with manufacturing standards. In addition, like manufacturing standards, preservation standards are often dependent on the existence of standard tests for physical, chemical, and other qualities.

NISO can avoid duplication of effort by closely coordinating with other relevant standards developers; in some cases it may be logical to develop joint standards. Relevant standards developers include, but are not limited to:

- Association of Information and Image Management (AIIM), which develops standards for the production, testing, and storage of photographic images, including archival quality microfilm.

- American Society for Testing Materials (ASTM), which develops specifications and test methods for an enormous variety of products. ASTM Standards exist for categories for permanent paper, including bond and ledger paper, file folders, and copying paper.

- Technical Association of the Pulp and Paper Industry (TAPPI), which develops standard procedures for testing the physical and chemical composition of paper products.

- The National Association of Photographic Manufacturers (NAPM), secretariat for ANSI PH and IT committees. Although NISO and other groups in the United States are leaders in the international preservation, any developments abroad should be tracked.

Other Groups as Sources for Standards

One justification for increased development of preservation standards is the existence of *ad hoc* standards throughout the profession. The work of professional associations represent an important first step in preservation work codification. In addition, the work of the preservation research and testing laboratories at the Library of Congress and the National Archives, contracted work to the Government Printing Office and the National Institute for Science and Technology (formerly NBS), and non-profit laboratories such as the Image Permanence Institute and the Institute for Paper Chemistry has already fed directly into formal standards. There is potential for greater activity.

Work of professional and other associations that should be tracked include the American Library Association (ALA), the Society of American Archivists (SAA), the American Institute for Conservation of Historic and Artistic Works (AIC), the Research Libraries Group (RLG), and the Association of Research Libraries (ARL).

Finally, trade associations such as the Library Binding Institute (LBI), the National Institute for Conservation (NIC), the Book Manufacturing Institute (BMI), and the American Society of Heating, Refrigeration, and Air Conditioning Engineers (ASHRAE) are possible sources for joint standards.

A Proposal for NISO Families of Preservation Standards

The NISO Preservation Study Area should include five families of preservation standards: archival storage; original media; book binding; physical treatment and condition of library and archival materials; reformatting. In some cases, NISO would be the principal standards developer; in other cases NISO would maintain contact with other standards developers or develop joint standards.

- **Archival storage:** The most important area for NISO preservation standards is developing standards for the storage and housing of recorded media. Libraries and archives collect information; the choice of original recording medium cannot be controlled by a library. However, the useful life of materials can be significantly extended by applying proper environmental and physical controls. Standards in this area include the macro-environment of the building, now being addressed by Standards Committee R, as well as specifications for housing and protective enclosures for material. In addition to general environmental conditions, NISO should develop standards for specific media or situations. ANSI PH1.43-1985, *Storage of Processed Safety Film*, is an example of a standard aimed at a particular medium; a standard for the storage of videotapes may be another. The work of Standards Committee MM on the environmental conditions for material on exhibition is an example of a particular storage situation; a standard for secondary storage facilities is another possibility. Requirements for storage conditions are also needed when libraries and archives reformat original materials to a secondary storage or preservation format, such as videotape to 16mm film under cold storage conditions, or reformat brittle books to microfilm.

- **Original media:** Although preservation standards for original media can overlap with standards for the composition and manufacture of recording media, preservation standards can be developed that concentrate on the preservation potential (performance) of media, including digital media. Preservation goes beyond the initial requirements for a recording medium (videotape recording of evening news broadcasts) to its performance over time (videotape collections on the history of broadcast news). ANSI Z39.48-1984, *Permanence of Paper for Printed Library Materials*, is an example of a standard covering certain aspects of production, but primarily concerns the preservation potential of paper for documents.

- **Book binding:** Libraries and archives collect materials in several recording media, with the book currently dominant. Binding standards are necessary both for the original binding (trade books, scholarly publications, reference books), the binding of books already owned by a library, and the binding of serials into volumes. NISO has made a start with the work of Standards Committee GG, which developed a draft for durable hard-cover binding. A joint standard for library binding will shortly be undertaken with the Library Binding Institute, a trade association of library binding companies. In addition, binding standards are needed for various categories of books so that librarian, publisher, and book manufacturer can agree about durability and usability requirements. An example of effective standards work in this area is the standard maintained by the National Association of State Textbook Administrators (NASTA) which publishes and promulgates a series of standards for the manufacture of textbooks.

- **Physical treatment and condition of library and archival materials:** Allied with the need for standards for book binding, but much more complex, is the need to develop a series of standards and standard practices to document the condition and specify requirements for the physical treatment of library and archival materials. For example, American librarians have launched a national "brittle books" program without a standard definition of a brittle book. Libraries, including the Library of Congress, are attempting to procure mass deacidification services without a standard for what such a process should accomplish. Hundreds of thousands of unique documents were encapsulated in archives before a standard practice was established to ensure deacidification before encapsulation. Libraries across the country and the world relegate their most valuable items for treatment without a standard for documenting current condition and specifying treatment. Fortunately, a significant body of work already exists in the library and archival communities to inform this standards work, but it must be tapped by working with the professional communities and vendors.

- **Reformatting**: Standards have been developed that specify standard procedures and products to reformat deteriorating library materials on microfilm. Additional work is needed to describe standards for the reformatting and copying of other media, including still photographs, motion picture film, and magnetic tape (videotapes, sound recordings, and electronic records); this work is especially needed for electronic formatting. Research has been done, but no standard has been written on specifications for preservation of xerographic copies. In addition to standards that describe how an item is reformatted to achieve preservation goals, standards are required to describe how copies are identified. Z39.32 and Z39.62 cover standards for eye-legible information on microfiche headings and microfilm leaders. Standards work will also be needed in the future when the optical disk technology is used as a reformatting medium. This latter area will require cooperation with other standards developers.

Action Agenda

Short-Term

Substantial work is already under way in preservation. However, additional actions are:

- Initiate new standards work items for library binding (joint standard with the Library Binding Institute) and requirements of a mass de-acidification process (including performance tests).

- In cooperation with professionals in the field, define an action agenda for each of the five families of preservation standards including a list of relevant standards and suggestions for new standards work.

- Appoint an expert to develop and distribute a list of relevant standards and guidelines (informal standards) for informing and stimulating the various professional communities.

- Appoint an expert to investigate the sufficiency of existing ANSI PH and IT technical and operational standards for copying cellulose nitrate motion picture film onto safety film.

- Recommend Z39.66, *Durable Hard-cover Binding for Books*, and the results of SC R study of environmental control as work items to the International Standards Organization, TC 46/SC 10, Physical Keeping of Documents.

Long-Term

- Develop a plan for monitoring the development of standards in this study area and seek to participate in the development of joint standards when appropriate.

- Encourage pre-standards work by ensuring that relevant professional organizations are aware of NISO's preservation agenda and monitoring pre-standards work in appropriate organizations so that whenever possible, NISO can form standards committees based on existing draft standards and guidelines.

- Examine implications of the relationship between the format and its preservation, e.g., for databases such as LEXIS and electronic products such as CD-ROM. A book can be reformatted for preservation onto preservation microfilm, digitized and disseminated in electronic format, and scanned and used in hardcopy. The use of digital media, in particular, needs investigation, but preservation implications exist in all of these activities.

Library Equipment and Supplies Key Study Area

Libraries of all types and sizes are major consumers of many pieces of equipment and numerous supplies. However, only a small number of these products are peculiar to libraries in their configuration or specific use. Office equipment and supplies are not specific to libraries, even though at one time there was a library standard keyboard in wide use. Furnishing and floor coverings are also general.

A few types of equipment are specific to libraries and hold promise for NISO involvement in standards activities. These are bookstacks, compact shelving, book trucks, book returns, and possibly book theft detection systems. In addition, photocopy machines that address specific needs of libraries are beginning to appear.

Areas for Development

A draft standard on library bookstacks was agreed upon by a Standards Committee of Z85 in 1985. It has no official standing, but has been cited many times in bid documents. It is currently the basis for a large-scale test program of thirteen models from eleven bookstack manufacturers. These tests results will be published [in 1991].

In a related area, two ALA Library Administration and Management Association members, Frank Bright (University of Wisconsin at Madison) and Gloria Stockton (University of California, Richmond facility) are writing a technical paper on moveable compact shelving used primarily for books.

Book trucks come in many sizes and configurations, however most problems occur with wheels or casters or with instability. Any standards work would require engineering expertise. Many vendors seem to be active, offering a variety of models.

A standard for book returns may not be feasible, since at present, a satisfactory [book return] is not available. If performance measures were to be established, however, it might encourage manufacturers to make such a product. There is some interest at Brigham Young University in creating an improved book return; this institution should be contacted.

Book theft detection systems may need standards. However, not many systems are available and performance varies.

One real obstacle to creating standards for equipment and supplies is the extensive and expensive testing that must take place to ensure compliance. Libraries do not have funds for this kind of activity; funding must be found elsewhere, presumably from vendors.

Coordination with Other Standards Developers

Microform and audiovisual equipment, used widely in libraries but not specific to them, are the responsibility of ANSI-accredited standards committees (PH5 for micrographics and sponsored by AIIM, and IT7 for A/V, sponsored by NAPM and ICIA). However, NISO should monitor their activities and be prepared to offer advice when the result of standards work affects libraries.

Ergonomics should also be investigated, as applied to library workstations. The Human Factors Society may be engaged in this work and NISO could contribute to it.

The ALA work on compact shelving should be tracked, as well as the activity at BYU on book returns.

Action Agenda

Short-Term

- Monitor the results of the *Library Technology Reports* bookstack test program. When the report is published in early 1991, decide whether a committee is needed to review the present draft in view of new findings. If so, appoint the committee; otherwise, proceed with balloting.

- Meet with the ALA/LAMA/BES Equipment Committee to solicit their assistance in identifying needed standards. Find out what has been accomplished by Bright and Stockton in regard to their LAMA/BES work on compact shelving.

- Investigate the need for a library workstation ergonomics standard. This is one of the issues that will be brought to the LAMA/BES committee.

Long-Term

- Secure vendor opinion on standards they think are needed. Send a questionnaire and follow up with a meeting, perhaps in conjunction with an ALA conference.
- Identify sources of funding for test programs that can feed into the standards process or for ways in which test results from other organizations can be utilized.
- Develop and implement a plan for identifying relevant international standards groups and for tracking their work.

Managing and Improving The Standards-Making Process

Currently, the process of identifying and developing new standards takes much too long. The standards development process depends on volunteer committees which meet infrequently to develop the standard, a commenting and voting procedure extending over 12 or more months, and the formal acceptance of the standard for publication. More often than not, this process requires 5-8 years. The entire procedure must be speeded up to meet the rapidly developing information and technological marketplace. Otherwise, other organizations will move ahead, creating formal or industry standards that may not meet the needs of the NISO constituencies.

NISO should consider several paths for streamlining this work: examine the balloting process; consider more intense work by Standards Committees; provide better coordination with international work; arrange for additional staff; use electronic conferencing for standards reviewing and committee work.

The NISO Standards Committees would benefit from a handbook that succinctly states the procedures. Those working with the Standards Committees need to be able to extract information about responsibilities, the outline of the process (with attendant time periods), a style guide for standards documents, and a description of the balloting process.

The procedures for the NISO standards process are documented in the *Operating Procedures*, 1986. The SDC is submitting recommended document revisions to the NISO Board of Directors. After the changes and additions to the procedures are adopted, several tasks remain before the goals of improving and streamlining the standards committee work and the balloting process are met.

Education, Marketing, and Monitoring

An education program goal is to make the consumers aware of standards and the positive effect these standards can have on institutions in each constituency. NISO must encourage the marketplace to demand adherence to standards; it is cost effective to take advantage of work done by experts in the area, for both the product or service quality, and for communicating information. If the market is willing to implement systems that do not adhere to standards, the vendor community will ignore standards. If institutions demand standards, then the process of standardization will increase.

In addition to education, existing standards need to be marketed to those who could benefit from using them; the publisher of NISO standards can help with this. Although some action items for study areas include review of existing standards, NISO needs to emphasize reviewing existing standards as they relate to other current standards and future directions. Standards may outlive their usefulness, due to changing needs or advances in technology. NISO also needs to find a way to determine the level of use of published standards in order to obtain information for the review process.

Action Agenda

Short-Term

- Develop and implement new balloting and tracking forms to support standards committee work and the changes to the balloting procedures. These forms include matrices for recording comments and votes, a style sheet, and templates for development milestones.

- Revise the NISO Operating Procedures to reflect the above changes. The format must be flexible so that relevant sections can be excerpted and given to Standards Committees.

- Develop and implement an orientation and training program for new standards committees. Consider the use of appropriate generic training materials.

- Investigate the possibility of developing a "Fast Track" method of standards development.

- Determine how tracking standards committee work and providing support for them should be divided up between SDC members and NISO staff. Create and submit a proposal to the NISO Board of Directors for additional staff required.

- Determine the feasibility of sponsoring a NISO Standards Week twice a year to cluster meetings of NISO Standards Committees and provide training to this cadre of volunteers.

Long-Term

- As standards become eligible for reaffirmation, give careful consideration to their relevance and level of implementation. Standards that are no longer needed or have not been implemented should be withdrawn. Consideration should be given to adopting appropriate international standards as U.S. standards rather than maintaining redundant national and international standards.

- Develop and implement a self-auditing program to demonstrate compliance with ANSI criteria for due process.

- Working with NISO's publisher, develop a model for marketing standards to NISO constituencies.

- Develop a plan to elicit greater involvement in and financial support of standards development from the vendor community.

- Develop and implement a plan for tracking international standards activity in all areas of interest to NISO constituencies. That plan should include organizing the liaison involvement and setting priorities.

Summary

The section above completes the *NISO Technical Plan*, which also includes a list of NISO standards grouped by subject area (not by key study area). The remaining comments are mine. This plan is an ambitious one; if NISO is able to carry it out, the organization will reaffirm its importance in the standards community and within its own communities of interest.

That's the challenge and the optimistic outlook. The challenge won't be met easily, particularly as NISO also struggles with finances and the difficulties of maintaining the existing body of standards. NISO must have the active participation and membership of more library vendors, publishers, major libraries and library associations, and other organizations in order to carry out its plans. Chapter 11 discusses NISO's membership and ways that people and organizations can be involved in or stay aware of its standards activity.

11

Library, Publisher, and
Agency Involvement

All standardization efforts rest on the same foundation: the intelligence, effort, and awareness of people. From the technical standards set down by a single artisan, through the relatively simple organization of NISO, to the elaborate structure of ISO, it all begins and ends with individuals. You can involve yourself in technical standards at several different levels, depending on your needs and those of your agency. Levels of involvement include:

- **Awareness:** Finding out what standards exist and are being developed, how they apply to your work, and how they can be used;
- **Use:** Acquiring the appropriate standards, using them, and supporting their use;
- **Professional involvement:** Helping to investigate the need for new standards through professional associations;
- **Informational agency involvement:** Joining appropriate standards organizations as an informational member, to keep up with developing standards;
- **Active agency involvement:** Joining standards organizations as a voting member, committing membership fees and staff support;
- **Active personal involvement:** Developing ideas for new standards, volunteering to serve on standards committees.

This chapter considers some paths through these levels. You and your agency must choose the one at which you will be most active.

Technical standards would cease to exist if nobody became involved; standardization efforts would become hopelessly complex if everybody in a profession was passionately involved in the process.

Awareness

Every library, library vendor, database supplier, and publisher should subscribe to *Information Standards Quarterly* ($40 per year from the National Information Standards Organization, P.O. Box 1056, Bethesda, MD 20827). That first move will keep you informed on developing and newly approved standards within NISO's purview, and will provide a wide range of useful articles about technical standards within libraries, publishing, and information sciences. Vendors should do more than subscribe; any serious library automation vendor or database supplier should be a voting member of NISO, as should many publishers.

Many larger libraries and most vendors should also subscribe to the *ANSI Reporter* and *ANSI Standards Action*. At $100.00 per year, the combined subscription is not cheap, but *ANSI Standards Action* does let you know what standards are being balloted and which ones have been approved, for all standards submitted for ANSI approval as well as ISO and IEC standards. In some cases, an organization can join ANSI for the same $100.00, showing their support and receiving the publications as well.

Every library automation vendor, and every librarian interested in technology, will also belong to ALA's LITA division. That membership brings with it the *LITA Newsletter* and the column "Standard Fare," as well as occasional standards-related articles in LITA's scholarly journal, *Information Technology and Libraries*. It's possible to subscribe to *LITA Newsletter* and *Information Technology and Libraries* without belonging to the division (which requires ALA membership), but at a combined cost of $60 or more (as compared to $35 personal or $50 organizational for LITA), it only makes sense if ALA membership is out of the question.

Use

Awareness should lead to use, which requires purchasing appropriate standards. If your agency is actively interested in the use of technical standards, as it should be, you should be acquiring those standards that appear to be directly relevant.

Although ANSI does not publish all American National Standards, you can purchase all American National Standards from ANSI, as well as ISO and IEC standards. ASC X3 publishes its standards through ANSI, so that it is the only means of acquiring them. ANSI is also the exclusive American distributor for ISO standards. NISO standards are available through ANSI and can also be purchased from NISO's own publisher, Transaction Publishers. *Information Standards Quarterly* carries a complete list of available NISO standards, with price and order information and a topical index, in each year's April issue.

When an agency moves from implicit reliance on technical standards to active use of technical standards, it should evaluate those it chooses to support. For each standard, a study should evaluate:

- **Currency and validity:** If your agency determines that the standard is out of date or invalid for your operations, you should not implement it, but should record the reasons for that finding, and (for NISO standards) inform NISO of the problem;

- **Changes necessary to implement it:** In the likely case that the standard will serve your agency well, but differs in some details from your current practice, a careful list of those differences and a plan to resolve them should be prepared;

- **Policy requirements to ensure its proper use:** Sometimes, this may involve some announcement that your agency will follow the standard as of a given date. (For new or less-used standards, this may even be a noteworthy announcement.) Proper use of a standard involves explicit reference to it so that new employees know where to go to check on requirements.

Explicit support of American National Standards makes sense for most agencies. Such support does not mean that an agency must adopt every standard without question. Deliberate choices to ignore certain standards are in keeping with the voluntary nature of standards in the United States.

The cost of using appropriate technical standards is relatively small. The newer the agency, the less difficult it will be to implement their use. Even a well-established agency should have little trouble implementing technical standards in emerging technology. An agency that fails to be aware of current standards and to use those that make sense is cutting itself off from a community of users. Such separation reduces the chance for efficiencies of scale and other advantages gained through sharing a common ground. Agencies should not blindly adopt all technical standards, but should certainly use those that can be beneficial.

If you're a writer or researcher, or work in a library or publishing house, you might consider purchasing a starter set of NISO standards. The sets suggested below are only examples, and include only NISO standards adopted by the end of 1990. Prices are omitted because they are subject to drastic change; a current list of standards with prices is readily available from NISO.

Standards for Writers and Editors

Five NISO standards, all described further in Chapter 12, deal with various issues of writing and editing:

- Z39.4, *Basic Criteria for Indexes*: Good suggestions for anyone compiling an index.

- Z39.14, *Writing Abstracts*: Most nonfiction articles deserve or require abstracts.

- Z39.16, *Preparation of Scientific Papers for Written or Oral Presentation*: Specifically intended for scientific papers, this standard is full of good advice for anyone preparing nonfiction papers or speeches.

- Z39.22, *Proof Corrections*: A clearly written explanation of standard proof corrections, with explicit examples.

- Z39.29, *Bibliographic References*: Any writer who has trouble establishing and maintaining a standard style for citations and references will find this standard helpful. Note that Z39.29 is not the standard specified by the *Chicago Manual of Style* or by many professional associations, but it is clear and consistent, with extensive examples and explanations.

NISO may very well move to combine some of these standards, several of which are guidelines or good advice, rather than proper technical standards, into appropriate handbooks. At that point, they might make better economic sense for the individual writer.

Standards for Libraries

Any medium-sized or larger public, special, or academic library should have the five standards listed above as a service to its patrons. Other standards will also help the patrons, and some specifically serve technical processing. In addition to Z39.4, Z39.14, Z39.16, Z39.22, and Z39.29, libraries may wish to consider some or all of the following:

- Z39.2, *Bibliographic Information Interchange*: The standard that underlies USMARC.
- Z39.5, *Abbreviation of Titles of Periodicals*.
- Z39.7, *Library Statistics*.
- Z39.9, *International Standard Serial Numbering*: Includes a clear explanation of ISSN check digits and how ISSNs are assigned.
- Z39.21, *Book Numbering*: The ISBN standard.
- Z39.23, *Standard Technical Report Number (STRN), Format and Creation*.
- Z39.30, *Order Form for Single Titles of Library Materials in 3-inch by 5-inch format*.
- Z39.43, *Identification Code for the Book Industry*: The SAN standard.
- Z39.44, *Serials Holdings Statements*.
- Z39.45, *Claims for Missing Issues of Serials*.
- Z39.46, *Identification of Bibliographic Data On and Relating To Patent Documents*.
- Z39.48 *Permanence of Paper for Printed Library Materials*.
- Z39.50, *Information Retrieval Service Definition and Protocol Specification*.
- Z39.52, *Standard Order Form for Multiple Titles of Library Materials*.
- Z39.57, *Holdings Statement for Non-Serials*.
- Z39.63, *Interlibrary Loan Data Elements*.
- Z85.1, *Catalog Cards*.

Larger public libraries and academic libraries should obtain complete sets of NISO (Z39) standards.

Standards for Publishers

Most publishers should have all five standards mentioned for writers. Some will find use for specific standards such as those for developing thesauri or for preparing library directories. Publishers should generally find the following standards useful:

- Z39.1, *Periodicals: Format and Arrangement*
- Z39.6, *Trade Catalogs*
- Z39.8, *Compiling Book Publishing Statistics*
- Z39.9, *International Standard Serial Numbering*
- Z39.13, *Describing Books in Advertisements, Catalogs, Promotional Materials, and Book Jackets*
- Z39.15, *Title Leaves of a Book*
- Z39.18, *Scientific and Technical Reports—Organization, Preparation and Production*
- Z39.21, *Book Numbering*
- Z39.26, *Advertising of Micropublications*
- Z39.41, *Book Spine Formats*
- Z39.43, *Identification Code for the Book Industry*
- Z39.48, *Permanence of Paper for Printed Library Materials*

Every agency must determine which standards will serve its own needs, but the suggestions above may serve as starting points.

Professional Involvement

Your interest in technical standards can lead to personal involvement through your professional associations. Professional associations make up over a third of NISO's voting membership, including most of the major national organizations in the library field. If you're a member of one or more of those organizations, you should be able to find the committee that studies technical standards. Some have more than one such committee.

You should be able to contact the association's representative to NISO, or the committee that advises that representative, for more information. For those associations that, like the American Library Association, mandate open meetings as a rule, you can attend committee meetings as an observer. This should show you the level of activity and interest within the association, and will probably lead you to ways in which you can help with standardization efforts.

American Library Association (ALA)

One national organization represents a broader range of library interests than any other: the American Library Association. If you're a professional librarian or otherwise involved in libraries, you should consider membership. ALA is a voting member of NISO, and the Library and Information Technology Association (LITA) of ALA is a voting member of ASC X3.

ALA also has a number of internal standardization activities, not all of them related to technical standards. Information on ALA membership is available from the association, Public Information Office, 50 East Huron Street, Chicago, IL 60611. All divisions are also reached through this address.

The standards committee of ALA develops procedures for ALA standards, which are largely professional and service standards rather than technical. This committee does coordinate standards efforts within all ALA divisions, and has liaisons to each division with any current standards effort.

Association for Library Collections and Technical Services (ALCTS)

ALCTS coordinates ALA's review of NISO standards and names ALA's representative to NISO, who reports to the ALCTS board. Reports on standards activity within NISO sometimes appear in the *ALCTS Newsletter*. ALCTS does not itself have a standards committee. The Reproduction of Library Materials (RLMS) section of ALCTS has a standards committee that considers the needs for standards related to the reproduction of library material. This committee works more through representation to the Association for Information and Image Management (AIIM) than through NISO.

Library and Information Technology Association (LITA) Technical Standards for Library Automation Committee (TESLA)

ALA LITA TESLA is the ALA committee most directly concerned with ANSI technical standards. The committee's function statement reads:

> To encourage and support the development of standards relating to library automation; serve as a clearinghouse for such standards and information about such standards. In the area of library automation, transmit proposed standards and recommendations to standards development committees through appropriate American Library Association representatives to American National Standards Institute (ANSI) Committees; arrange for appropriate standards publicity; cooperate with the American Library Association Standards Committee; and encourage and support technical communications between the library community and its suppliers in the business machine and computer industries.

> The LITA representative to the ANSI X3 Committee is an ex officio member of this committee.

TESLA has operated for more than a decade as an active, informal combination of appointed committee members and others who are interested in its work. It carries out its charge by such activities as the following:

- **Program sessions:** Once every year or two, TESLA organizes a program at ALA's annual conference. These programs have covered topics as diverse as bar-code standards, library-computer center relations, and the Linked Systems Project (LSP).

- **"Standard Fare":** Every issue of the *LITA Newsletter* features a column edited by the pseudonymous "Pierre Badin LaTes," a name used by a succession of editors from TESLA. Each column features news of TESLA's activities and developments in the standards field, with emphasis on NISO and X3; some columns also feature signed sections by guest columnists.

- **Checklists and other articles:** TESLA has encouraged members and observers to develop useful articles. Several articles based on TESLA work have appeared in *Journal of Library Automation, Information Technology and Libraries* and *Library Hi Tech*.

- **Needed standards:** TESLA gathers suggestions for needed standards, and attempts to interest other committees and agencies in developing those that appear promising. At the same time, TESLA maintains sufficient continuity and balance to answer many suggestions with information on existing standards, or with comments on the inadvisability of standards within a particular area.

TESLA has always been open, and has always acted on the basis that whoever attends a meeting is a functioning TESLA participant. Past, future, and possible members of the committee can be as involved as current members; future members almost always come from the ranks of active observers. TESLA meetings can be an interesting and easy way to get more involved in technical standards. TESLA maintains formal liaison with the LITA representative to X3, and attempts to maintain liaison with NISO as well; it has had good, informal summaries of recent NISO and X3 activities at each ALA conference and midwinter meeting during the past decade.

Informational Agency Involvement

A library may join NISO as a nonvoting informational member for $100 per year. This fee pays for press releases, *Information Standards Quarterly*, and copies of draft standards in the process of development. Informational members are free to comment on such standards.

Informational membership is a first step toward full membership in NISO. If your library is uncertain about its need for, or commitment to, an active role in standards, $100.00 per year will allow you to keep up with new standards as they are being developed. For many libraries, informational membership may be the most active level of organizational involvement.

Active Agency Involvement

If your library, company, or other agency finds that it has a vital interest in technical standards, it should become a full member of the appropriate standards agency or agencies: NISO, X3, or others.

Membership in NISO costs $1,000 to $4,500 per year, depending on the agency's budget for libraries, information services, and publishing. Membership involves some responsibilities. A voting member is expected to review all proposed standards carefully and to vote responsibly on them. An agency that votes to approve standards without careful review is betraying the process. When an agency votes against a standard, it is expected to state reasons; negotiation is used to resolve negative votes.

The NISO representative in an agency may expect to spend considerable time dealing with drafts and ballots. The representative may have to circulate draft standards for review, and collate responses into a single agency response. Many NISO members have representatives and alternates; the alternate shares the load of active membership.

Voting membership in NISO commits an agency to review, respond, and probably devote time and travel to carry out the standards process. Membership does not commit an agency to adopt all NISO standards. Some will be irrelevant, others may have been adopted over the objections of the agency, or may simply not meet an agency's needs.

Every library automation vendor should be a voting member. More publishers should belong, particularly those that believe in the future of the printed book and the significance of standards for print publishing.

Current Membership

The following institutions are Voting Members of NISO as of December 1, 1990:

American Association of Law Libraries

American Chemical Society

American Library Association

American Psychological Association

American Society for Information Science

American Society of Indexers

American Theological Library Association

Apple Computer, Inc.

Art Libraries Society of North America

Association of American Publishers

Association of American University Presses

Association of Information and Dissemination Centers

Association for Information and Image Management

Association of Jewish Libraries

The Association for Recorded Sound Collections

Association of Research Libraries

Baker & Taylor

The Blue Bear Group, Inc.

Book Manufacturers' Institute

CAPCON Library Network

Catholic Library Association

CLSI, Inc.

Colorado Alliance of Research Libraries

Council of Biology Editors

Council of National Library and Information Associations

Data Research Associates, Inc.

Dynix

EBSCONET

Engineering Information, Inc.

Faxon, Inc.

Gaylord Information Systems

IBM Corporation

Indiana Cooperative Library Services Authority

Information Workstation Group, Inc.

Library Binding Institute

Library of Congress

Medical Library Association

MINITEX

Music Library Association

National Agricultural Library

National Archives and Records Administration

National Commission on Libraries and Information Science

National Federation of Abstracting and Indexing Services

National Institute of Standards and Technology, Research Information Center, Information Resources and Services DivisionMINITEX

National Library of Medicine

National Technical Information Service

OCLC, Inc.

OHIONET

Optical Publishing Association

PALINET

Pittsburgh Regional Library Center

Readmore, Inc.

Reference Technology, Inc.
Research Libraries Group, Inc.
Society for Technical Communication
Special Libraries Association
SUNY/OCLC Network
Unisys Corporation
U.S. Department of Commerce, Printing and Publishing Division
U.S. Department of Defense, Army Library Management Office
U.S. Department of Defense, Defense Technical Information Center
U.S. Department of Energy, Office of Scientific & Technical Information
U.S. ISBN Maintenance Agency
University Microfilms, Inc.
UTLAS International U.S., Inc.
VTLS, Inc.
H.W. Wilson Company

Active Personal Involvement

Your involvement need not be at the same level as your employer's. Many of the members of NISO standards committees, and some of the chairs, are from agencies that are not currently voting members. Standards organizations look for expertise and availability. For example, members of NISO committees frequently come from university libraries. None of these libraries is a voting member of NISO, although most of the librarians are members of associations that have NISO membership.

You can be personally involved in your professional associations, as noted above. You can also serve more actively, typically in two ways:

- Serving on standards committees in areas where you have expertise. Such service requires travel and available time to work on research and drafts; good standards involve careful and extensive preparation.

- Proposing new technical standards, preferably with sufficient background and detail to simplify the work of the standards committee. This may well lead to a request that you chair the committee to work on the proposal. If you're serious about a needed standard and have the skills required to make a careful proposal, you should either be prepared to accept such a request, or have another individual in mind.

You may also review and comment on draft standards without other involvement; most of them are widely publicized to elicit review and comment.

If an area of standardization is important to you, don't assume that someone else will take care of it, or that if they do, the results will be to your liking. The way to ensure that your concerns are heard is to become involved, personally and organizationally. NISO needs more members; it also needs more committed, enthusiastic volunteers.

Summary

Technical standards save money and time, avoid redundant effort, and encourage both sharing and competition. People make technical standards; time, effort, and knowledge go into useful ones. Your awareness of existing standards may make you and your agency more effective. Your involvement and that of your agency can make technical standards more effective.

12

Current NISO Standards

This chapter provides brief summaries of all NISO standards available as of February 1991, including those in draft stage. Summaries include notes on revisions, when such notes are appropriate. Each summary in these chapters includes some or all of the following:

- **Identification:** Number and brief title of the standard;
- **Purpose, use, and scope:** What the standard is for, who would use it, and its intended scope;
- **Details:** Some details of the standard;
- **Related standards:** Notes on other standards related to this one;
- **Notes:** Subjective comments on the document and on the standard as implemented;
- **Status:** When the standard will be reviewed or the status of revision or development.

Summaries in these chapters should not be used in place of the standards. In every case, the summary is just that: an abstracted idea of what is in the standard. Technical details are generally not included. These summaries are purely informational, intended to guide you to those standards that are useful for your activities. Once you've located useful ones you or your organization should purchase them from Transaction Publishers, Department NISO Standards, Rutgers—The State University, New Brunswick, NJ 08903. You can obtain a current price and availability list from NISO or from Transaction Publishers.

NISO standards are discussed in numeric order. Within text, the shorter form of a number is used except where changes within a standard are being discussed. Z39.2 always refers to the current edition; any other editions will be specifically identified (e.g., Z39.2-1971).

Every American National Standard includes some caution notice; the following, taken from Z39.48, is one of the more complete. These notes and cautions generally apply to all standards discussed in this chapter.

Approval of an American National Standard requires verification by ANSI that the requirements for due process, consensus, and other criteria for approval have been met by the standards developer.

Consensus is established when, in the judgment of the ANSI Board of Standards Review, substantial agreement has been reached by directly and materially affected interests. Substantial agreement means much more than a simple majority, but not necessarily unanimity. Consensus requires that all views and objections be considered, and that a concerted effort be made toward their resolution.

The use of American National Standards is completely voluntary; their existence does not in any respect preclude anyone, whether he has approved the standards or not, from manufacturing, marketing, purchasing, or using products, processes, or procedures not conforming to the standard.

The American National Standards Institute does not develop standards and will in no circumstances give an interpretation of any American National Standard. Moreover, no person shall have the right or authority to issue an interpretation of an American National Standard in the name of the American National Standards Institute. Requests for interpretations should be addressed to the secretariat or sponsor whose name appears on the title page of this standard.

CAUTION NOTICE: This American National Standard may be revised or withdrawn at any time. The procedures of the American National Standards Institute require that action be taken to reaffirm, revise, or withdraw this standard no later than five years from the date of approval. Purchasers of American National Standards may receive current information on all standards by calling or writing the American National Standards Institute.

Z39.1-1977
Periodicals: Format and Arrangement

Z39.1 establishes certain standards for periodicals, such as information on the cover, spine, contents, and masthead; pagination; and issue and volume identification. Publishers can apply this standard to all periodicals and to some monographs.

Details

Several sections give specifications (required and suggested) to be followed in different areas, for example:

- **Pages:** Each double page should include running heads or footlines including title, volume and issue or date, and page numbers. Pagination should be sequential within an issue or volume; the inner margin should be a full inch and not less than three-quarters inch, and the outer margin should be at least one-half inch. Errata should appear in a fixed location.

- **Cover and spine:** The cover should include title, subtitle, number of volume and issue, date, ISSN, and (optionally) location of the table of contents and name of the publisher and sponsoring body. Presence of an index should be noted; covers should not be paginated; if the cover contains the table of contents, that table should also appear inside; if the title has changed, the previous title should appear for at least one volume. Periodicals with flat spines should show the title, volume and issue number, date, and pagination on the spine.

- **Table of contents and masthead:** The table of contents should contain the title, volume, issue, and date. The masthead should include title, ISSN, publisher (and address), sponsoring body (and address), editor or staff, frequency of issue, complete subscription price schedule, copyright notice, postal notice, and procedure for filing change of address.

- **Volume:** A volume should include a special volume title page and full-volume index. "If the issues published in a single year make up too bulky a book for convenient use if bound as one volume, the publisher should divide the issues for one year into two or more volumes."

- **Other cases:** A periodical should only change size at the beginning of a volume; titles "should rarely be changed once established" and should be changed only at the start of a volume. A new title requires a new ISSN. Changes in title, frequency, or size should be announced in advance and on the title page of the first year's worth of post-change issues. Interruptions, extra issues, and divided issues should be labeled prominently and clearly.

- **Supplements:** Supplements should be the same size as the periodical, should have separate volume numbering (unless intended to be bound with the main item), and sometimes (in cases spelled out within the standard) should be treated as an independent serial.

Definitions clarify the provisions of the standard.

Related Standards

Z39.1 refers to standards Z39.4, Z39.5, Z39.9, Z39.14 and Z39.29—discussed in this chapter—and to BS 2509-1970, *British Standard Specification for the Presentation of Serial Publications, including Periodicals*; ISO 4-1972(E), *International Code for the Abbreviation of Titles of Periodicals*; ISO 833-1974, *International List of Periodical Title Word Abbreviations*; and ISO/R8-1954, *International Standard Recommendation for the Layout of Periodicals*.

Notes

The standard is straightforward but not universally followed by any means. Many periodicals that carry contents on the cover do not repeat the information inside. Many periodicals with flat spines do not carry pagination on the spine. Many periodicals, probably including most nonscholarly periodicals and many in the library field, do not print a separate volume title page. Periodical volume sizes have little to do with binding abilities: the reasonable binding limit is exceeded by any five issues of *PC Magazine* (with 22 issues per volume) or any five issues of *Byte* (with 12 to 14 issues per volume).

The only area in which periodicals tend to follow the standard is in the masthead; since much of a masthead's contents is required by the U.S. Postal Service if a periodical is to retain special mailing rates, this conformance is less to Z39.1 than to government requirements. Relatively few of those checked had full-inch or even ¾-inch binding margins; some have as little as ¼-inch inner margin. *Information Technology and Libraries* has a ½-inch inner margin.

Z39.1-1967, which called for inclusion of abbreviated title and a bibliographic strip on the cover, was a standard whose apparent costs of implementation outweighed its apparent benefits, at least to those who would bear the costs. Z39.1 primarily benefits libraries and indexing and abstracting services, and the benefits to these agencies are somewhat nebulous. Except for scholarly journals that rely on library subscriptions, most periodical publishers do not consider libraries to be a primary market.

The current version of Z39.1 is much less onerous to implement, but still adds some costs to publishing and reduces flexibility. The added paper cost of wide binding margins may not appear justified (and may restrain the creativity of magazine designers); still, the specified margins are necessary if periodicals are to survive binding without loss of legibility. Repeating a cover table of contents inside the issue seems a clear waste of space; many publishers would be appalled by the argument that they should do this because issue covers may be removed during library binding.

For Z39.1 to be widely used, agencies that would benefit from its provisions would have to make a convincing economic case to publishers. My quick survey included publications from most of the library specialist publishers (ALA, Haworth, Ablex, Pierian, Bowker, etc.); even within this narrow field, the case clearly hasn't been made.

Status

Z39.1 has passed the 10-year point at which standards cease to be considered active, and ANSI has withdrawn the 1977 version. Revision has proved to be lengthy and difficult; the first edition of this book assumed incorrectly that a revised 1984 version would become a published standard. In fact, revision continued through 1990, due partly to conflicting motives: on one hand, the desire to specify attributes that would make a serial as useful as possible in a library setting; on the other hand, the desire to achieve a standard that will be widely used.

The latest revision, labeled ANSI/NISO Z39.1-199x, *Proposed American National Standard for Periodicals: Format and Arrangement*, went out for ballot from July 15-October 15, 1990. The ballot resulted in three no votes and seven yes votes with comments.[1] This draft has a rather small number of mandated provisions and a much larger number of recommendations delineating desirable but not mandatory attributes of a standard periodical.

For example, the new draft regards the following as mandatory for a title: it must be clearly distinguishable on the cover and title page; it must be consistent and complete there and in the table of contents, masthead, running title and on volume title pages and indexes; abbreviated titles must not appear on the cover, masthead or volume title page, and abbreviated titles used "for bibliographic identification purposes" must be in accordance with Z39.5; a periodical title "must not be modified in any way unless a deliberate title change is intended"; and new titles must be made at the start of volumes and must be accompanied by new ISSNs. Additional non-mandatory recommendations are that the title should define the content of the periodical, be as short as possible, and be unique; derived acronyms should not be used for bibliographic identification.

The new draft includes reasons for most of the provisions, and goes to some pains to weaken recommendations that would reduce usage. For example, the title *Information Standards Quarterly* would have violated most earlier drafts because it (quite deliberately) includes a frequency; in the latest draft, after noting that a change in frequency would cause a title change, the advice is that "the use of words indicating frequency or year should be carefully considered."

Explanations make the new draft much more convincing; at the very least, publishers will understand why something is requested and the significance of ignoring the provisions.

---

1 Here and throughout this chapter, ordinary yes votes, typically the majority of all votes received, are not included. For example, Z39.1 also received 28 yes votes and 2 abstentions.

In all, the current draft represents a more useful and more understandable standard than Z39.1-1977. Unfortunately, it still contains mandatory criteria that, while perfectly reasonable from a library perspective and well-argued in the standard, will prevent it from being as widely adopted as might otherwise be the case:

- The period of publication for a volume must fall within a calendar year. Good advice, but certain to be ignored by many academically oriented publications.

- Permanent paper must be used for periodicals. Somehow it seems unlikely that the average newsletter or current-affairs publisher will go to great pains to do this.

- The inside or gutter margin must be at least 1 inch (2.5 cm.).[2] The reasoning is clear: that much space is required for trimming and binding. But 1 inch (leaving a 2-inch gutter in the page spread) or even ¾ inch (leaving a 1½-inch gutter) is more space than many publishers will willingly give up. NISO's own publication, *Information Standards Quarterly*, is only slightly shy of the ¾-inch mark. In an informal scan of 20-odd periodicals, journals, and newsletters received at home, I found *none* that met the 1-inch standard, and only one newsletter that met the ¾-inch escape clause. Given that good page design tenets (frequently ignored in periodicals) call for *wider* outside margins to provide visual balance for the double-width gutter margin when looking at a page spread, this provision faces an uphill battle in any widely circulated periodical; economics typically mean that magazines and journals just won't use that much extra paper.

The new draft is far better than the current standard, and offers quite a bit of useful advice for publishers who want their serials to be useful within libraries. Still, I believe, it is doomed to be (at best) only partially respected even by publishers that are aware of its provisions. That may not be desirable, but it's reality.

---

2 But the explanation includes an exception: issues formatted as a single group of folded pages may have a gutter margin of 3/4 in.

Z39.2-1985
Bibliographic Information Interchange

Z39.2 establishes a structural basis to support machine-readable bibliographic records. USMARC and other MARC formats are based on the record structure defined by Z39.2 and the related ISO 2709. The standard is intended for interchange of records between systems, not for processing within a system, and should be used by programmers and others building systems for bibliographic records. It defines a structure, but does not specify content or content designation (with some exceptions).

Details

Z39.2 specifies a record format beginning with a 24-character leader. Several leader positions are specified: record length, status, type of record, bibliographic level, indicator count, identifier length, base address, and entry map. Definitions for indicators, delimiters, and other elements work with the leader specifications to correctly define the structure of a Z39.2 record.

The standard also specifies the directory, reserves tags for control fields, and specifies placement of indicators and data element identifiers within a record. An application may use numbers and either capital or small letters—but not both—for tags; data element identifiers and indicators may be any ASCII graphic character. Specific characters are defined to serve as element, field, and record delimiters.

Related Standards

The standard refers to, and relies on, ANSI standards X3.4-1977, X3.22-1983, X3.39-1973, X3.54-1976, and X3.27-1978: ASCII, three standards for magnetic tape, and a standard for tape labels. Z39.2-1979 conforms to ISO 2709, *Documentation - Format for Bibliographic Information on Magnetic Tape.*

Notes

Z39.2 specifies a basic structure, sufficiently explicit that a generalized computer program could read any record format based on it and select fields, subfields, and indicators. It deliberately allows a range of options for such factors as number of indicators per field and length, or presence, of subfield codes (or data element identifiers). As a result, two different implementations can be extremely different in details, and a generalized program might not be able to make sense of the elements extracted.

As implemented in USMARC, OCLC MARC, RLIN MARC, and related formats, Z39.2 is widely used: tens of millions of MARC records have been distributed. Non-MARC Z39.2 formats also exist, including a recently developed variable-length format for transmitting book orders, Z39.49. Z39.2 is successful as a standard for bibliographic interchange among libraries, but is less successful in the abstracting and indexing industry, where most record formats do not follow Z39.2 guidelines.

This standard establishes a sound and flexible structure; it provides essential information to agencies using or creating MARC records, and should be considered by agencies creating other formats for bibliographic information.

Status

Because of comments and votes during a reaffirmation ballot in 1990, revision of Z39.2 will take place during the early 1990s. Most probably it will broaden the scope of the standard beyond bibliographic data, and presumably not weaken its concise, precise nature.

Z39.4-1984
Basic Criteria for Indexes

"This standard provides guidelines and a uniform vocabulary for use in the preparation of indexes." It deals with principles of indexing, the nature and variety of indexes, and organization, style, and means of preparation. Z39.4 is suited for use by authors, editors, and others who plan or prepare indexes, and covers all forms of material and indexes as narrow as back-of-the-book or as broad as library catalogs.

Details

A set of definitions with clearly labeled examples clarifies terms used in the standard, which goes on to define the function and nature of an index. Brief discussions of various types of indexes include suggestions for style and arrangement. A discussion of scope sets forth useful guidelines for what should and should not be indexed: for instance, a back-of-book index would not normally include the dedication, bibliographies, or table of contents, but should cover forewords, appendixes, and illustrations.

The longest portion of Z39.4 discusses factors influencing index structure: what's being indexed, level of indexing, arrangement of entries (alphanumeric, classified, chronological), term coordination, vocabulary control, and special problems of indexes in parts. Guidelines for entry structure include comments on choice of terminology, use of singular and plural forms, use of inverted terms, specificity, differentiation, and precision of locators. An example of the guidelines: "If the number of locators at a given heading is large, additional headings or levels of subheadings or modifiers should be introduced as needed. The point at which this should be done depends on the ease with which items may be located, but more than ten undifferentiated entries is probably always a disservice to users."

A careful treatment of syndetic structure (cross references and explanatory information) covers all major aspects of this topic and includes notes on qualifying expressions (e.g., to distinguish "seals (animals)" from "seals (mechanical)"). The section advises against "see" references in short indexes, preferring duplicate locators to save time for the user.

The final section of Z39.4 discusses physical format, with useful guidelines on indentation, punctuation, style, and separation of letter groups within an index; and comments on microform indexes and indexes stored in machine readable form complete the section.

A brief bibliography includes source materials used in compiling the standard, and is referred to within the standard as a source of textbooks on indexing. The index is exceptionally long, over two pages for a document of 21 pages, as it is "designed to exemplify the application of relevant provisions of this standard." "It is the nature of a standard to contain a high density of information, and the index to a standard for indexes should be full; hence, this one is much larger than would be expected, based simply on the page count of the standard." (Many standards lack indexes.)

Related Standards

Z39.4 cites no related standards within the text, but ANSI Z39.19-1980 and ISO 999 are included in the bibliography. The bibliography itself follows ANSI Z39.29-1977, although with some inconsistency in capitalizing monographic titles.

Notes

Z39.4 sets forth criteria and guidelines, and presents an exceptionally clear and concise view of good indexing. It should be useful for anyone planning an index of any sort, but is not the sort of technical standard that is implemented as such. Unless a publication explicitly credits Z39.4 as a basis for indexing, there would be no way to determine that the standard was used; such explicit credit is rare. Certainly an abundance of indexes do not meet the criteria of Z39.4, and it is fair to assume that most of these were developed in ignorance of the standard's existence.

Z39.4 is readable and lively in spots, and presents a large amount of useful information in a small amount of space. It can't help overcome the most serious problem with indexing (total lack), and the writers of the standard would probably agree that a bad index is better than no index at all.

Status

When this standard came up for reaffirmation in early 1989, six of the voting NISO members voted against reaffirming and six others added comments to their yes votes. As a result, the standard will be revised. That work had not begun as of February 1991. This may be a case where the standard would be more useful as part of a handbook on good writing and publishing practice.

Z39.5-1985
Abbreviation of Titles of Periodicals

Z39.5 specifies rules for forming the shortest possible abbreviated form of serial (and some nonserial) titles, so that an abbreviated form never refers to more than one publication. The standard should be used by publishers, abstracting and indexing agencies, and others who must abbreviate titles. The specification should result in the same abbreviated form when applied to the same title at different times; that is, consistent application of the specification should yield consistent, unambiguous results. The standard applies to serial publications and other title or corporate author entries in library records, can be used for nonserial publications, but is not a method of establishing entries as such.

Details

The standard specifies explicit and generally unambiguous rules for abbreviation. The rules depend on an external list[3] of words and abbreviations. Except for words on the standard list, abbreviations must always be formed by truncating final letters, and no words may be omitted (except that articles, conjunctions, and prepositions are usually omitted).

Capitalization and periods may follow any of a limited number of patterns, such that IND. ENG. CHEM., Ind eng chem, and Ind. Eng. Chem. are all equally valid abbreviations for *Industrial and Engineering Chemistry*—but ind. eng. chem. is not. Commas have the specific purpose of separating segments of the abbreviated entry, hyphens are always retained, and other punctuation may be used or omitted at will. Special characters are always retained.

The foreword, not part of the standard, explicitly states that "it is not possible to set down rules that will in every instance assure unassisted reconstruction of the original title... authors, editors and

---

3 *International List of Periodical Title Word Abbreviations*, maintained and published by the Centre International d'Enregistrement des Publication en Series (ISDS), 20 Rue Bachaumont, 75002 Paris, France.

organizations making extensive use of title abbreviations in their publications are encouraged and urged to make available to their readers, at frequent intervals, lists of the abbreviated titles they use with corresponding equivalent unabbreviated titles."

Notes

The key to Z39.5 is the word abbreviation list. That list is vital to anyone who intends to abbreviate a title, and equally vital to those wishing to recreate a title from an abbreviated form. Reference librarians are well aware that researchers frequently arrive with citations in abbreviated form, with no clear memory of the source of the citation and thus, no clear list for expansion of the abbreviated form. If the source followed Z39.5, and the library has the word abbreviation list, chances of restoring the original title are considerably improved. Cases of ambiguous abbreviated forms are legion; some of these may result because Z39.5 is not widely used, whereas others may result because abbreviated citations are transcribed incorrectly. For instance, *J. Math. & Phys.* might well be transcribed as *J. Math. Phys.*, but the former refers to the *Journal of Mathematics and Physics* and the latter to the *Journal of Mathematical Physics*.

The standard is quite explicit in most specifications, and appears to be a useful tool for creating abbreviations and deciphering them. In both cases, the standard is nearly useless without the word abbreviation list. The second use assumes that most abbreviated terms are on the list; the standard allows for truncation of other words as well, requiring only that "the same abbreviation is not to be used for unrelated words" and that "words consisting of a single syllable or of five or fewer letters shall not be abbreviated," in both cases, except as found on the word abbreviation list. The problem with the first provision is that it will only apply within a given agency; different authors and agencies with different sets of referenced titles may well use the same abbreviation for different, unrelated words. In sum, while the standard should result in an unequivocal abbreviation for each title *within a single list*, it cannot be expected to result in universally unequivocal abbreviations unless the word abbreviation list is readily available and used consistently.

Status

When this standard came up for reaffirmation in 1990, 5 of the 37 NISO members who voted, voted to revise the standard; 5 others voted to reaffirm, but with comments. At least one member called the existence of the standard into question: "There was some concern that title abbreviations . . . are not beneficial, and that with current technology there is little to be gained by the abbreviation process."[4] The standard will be revised during the early 1990s.

Z39.6-1983
Trade Catalogs

This standard specifies size and suggests good practice for trade catalogs, and is "intended to assist in producing trade catalogs that will contain the maximum amount of necessary information in a form that can be used easily."

Details

After defining methods of printing and binding, the standard specifies what information should be provided on the cover, in the index, and in each product listing to make a catalog useful. The standard calls for a narrow range of page sizes (from 7½ by 10½ inches to 8½ by 11 inches), calls for body type 8 points or larger, recommends against gatefolds, and calls for consistent and visible page numbers. The standard specifies normal paper weights and lists typical printing methods with notes on their applicability. Binding methods are also discussed with specific advantages and disadvantages listed for each, and with suggestions for appropriate cover stocks.

Title 37 of the Copyright Code (Section 201.20,37 Code of Federal Regulations, Chapter II), concerning placement of copyright notice, is included as an appendix.

---

4 "Yes With Comments: Notes from the Field," *Information Standards Quarterly* 2, no. 4 (October 1990): 30.

Notes

Z39.6 includes valuable checklists for data that should appear in trade catalogs, and has brief but useful advice on printing and binding methods. Observation suggests that most trade catalogs do use standard letter-size pages and meet many other criteria of Z39.6, but that many industrial catalogs use type smaller than 8 points.[5]

Status

Revision for this standard will begin in 1991. This may be another candidate for inclusion in some guide to good practice, rather than separate publication as a technical standard.

Z39.7-1983
Library Statistics

This standard aims "to provide a pool of defined statistical data items about libraries, from which various surveys and studies may be designed by selecting the information most valuable to collect for their purposes." It defines many items, "more . . . than any single survey or study is expected to use nationally in the future," but sets forth explicit categories so that sets of data will be comparable and can be aggregated. Z39.7 is intended for use by libraries and agencies who survey library statistics, and applies to all types of libraries in the United States.

Details

The standard begins with a set of six general principles: categories should be mutually exclusive; collections should be reported as intellectual and as physical resources; equipment needed to use materials should be reported; all major forms of income (including in-kind and contributed services) should be reported; estimates should be made

---

5 Eight-point type with one-point leading will yield eight lines per inch. Many industrial catalogs run 10 to 14 lines per inch, using type as small as five points.

when exact figures are not known; and statistical data should be collected annually and be published within a year of collection.

Seven detailed sections follow, stating categories of information and defining them and how they can be measured:

- **Identification and description** of the reporting library;

- **Personnel resources:** 28 statistical categories, including employees by category, employment status, work week and year, salaries and fringe benefits;

- **Collection resources:** 53 categories, showing units added, withdrawn and held, and titles held, by material format;

- **Facilities and equipment:** 15 categories, including "stationary service outlets" (e.g., branches), microcomputers, seats, and shelves;

- **Finances:** 43 categories of income and expenditure;

- **Services and use:** 18 categories, such as public service hours, reference transactions, cultural presentations, interlibrary loans, and circulation;

- **Computer use:** 32 possible categories, consisting of 8 applications as supported by 4 categories of computer access.

These sections take up 10 pages of the standard; another 16 are used for definitions of words and phrases used in the standard. Six appendixes give additional suggestions and guidelines for gathering, reporting, and aggregating library statistics.

Notes

This standard provides an explicit and fully detailed basis for standardized reporting of library statistics. Any library that reports statistics (that includes almost any library in the United States) and any surveying agency should be using this standard if they are not already doing so; it allows for generally clear and unambiguous statistical measures. It was developed in cooperation with statistics committees of ALA and other major national library associations in the United States, and draws on reports of recent national library statistical projects. Since the standard is in line with current use, it should see extensive use in the future.

Status

Work toward a revised standard began in November 1988. The new standard will focus on national-level reporting and will include data categories of two types:

- **Basic:** Where public, academic, school and special libraries report the same data;
- **Specific:** Where different sizes or types of libraries may collect and report different data.

The revision will include data categories only if there is evidence that most libraries can or do provide such data; will specify what and how to count for a limited basic set of elements; and will recommend collection of data on both what the library has (input or resources) and how the resources are used (output or performance).

The committee met actively during 1989 and 1990; a preliminary draft was circulated for comment in late 1990. A revised version should go out for ballot by the end of 1991; the revised standard should be adopted in the early 1990s.

Z39.8-1977 (R1984)
Compiling Book Publishing Statistics

This standard establishes definitions and subject categories for book publishing statistics in the United States, in confirmity with UNESCO recommendations for such statistics. It is for use by those who provide or collect book publishing statistics, and applies to printed books and pamphlets, excluding periodicals, advertising publications, timetables, calendars, telephone directories, maps, and musical scores.

Details

Definitions clarify what constitutes a book, a reprint, a title, and a translation. Title counts (rather than volume counts) are preferred, and the meaning of "title" in this case is defined. Twenty-three subject categories are defined, with Dewey Decimal and UDC numbers for nonfiction categories. Annual tables are called for, and various subcategories that could be counted are mentioned. The *Publishers Weekly* report on "American Book Title Output—1976-1977" is included as an appendix to show use of the standard.

Notes

Z39.8 provides a consistent method for reporting publishing statistics; its use by Bowker assures that such statistics can be compared meaningfully. Inclusion of UDC but not LC classification numbers is unusual for an American standard.

Status

The standard went out for revision at its most recent review period. It is being revised to align it more closely with its ISO counterpart; the revised standard will be balloted in 1991.

Z39.9-1979 (R1984)
International Standard Serial Numbering

This standard defines the International Standard Serial Number, how it is formatted, how the check digit is calculated, and how numbers will be assigned and disseminated. ISSNs are applicable to all serial publications, including monographic series; for instance, ANSI Z39 standards now carry an ISSN.

Notes

The original Z39.9, *Identification Number for Serial Publications*, concisely stated a number format and how the number would be assigned. The number was adopted by ISO in 1974 as standard ISO 3297, creating the International Standard Serial Number and establishing the International Serials Data System to administer the number. The ISSN, unlike ISBN, is an "idiot number," with no meaning assigned to any portion of the number except the check digit.

The ISSN is an outstanding success in the publishing field. The standard is terse (the text is less than one and a half pages long) but adequate. Between 1971 and 1979 the number was adopted as an international standard, Bowker assigned tens of thousands of ISSNs based on its files of serial publications, and a network of agencies was created to assign and control ISSNs, including the National Serials Data Program at the Library of Congress. While the meaningless nature of the number limits its extended usefulness, and the decisions of assigning agencies may sometimes be questioned, the ISSN has unquestionably succeeded, both in becoming well established and in making it easier to uniquely identify serial publications.

Status

Although the usefulness of the ISSN does not appear open to question, the wording of the standard itself may not be so clear cut. No NISO member voted against reaffirmation in an early 1989 ballot, but five did have comments. The standard should appear in a revised form in the early 1990s; revisions will probably be minor. One question that does arise is whether Z39.9 should exist as a separate standard, since it essentially duplicates ISO 3297.

Z39.10-1971 (R1977)
Directories of Libraries and Information Centers

This standard sets forth detailed and ambitious specifications for directories of libraries and information centers. It is intended to apply to all directories at the national, regional, or local level.

Details

The introduction recommends that questionnaires for directories be based on the applicable specifications, clearly and concisely stated, use standard terminology, and allow enough space for answers. Five short sections define directories; give content specifications for the cover, title page, and foreword; recommend geographic arrangement for most directories (and subject or alphabetic arrangements in certain cases); recommend placement and standards for table of contents and indexes; and specify format: no larger than 8¾ by 11½ inches, no thicker than 2½ inches, durable binding, 8-point or larger type, well laid out, and on 40- to 80-pound book paper.

The heart of Z39.10 is section 7, "Individual Entries." This section specifies a list of information to be included for each of seven types of libraries and information centers. Each list is explicit and quite extensive. The simplest, that for regional libraries, cooperative systems, and processing centers, contains 12 items such as name and address, telephone, Centrex, TWX, purpose and scope, name and title of the head, number of staff, and total annual income. The longest lists, for public libraries and college and university libraries, include over 30 items, including number of volumes, important special collections, and details on automated operations actually in use.

Related Standards

ANSI Z39.4, *Basic Criteria for Indexes*, is referred to; ANSI Z39.7, *Compiling Library Statistics*, is essential to this standard and contains definitions for many of the terms used in Z39.10.

Notes

This brief standard is clear and unambiguous, and provides a fine checklist for anyone preparing such a directory. Common American library directories appear to follow the standard in most of its details, although some items may be omitted. Certainly, any local or regional agency wishing to build a useful directory would be well advised to purchase and follow Z39.10; by doing so, the agency could assure a complete and useful directory, and one that would be comparable to other directories.

Status

A revised version, which provides a more uniform approach to directory compilation and includes data elements for SAN, fax numbers, and electronic mail addresses, was balloted in 1989. Based on the results of that ballot (2 negative votes; 10 yes votes with comments), the new version will be revised further. ANSI withdrew the existing standard in 1990; a new one should appear in the early 1990s.

Z39.11-1972 (R1983)
System for the Romanization of Japanese

"This standard establishes a system for the romanization of the Japanese written language. Unrestricted application of the system requires that the romanizer possess a detailed knowledge of the language in its modern and historical written forms."

Details

The standard uses modified Hepburn romanization techniques, and consists of four general rules and four romanization tables. As noted in the statement of purpose, the standard is not intended for use by persons who don't read Japanese. Figure 12.1 shows a portion of one of the romanization tables.

No.	H	K	R	No.	H	K	R
1.	あ	ア	a	2.	い	イ	i
6.	か	カ	ka	7.	き	キ	ki
11.	さ	サ	sa	12.	し	シ	shi
16.	た	タ	ta	17.	ち	チ	chi
21.	な	ナ	na	22.	に	ニ	ni

Figure 12.1: Portion of Japanese Romanization Table

Status

While this standard was reaffirmed in 1988, the reaffirmed version has not yet been published. The status of all NISO romanization standards is being considered by the Standards Development Committee, which may recommend that these standards be withdrawn in favor of the simple statement that United States libraries use the romanization schemes established by the Library of Congress.

Note that this standard has nothing to do with transcribing Japanese characters themselves into machine-readable form; another NISO standard (Z39.64) addresses that issue.

Z39.12-1972 (R1984)
System for the Romanization of Arabic

Z39.12 provides a romanization scheme to render Arabic personal, corporate, and place names, titles, and other items into the Roman alphabet for use in catalogs, bibliographies, citations, and the like. The standard is applicable to all languages written in Arabic writing and is designed to be fully reversible.

Details

The standard consists of three tables: letters of the alphabet, vowels and diphthongs, and other orthographic symbols. Each table shows Arabic character, name, romanization, and examples of words containing the character and appropriate romanized forms. Letters of the Arabic alphabet are shown in all four possible forms: initial, medial, final, and free-standing. Figure 12.2 shows a portion of one of the tables.

Letters of the Alphabet					
Initial	Medial	Final	Alone	Name	Romaniz
ط	ط	ط	ط	ṭā'	ṭ
ظ	ظ	ظ	ظ	ẓā'	ẓ
ع	ع	ع	ع	ʻayn	ʻ
غ	غ	غ	غ	ghayn	gh

Figure 12.2: Portion of Arabic Romanization Table

Since this is a symbol-by-symbol scheme, those who do not read the language being romanized should still be able to carry out the romanization (which is not the case with Japanese, for instance). The scheme requires diacritical marks to ensure full reversibility.

Status

As with Z39.11, this standard was reaffirmed in 1988, but its status is under review by SDC. ISO 233, *Documentation—Transliteration of Arabic characters into Latin characters*, is not identical to Z39.11, although the two include many of the same transliterations..

Z39.13-1979
Describing Books in Advertisements, Catalogs, Promotional Materials, and Book Jackets

Z39.13 defines a set of 22 different pieces of information about a book, a set of 10 different types of promotional media, and 4 different markets. An appropriate subset of the 22 items is recommended for each medium in each market. Publishers, ad agencies, and others preparing promotional material may use Z39.13 for guidelines. The standard covers all books offered for sale.

Details

The 10 media, such as direct mail, display advertising, book jackets, and seasonal catalogs, are briefly but clearly defined. The four markets are consumer, educational, institutional, and trade; bibliographic items include author, title, copyright date, ISBN, and the like. The list of bibliographic items is clear and reasonable, as are the recommendations for which items should be included in each medium. The standard gives a textual summary for each medium, and includes all 40 possibilities in a one-page table.

Notes

The definitions and inclusions are sensible, and can serve any publisher as a quick and easy checklist to make sure that any promotional material includes enough of the right information to be useful to prospective purchasers. Adherence to the standard would be hard to measure, since its recommendations fit so neatly with common sense. This may be an example of a standard that cost more to develop than it is likely to save. Its relatively modest price ($10.00 in 1990) makes it a useful working document for any new publisher.

Status

A reaffirmation vote in 1989 resulted in three negative votes and three yes votes with comments; one of the negative votes was from the Association of American Publishers, representing the most likely users of the standard.

Since that vote, the standard has been scheduled for revision, but as of this writing no activity has taken place. A call went out in October 1990 for volunteers to work on the revision; in the absence of volunteers, the standard will be withdrawn. This standard may be an ideal candidate for inclusion in a handbook of guidelines for good practice and withdrawal as a formal standard.

Z39.14-1979 (R1987)
Writing Abstracts

This standard provides guidelines for abstracts, including a variety of examples. It can cover any form of nonfiction publication but appears most suited to scholarly journals and scientific and technical publications. It is intended for use by authors and editors, and recommends that authors (rather than editors) prepare abstracts.

Details

After a five-paragraph abstract, which violates the standard itself ("write most abstracts in a single paragraph, except those for long documents"), an unusually long statement of scope and definition defines abstracts on their own terms and by distinguishing them from annotations, extracts, summaries, and synoptics. An abstract is "an abbreviated, accurate representation of the contents of a document."

A section on purpose and use includes specific recommendations for journals, reports and theses, monographs, patents, and access publications; for example, *"Journals*. Include an abstract with every journal article or synoptic, essay, and discussion. Notes, short communications, editorials, and 'letters to the editor' that have substantial technical or scholarly content should also have brief abstracts."

"Treatment of Document Content" gives guidelines for preparing a proper abstract in terms of content; "Presentation and Style" gives stylistic advice ("make the abstract self-contained," "begin the abstract with a topic sentence that is a central statement of the document's major thesis . . . ").

An appendix shows 26 different abstracts broken down into six different categories, such as "typical informative abstracts," "abstracts of monographs and chapters," and "order of document-content subject elements."

Related Standards

Z39.14 is directly related to *ISO 214-1976, International Standard on Abstracts for Publications and Documentation*, which was based largely on the 1971 edition of Z39.14. It refers users to seven other Z39 standards, all described elsewhere in this chapter: Z39.1, Z39.5, Z39.15, Z39.16, Z39.18, Z39.29, and Z39.34.

Notes

Z39.14 is long, detailed, and directly usable by any nonfiction writer. Combined with the other Z39 standards referenced (particularly Z39.16,and Z39.29), it can give a new author a considerable advantage in producing abstracts that will be accepted and used. The foreword to the 1979 edition indicates a belief that abstracts have improved since 1971, and that Z39.14 is part of the reason for that improvement. Certainly, the standard should help to generate abstracts that are directly useful in secondary publications (abstracting and indexing services); defensively, an author's preparation of a good abstract is likely to prevent abstracting by some less knowledge-able reader.

Status

The 1979 standard was reaffirmed in 1987 and will come up for review in 1992.

Z39.15-1980
Title Leaves of a Book

This standard specifies items that should be included on the title leaves of a book and, in some cases, whether the items should appear on the verso or recto of the full title leaf. The standard is for use by publishers, and applies to all books.

Details

The list of essential information is well defined and sensible, with one possible exception: "abstract of contents, in accordance with American National Standard for Writing Abstracts, Z39.14-1971." Other items are standard, although specifications for placement may not be. In practice, nearly all books meet about half the standard, and most contemporary books meet most of it.

Notes

Common deviations from Z39.15 seem to fall into three categories:

- **Date of publication:** According to the standard, this should appear on the recto (front). Publishers appear to be evenly split as to placement of publication date.
- **Edition statement:** Relatively few publishers among those sampled show "first edition" explicitly.
- **Abstract:** Z39.15 calls for an abstract to appear "on the verso of the title page or on the right hand page following it; separate abstracts of chapters should appear on or preceding their first pages." This recommendation only affects nonfiction books and monographs, but none of the books sampled included leading abstracts.

The call for abstracts is somewhat unrealistic in books other than textbooks, and has gone largely unheeded, at least by publishers in the library field. The virtue of consistent placement of year of publication on the front of the title leaf is also unclear, although clearly it is necessary to include the date.

Inclusion of ISBN and LCCN is an enormous aid to librarians trying to find cataloging copy; all books checked in an informal sample, even those without Cataloging In Publication (CIP) data, did contain both ISBN and LCCN on the verso. In each case where CIP data was not included, the LCCN was explicitly labeled; most books containing CIP data did not separately label the LCCN.

This standard was originally based on ISO 1086, *Documentation—Title leaves of a book*. That standard, which does not call for an abstract or specify on which side of the title leaf elements should appear (except for title and ISBN), works as a brief list of essential elements.

Status

Z39.15 seems to be a mystery standard. It was balloted for reaffirmation in 1986, but no report of that ballot ever appeared in *Voice of Z39*, the "(R1986)" does not appear in the available publication, and it has never been scheduled for revision.

This seems to be an excellent candidate for withdrawal or inclusion in a handbook of guidelines for publishers. Even within such a handbook, some requirements in the current standard, although possibly desirable from a researcher's or librarian's perspective, almost assure that the standard will not be adopted. The publishers that might be aware of NISO standards know how to prepare title leaves; those that do not are unlikely to be aware that NISO even exists.

Z39.16-1979 (R1985)
Preparation of Scientific Papers for
Written and Oral Presentation

This standard sets guidelines for scientists: when and how papers should be prepared, and how oral presentations differ from papers. Intended for all fields of pure and applied science, the standard is primarily useful for authors but includes some special recommendations for editors. Its advice will serve almost any nonfiction writer or speaker.

Details

"The purpose of this standard is to help all scientists in all disciplines to prepare papers that will have a high probability of being accepted for publication and of being noticed, read, and completely understood when they are published." After expanding on that purpose and counseling flexibility in applying the standard, a series of general recommendations are presented. Each recommendation is one or more paragraphs; they boil down to:

- **Have something to say:** "If the proposed contribution to knowledge is minor, the author should postpone publication until he has a more significant contribution to offer."

- **Put it in context:** The author should show how the work fits into what is already known and how the conclusions affect further investigation or technology.

- **Don't repeat yourself:** Publication of the same work twice is only acceptable when the first publication was preliminary or was for an entirely different audience; duplicate submission is rarely reasonable.

- **Say it all at once:** One set of experiments should result in one paper, not a series of them, except in some cases where experiments take years.

- **Know your audience and journal:** The author should select the proper journal, study its requirements, and plan the paper to suit it.

- **Use an appropriate form:** Later sections of Z39.16 describe nine different forms of written presentation; one of those nine should be chosen except in cases where a hybrid form is most appropriate.

- **Consider secondary readers**: An author should assume that people with less specialized knowledge may have to consult the paper, and should make the material clear enough so that it can reach such people.

Ten forms of presentation are described briefly but clearly, nine written (including original articles, letters to the editor, tutorial papers, and theses) and one oral. Seven sections give detailed recommendations for aspects of written presentation:

- **Title, by-line, abstract**: Titles should be descriptive and avoid empty words like "Studies on . . . "; authors should use the words that they would assume to be included if they were searching for the article. All who have substantially contributed to the work should be included in the by-line, and each should adopt a single consistent version of his or her name for publication. Affiliations should be current for the time the work was done; as published, it should be clear that publication does not represent endorsement by the organization. Manuscripts should always begin with a self-contained abstract suitable for direct use by abstracting and indexing services.

- **Body**: Two pages discuss organization, description of materials and methods, presentation of results, illustrations, discussion, and summary.

- **Style**: Good technical writing isn't much different from any other good nonfiction writing: active voice, verbs rather than abstract nouns, simple language, concise but not cryptic, and so on. Use of the first person is occasionally helpful but can be distracting; use of more than three modifiers for a noun can "impede comprehension and . . . contribute to ambiguity," as in the example "heavy beef heart mitochondria protein."

- **Terminology**: Use standard abbreviations and symbols; explain all nonstandard abbreviations and acronyms (and avoid excessive use); use International System of Units measures (metric), but add conventional (inch-pound) measures in those fields that still use it.

- **References**: References must be cited; other items belong in a separate bibliography. References should be to published material if possible, and should include availability where documents are not readily available. If an author can't cite a classified document in such a way that the reader doesn't have to consult the document, it shouldn't be cited at all.

- **Acknowledgments, footnotes, appendixes:** Keep acknowledgments brief, don't use many textual footnotes (as opposed to references), and use an appendix if necessary.

- **Submission:** Type everything double-spaced, check the final draft, and make everything clear for typesetting. Try to have the draft reviewed locally before submitting it. Follow the rules of the journal: duplicate or triplicate copies, as required. Editors should acknowledge submissions when received, and should handle them promptly.

A final section gives guidelines for oral presentations, and points out that different methods are required for effectiveness. Simplicity is even more important when speaking, and repetition of the major theme is good for talks but bad for papers. Slides should be simple, clear, and kept to a reasonable number, and people shouldn't be expected to look at slides throughout the talk. The speaker should try the talk out before giving it.

Related Standards

Several American National Standards, one IEEE recommended practice document, and several style manuals are cited. Z39 standards cited are Z39.14, *Writing Abstracts*; Z39.34, *Synoptics*; Z39.29, *Bibliographic References*; and Z39.5, *Abbreviation of Titles of Periodicals*. Other American National Standards cited define symbols and standard practice, such as Y15.1, *Illustrations for Publication and Projection*; Y10.5, *Letter Symbols for Quantities Used in Electrical Science and Electrical Engineering*; and Y32.14, *Graphic Symbols for Logic Diagrams*.

Notes

The standard is self-contained in matters of style and content, and provides an excellent, concise standard for scientific and technical papers (the body of the text is only eight pages). Its use by writers and editors seems designed to ensure the greatest amount of communication with the least difficulty and fewest superfluous publications.

The standard does not apply to library and information "science" as such, although some of its recommendations would certainly help to cut the amount of excess and redundant publication in the field. Most likely, the standard is not as well used or well observed as it should be. Certainly, any scientist (or librarian) would do well to consider Z39.16; even if some of its provisions are inapplicable to a field, its general advice is sound, well written, and concise.

Status

A reaffirmation ballot in 1990 resulted in three negative votes and seven yes votes with comments. The balloting will be reviewed to determine whether the standard should be reaffirmed or revised.

This material would be excellent as part of a concise handbook for writers and editors, and might be more useful in that form than as a technical standard, since, in fact, it does not meet the norms for formal technical standards, being rather a set of guidelines.

Z39.18-1987
Scientific and Technical Reports—
Organization, Preparation, and Production

Where Z39.16 gives guidelines for content and presentation of reports and articles, Z39.18 gives guidelines for the organization, preparation, and production of scientific and technical reports. It is to be used by those who prepare reports for dissemination, including publishers; it "was developed to foster uniformity in such reports, while allowing for diversity of subject matter, purpose, and audience." Most of its recommendations apply only to reports intended for dissemination, whether in manuscript, reproducible copy, duplicated or printed form, or microform.

The latest version of the standard, almost three times longer than the previous version, includes a number of relevant illustrations and a detailed table of contents, glossary, and index. It also offers specific comments on reports prepared using desktop publishing systems and other contemporary technology.

Details

This standard gives specific guidelines for the order of elements within a technical report. The front cover is specified in detail, with elements and their order, specified from report number through name and address of the sponsoring organization (if different from the performing organization). Z39.18 specifies a standard report documentation page to appear after the front cover; an appendix describes each element of the standard page and includes a blank form intended for reproduction.

In addition, the standard discusses and describes the remaining elements of a proper technical report: abstract; contents (when needed); lists of figures and tables; foreword (optional); preface and acknowledgments; lists of symbols, abbreviations, and acronyms (if needed); body matter; and back matter.

Body matter is broken down into seven subcategories with brief descriptions: summary; introduction; methods, assumptions, and procedures; results and discussion; conclusions; recommendations; and references. Back matter includes appendixes, bibliography, glossary, index, and (if appropriate) a distribution list.

The second portion of the standard provides guidelines for *preparing* the manuscript, as opposed to the earlier guidelines for *organizing* it. The preparation section includes notes on report format (subheadings and pagination), terminology (defining terms, using consistent units of measurement), formulas and equations, graphic and tabular material, explanatory footnotes, and the mechanics of keyboarding. The advice is extensive, well written, and all aimed at achieving clarity and consistent organization for technical reports.

A section entitled "Production of Report" deals with graphic design (image area, column layouts, margins, line length and character density), typography, layout and assembly, reproduction (printing processes, paper and ink, "reimaging" [what happens when a report has been microfilmed and is then printed from microfilm]), and binding. Most of the section is advisory rather than prescriptive, and most of it is quite sensible.

Appendixes include a blank Report Documentation Page with instructions for completing it and a selected annotated bibliography.

The bibliography includes 37 different standards, 5 of them Z39 standards.

Notes

Since the standard includes and explains a reproducible Report Documentation Page and clearly explains the guidelines, it requires no other documents (except those standards cited) for direct implementation. Its use appears to improve accessibility to technical reports, and the standard (and standard Report Documentation Page) does seem widely used.

Z39.18 is more concerned with form, whereas Z39.16 is primarily concerned with content. The two work together to improve the quality and accessibility of scientific and technical presentations.

The latest version of Z39.18 provides a wide range of useful guidance, most of it applicable to internally published documents other than technical reports.

At least one recommendation won't work for modern typography: "Ideally, text matter intended for continuous reading ... should be set in lines 40-43 picas wide, allowing 65-72 characters per line in a single-column format." While 40 picas is a reasonable width for a standard page, this advice conflicts flatly with the later recommendation to use 10-point type: a 40-pica line will contain considerably more than 72 characters in any proportional typeface that I know of.

That's nit picking, however, particularly since this version was published in 1987 and completed during 1986, early in the history of desktop publishing.

Status

This standard will come up for review in 1992. It is in excellent shape at the moment. Portions of it can function as a proper technical standard, although the bulk of the document—and perhaps the most valuable portions—are well-written guidelines for good practice, rather than standard provisions.

Z39.19-1980
Guidelines for Thesaurus Structure, Construction, and Use

Librarians and information specialists design and use controlled vocabularies or "authority lists." This standard presents rules and conventions for building and maintaining such a vocabulary, including necessary references and scope notes. It can be used to build a thesaurus of terms for any use and in any field.

Details

In common and dictionary use, a thesaurus is specifically a dictionary of synonyms. The first task of Z39.19 is to use the different definition common to library and information science: "a compilation of words and phrases showing synonyms, hierarchical, and other relationships and dependencies, the function of which is to provide a standardized vocabulary for information storage and retrieval." The key difference is that a common thesaurus would suggest synonyms, where a thesaurus for vocabulary control specifies which synonyms are used and which are not.

A term should represent a single concept and may use more than one word. Nouns are better than verbs, singular forms should be used except for classes of things (e.g., "painting" is process or method, whereas "paintings" are objects). Multiword terms should appear in natural order, with cross-references from the inverted form if appropriate. Punctuation should be minimal. Relationships should be specified as broader term, narrower term, use, used for, or related term. Scope notes and qualifications should be used as needed. Terms should appear in alphabetic order; hierarchical, network, and permuted displays may be added. Alphabetic order can be letter by letter or word by word, and the choice should be stated.

A lengthy section concerns the process of identifying concepts, selecting terms, and determining relationships. It recommends that a draft thesaurus be used for some period, and recommends a process for maintenance of the thesaurus, including a sample Thesaurus

Term Review form. Appendixes show a sample terminology chart and a thesaurus term review form suitable for reproduction.

Notes

The standard is well constructed and quite explicit, and provides sufficiently clear guidelines to design a thesaurus. While there are some examples, most users would also want to examine a sampling of existing thesauri before developing a new one. Naturally, librarians and information specialists working in a field should check for availability of a thesaurus before setting out to build a new one. Even with clear guidelines, building a controlled vocabulary is slow and expensive; it makes sense to use existing sources where practical, and to use an existing thesaurus as a basis for a new one if possible. Z39.19 is also useful here; its guidelines for maintaining a thesaurus are clear, and the sample form appears useful.

Status

When the 1980 standard was balloted for reaffirmation in late 1985, two organizations voted for revision. After a default ballot in 1987, a committee was formed to revise Z39.19. That revision effort has been unusually well publicized. Dr. Bella Hass Weinberg, chair of the revision committee, published "Issues in the Revision of the Thesaurus Construction Standard" in the *Bulletin of the American Society for Information Science*, December/January 1989, pp. 26-27, and presented a paper on progress of the revision at the 1989 ASIS annual meeting. The committee reported on its progress and frequent meetings in each issue of *Information Standards Quarterly* from April 1989 through October 1990.

The proposed revision, 113 pages in the comment round version circulated in early 1990, is far more ambitious and less prescriptive than the 1980 standard. The new draft eliminates "use" from the title (after all, why should a standard tell people how to use a document?) and adds "monolingual," since there is an ISO standard (ISO 5964) for multilingual thesauri. The revision does not take a monolithic approach to thesaurus structure and display, but points out the pros and cons of various formats; it includes an extended discussion of online displays, totally ignored in the 1980 version. More than 800 specific comments were received during the comment round.

When a final new version is adopted, sometime in the early 1990s, it is likely to be an extremely useful, wide-ranging basis for the construction of all sorts of monolingual thesauri. Is it really a technical standard, or is it a self-contained handbook? That's a more difficult question.

Z39.20-1983
Library Materials—Criteria for Price Indexes

Z39.20 provides criteria for developing price indexes for library materials, to measure change in average list price over time. It applies to seven categories of materials: hardcover and paperback books, periodicals, serials services, newspapers, nonprint media, and library-produced microfilm. Trade catalogs, scores, maps, school textbooks, multivolume encyclopedias, and some "transitory" materials are specifically excluded.

Details

General specifications include full definition of materials and time covered, country or countries of publication, subject classification (for indexes arranged by subject), and methodology. These specifications also call for all prices to be stated in a single currency.

Specific guidelines follow for each of the seven types of materials. For instance, a "book" has at least 49 pages, "periodicals" exclude annuals, and a "daily newspaper" must be published "on five consecutive days of each week of the calendar year, except major religious, local, or national holidays that occur on weekdays."[6] Methods of determining prices and averages are also stated. Some, but not all, indexes are specified as broken down by subject.

---

6 College newspapers are apparently not daily newspapers by this definition.

Notes

The standard is clearly written and suitable for use by any library wishing to maintain its own price indexes, and would allow a library to make sensible comparisons of its own indexes with nationally published indexes. The standard is being used by agencies that prepare national price indexes for library materials.

Status

The 1988 reaffirmation ballot resulted in four negative votes and eight yes votes with comments. The standard is being revised, with no date yet set for balloting.

Z39.21-1988
Book Numbering

This standard specifies construction of an ISBN. It is intended for use by all publishers; ISBNs are useful for all who buy, sell, distribute, or retrieve books. The ISO equivalent is ISO 2108. The scope of Z39.21 now includes books and other monographic publications, including microcomputer software and other nonprint publications.

Details

The standard itself is very short (two pages). It specifies the construction of an ISBN (group identifier, publisher/producer identifier, title identifier, and check digit), how it should appear in written or printed form (preceded by "ISBN" and with hyphens between the portions), and definitions for each portion. It specifies where the ISBN should appear on printed material, where it should appear on other monographic publications, and how it should be displayed. A previous specification that it should appear in OCR-A type has been removed.

Three appendixes provide procedures for calculating the check digit; instructions for hyphenation when the first digit is 0 or 1 (the only first digits used for American publications); and functions of the maintenance agency (R.R. Bowker), including a specific statement of what publications are covered. The list includes books on cassette, microcomputer software, and maps, but explicitly excludes serial publications and music sound recordings "because they are covered by other identification systems." There is an International Standard Recording Code (ISRC), ISO 3901-1986; I have never seen it used in the United States (even on European recordings). Within the United States, the de facto standard number for most new recordings is the Universal Product Code (UPC), as it appears in a bar code.

Status

This concise standard is one of the first NISO-published Z39 standards and will be up for review in 1993. The chief question may be whether a separate American standard serves any purpose.

Z39.22-1989
Proof Corrections

Z39.22 describes proofreaders' symbols for use in the United States. It applies only to proofreading (correcting impressions of typeset text), not to copyediting and copyreading. It is suitable for use by anyone doing proofreading, including authors.

Details

After an introduction giving some of the background of correction symbols, the standard distinguishes proofreading from copyreading. Since proofreading is to correct errors in lines of type, corrections are always called out in the margins; when copyreaders use proofreaders' symbols, they place them directly within the typescript rather than in margins.

"Every proof correction requires two marks, one in the margin of the proof showing what is to be done, another in the printed line showing where the change is to be made." The bulk of Z39.22 is an 11-page illustrated table of proofreaders' marks. For each, the marginal mark, in-line mark, and meaning are accompanied by a simulated proof paragraph showing use of the marks. The table is organized logically; a four-page index covering the table provides an alphabetic (and symbolic) reference.

Notes

The standard is explicit, clear, and self-contained. It was written by representatives from a university press, a commercial typesetter, and a trade publisher; it reflects current use and provides a sound reference for those new to the field. Proofreaders' marks have been relatively stable for some time, and are included (to some extent) in a number of style manuals and other publications. This separate publication is a handy reference and a careful exposition of proper technique for marking proofs; it should be useful for any author who reads proofs.

Status

The current version, approved in 1989 and published in 1990, will be up for review in 1994.

Z39.23-1990
Standard Technical Report Number (STRN), Format and Creation

This standard establishes a standard number for technical reports. All technical reports, including those produced on nonprint media, are included in its scope.

Details

After defining "technical report," Z39.23 defines the STRN: a two-part code consisting of a report code (from 2 to 14 characters) and a sequential group (from 1 to 7 characters), separated by a hyphen. Additional definitions cover each portion: what characters may be used, what punctuation is allowed, an optional local suffix and how it is marked.

The remaining portions of the standard show how STRNs are formatted and used, specify uniqueness, and specify that a maintenance agency shall monitor the system and coordinate assignment of report codes (not sequential groups). A brief appendix establishes the National Technical Information Service (NTIS) as the maintenance agency.

Related Standards

Z39.23 specifies placement of the STRN in terms of the format called for in ANSI Z39.18-1974, *Guidelines for Format and Production of Scientific and Technical Reports.*

Notes

Like ISBN and unlike ISSN, the STRN carries significance within its structure; because it is alphanumeric, an STRN can be partly mnemonic. Unlike most other standard numbers, it varies in length (from 4 to 22 characters). It was devised "in an attempt to bring order and consistency into a heretofore uncontrolled and chaotic bibliographic field." With good publicity from NTIS and good support by other agencies, the standard can help to achieve that goal.

Two key steps in implementing STRN were the establishment of the maintenance agency and provision of a USMARC field to store the STRN in bibliographic records. Field 024 was defined for Standard Technical Report Numbers when the USMARC Books format was extended to cover technical reports. Subfield ‡u, as defined in Field 773 (Host Item Entry) and some other linking entries, allows storage of an STRN.

Status

A revised version of Z39.23, which allows for more characters, greater variability of separators, and coordination of volume and set numbers, was approved in 1990. That version will be up for review in 1995.

Z39.24-1976
System for the Romanization of
Slavic Cyrillic Characters

Z39.24 provides for standardized romanization of Cyrillic letters used in Russian, Ukrainian, Byelorussian, Serbian, Macedonian, and Bulgarian. The standard consists of a romanization table for the modern Russian alphabet followed by a romanization table for Slavic Cyrillic alphabets, with a small number of deviations depending on the source language. Footnotes provide further variations "when it is desirable to respect particular characteristics of Ukrainian, Byelorussian, and Bulgarian." Figure 12.3 shows a portion of one of the tables.

Russian			Roman-iza-tion	Cyrillic
Printed	Written			
ы	ы *ы* *ы*		y	был
ь	ь *ь* *ь*		'	белье
э	э *э* *э*		ė	это
ю	ю *ю* *ю*		yu	южный

Figure 12.3: Portion of Cyrillic Romanization Table

Related Standards

This standard is based on ISO Recommendation R-9 1968, *International System for the Transliteration of Slavic Cyrillic Characters*, incorporating variations pertinent to the United States. That standard has been replaced by ISO 9-1986, which (unlike Z39.24) does not separate modern Russian from other Slavic-Cyrillic alphabets.

Notes

Transliteration of Russian names has been a problem for many years, as traditional transliterations vary and tend not to match standard ones. This scheme is written, straightforward, and as easy to apply as any other scheme. It uses a minimum of diacritical marks, and appears to be usable by a nonspeaker, though precise use requires that the user at least know what language a work is in.

Status

The standard is theoretically being revised, but no recent activity has been reported and ANSI has withdrawn it.

As noted for earlier romanization standards, it is quite possible that this one will be withdrawn in favor of a reference to Library of Congress practice.

Z39.25-1975
Romanization of Hebrew

This standard provides four different systems of romanization, depending on intended use of the romanized version. It is intended for use by anyone doing romanization, including scholars, journalists, librarians, and religious functionaries.

Details

A lengthy introduction considers the historical difficulties of romanizing Hebrew, where different systems are used depending on different needs: whether pronunciation should be represented, whether reversibility is important, and the like. Rather than the usual single ANSI standard, a set of styles is presented and suggests that "actual need be the factor that determines which style to use."

An important limitation is noted: while unpointed Hebrew (written without vowels) may be romanized by any careful worker, pointed Hebrew can be romanized only by someone who reads pointed Hebrew. Unpointed Hebrew can only be turned into a voweled romanized form by one who knows Hebrew very well.

The general-purpose style appears first, recommended for use in books, newspapers, teaching materials, and "wherever philological fine points are not in question and where reconversion to Hebrew is not called for." The table of equivalents is accompanied by notes on pronouncing the romanized forms; for instance, "th" would always be "as in nuthatch", and "g" is "as in get, not as in gem." A number of options speak to expert use of the table, to choices that were made among existing systems, and to some exceptions. Figure 12.4 shows part of one table.

Consonants		Vowels	
א	'	ֵ	ā
בּ	b	ַ	a
ב	b̲	ֲ	ă
גּ	g	ֶ	ē
ג	g̲	ְ	ê

Figure 12.4: Portion of Hebrew romanization table

A more exact style follows "where Hebrew orthography is considered important"; this style is reversible for consonants but not vowels. The third style, "narrow transliteration," allows complete reversibility. The final style, "keypunch-compatible transliteration," stores all Hebrew consonants and vowels as capital letters, symbols, or letter-symbol combinations.

Status

A new version of this standard should be balloted in 1991. The current version has been withdrawn by ANSI. As with other romanization standards, Z39.25 may be withdrawn, since American libraries normally follow LC practice.

Z39.26-1981
Advertising of Micropublications

This standard specifies the data elements that should be included in advertising and promotional materials for micropublications. It applies to brochures, catalogs, ads, and the like, but not to the micropublications as such. Scope is limited to those publications "intended to be retained and used over a long period of time" that "are usually available directly from the micropublishers," excluding services that are periodically updated and distributed to a controlled readership.

Details

Z39.26 has two major sections in its two pages of text. The first is a set of data elements, some of which are considered basic. Twenty-two elements describe the micropublication itself (title, name, and address of micropublisher; price(s); size and type of microform; description of retrieval aids), 13 of which are considered basic. Two groups of elements describe the content of the micropublication; each member of each group is basic "as applicable," including such elements as original publisher, identifying numbers, and conference information. The standard calls for advertising to state when any basic element is missing, and why it is missing.

   The second section expands on one of the basic elements in the first section, "Standards to Which the Microform was Produced." Twenty-two ANSI standards, two National Micrographics Association standards that were not also ANSI standards as of 1981, and two Library of Congress specifications are listed.

Related Standards

This standard relies heavily on other standards: the 24 cited as applicable standards for production of micropublications, and 3 more cited in footnotes: ANSI Z39.21, ANSI Z39.9, and ANSI Z39.23, all of which specify standard numbers.

Notes

The standard is clearly written and should be easy for any micropublisher to implement. The original Z39.26, which did not require that advertisements specify standards followed, was established in 1975. "From 1977 to 1979, the American Library Association's Ad Hoc Subcommittee on Monitoring of Microform Advertising of the Microform Publishing Committee, Resources and Technical Services Division, made a study, the purpose of which was to encourage publishers of microform material to observe, where practical, ANSI Z39.26-1975 in their advertising literature. The subcommittee found that the standard had been well received and was widely used by micropublishers." This situation probably has not changed.

Status

This standard was due for review in 1986. A call went out for volunteers to revise it in October 1990. If volunteers do not appear, it will be withdrawn.

Z39.27-1984 [withdrawn]
Structure for the Representation of
Names of Countries, Dependencies, and Areas of
Special Sovereignty for Information Interchange

This former standard[7] "provides a structure for the representation of names of the basic geopolitical entities of the world for purposes of general information interchange." NISO voted to withdraw it in 1990.

Details

Z39.27 specified two standard codes: a two-character alphabetic code "recommended for purposes of international information interchange" and a three-character alphabetic code "that is derived from

---

7 Included here as historical record.

the entity name and serves the requirements for visual and mnemonic value." Two-letter and three-letter codes beginning AA, XA-XZ, and ZZ, are reserved for private use and provisional codes. The standard provided that a list of current names and codes would be maintained by the National Bureau of Standards.

Related Standards

The basis for this standard was ISO 3166-1981, *Codes for the Representation of Names of Countries*, although the NBS list added additional codes.

Notes

The following paragraph appeared in the first edition of this book:

> The standard is essentially useless by itself, depending entirely on the list maintained by the National Bureau of Standards. Notably, the USMARC codes for Place of Publication or Production does not conform to Z39.27, at least in most MARC records: for the United States, Great Britain, the USSR, and Canada, three-character codes are used in which the first two characters represent a political subdivision (state, province, republic), and the third character represents the larger body. Thus, for the largest single use of information interchange within the library community, Z39.27 is not in use and is not likely to be used.

That continues to hold. Meanwhile, ISO 3166 has been replaced with a 53-page 1988 version providing two-character, three-character, and three-digit codes.

Status

A reaffirmation ballot in early 1989 resulted in three no votes and two yes votes with comments. A year later, the standard was balloted for withdrawal, with only one dissenting vote, since resolved. The standard did not appear to serve any use within the library community.

Z39.29-1977
Bibliographic References

This standard provides guidelines for preparing bibliographic references: citations and entries in bibliographies and in abstracting and indexing publications. It should be used by writers, editors, and publishers. The scope is limited to bibliographies, citations, and the like: catalogs, union lists, and so on., are not covered. Scope of materials covered in the rules for citation include anything "in some finite form recoverable by the reader". This includes all media, but excludes unrecorded interviews or speeches for which neither recordings nor manuscripts exist.

Details

An extensive 17-page glossary defines all terms relevant to the standard, including each bibliographic element considered suitable for citations. After the glossary, six pages of principles and guidelines provide rules and rationale for the standard. The standard provides for hierarchical levels (article within journal, chapter within book within series); for distinctions between essential, recommended, and optional elements for citations; and for citations in author-first and title-first form.

Guidelines include recommended sources of bibliographic elements, methods for showing missing information, methods for handling nonprint media, and the sequence of bibliographic elements within a reference. Rationales are stated for the order of elements. A limited and unambiguous set of punctuation marks is defined. The standard as stated recommends that "bibliographic references be presented in a single typeface for the sake of simplicity and convenience," but leaves choice of typeface and use of underscores or italics to the publisher or user. Capitalization may follow either of two standard rules: capitalize each significant word in a title, or only the first word and proper nouns. Quotation marks for articles or chapters within larger works are not required, but may be used optionally.

The guidelines of Z39.29 are somewhat dense for everyday use. Appendix A, Applications of the Standard, makes it easy to implement. The appendix is 50 pages long, a superb piece of work with fine organization and many carefully annotated examples. Dozens of simple and complex situations are analyzed, using real examples that make clear the application of the rules.

Appendix B, Matrices of Bibliographic Elements, shows sequence, level of importance, and punctuation for each element as appropriate for each of 12 types of material. Appendix C is a bibliography of works consulted, providing another set of examples of the standard in action.

Related Standards

Z39.29 refers to a number of other standards: ANSI Z39.1, Z39.5, Z39.9, Z39.16, Z39.23, and X3.30-1971; ISO R30-1956(E), R690-1968(E), 832-1968, 833- 1974, 2108-1972(E), 2145-1972, and others.

Notes

Z39.29 is a clear standard, but no strong case was ever made for publishers, writers, and editors to change their long-established practices.

Three problems with Z39.29 may have slowed or prevented its acceptance. First, the default and recommended form of standard references is clumsy because it does not use quotation marks or italics. The two citations that follow are both legitimate Z39.29 citations. The second is much easier to read than the first, but the first is the preferred form:

> Frase, Robert W. Procedures for development and access to published standards. Library Trends. 31(2): 225-236; 1982 Fall.

> Frase, Robert W. "Procedures for development and access to published standards." *Library Trends*. 31(2): 225-236; 1982 Fall.

The second problem is one of history and inertia. Most publications and publishers have long-established house styles for citations, many of them based on *The Chicago Manual of Style*. Z39.29 was not widely publicized or promoted.

The third problem is that Z39.29 was a relatively expensive, relatively obscure publication that provided one way of solving a real problem; meanwhile, software developers came up with other ways to solve the same problem without requiring publishers to change existing practice. Programs such as ProCite and NoteBook can store and manipulate references as records made up of separate fields; when the time comes to prepare a bibliography or set of citations, the software can format according to any one of dozens of different styles. Thus, Z39.29 failed to provide any real economic or intellectual advantage to writers or publishers.

The Fall 1982 issue of *Library Trends*, on Technical Standards for Library and Information Science, carried this foreword:

> In an effort to get this issue to its readership in a timely manner, and because our standard for bibliographic citations has always been *The Chicago Manual of Style* (University of Chicago Press), we have not followed Issue Editor Rush's request to use the newer ANSI standard for citation formats. Although individual authors were asked to follow the ANSI standard, they either could not or would not do so, and we therefore chose to follow our past policy and practice. Let the record show that Dr. Rush would have preferred the ANSI standards—one of life's little ironies.[8]

Five years after Z39.29 was published it was still "the newer ANSI standard" and largely unused. This status continues today, to the point at which an author may still expect to argue if he or she wishes to use Z39.29 style. Although I successfully argued for Z39.29-style citations in the first edition of this book, citations in this edition do not follow the standard. I no longer see the point in following the standard for the sake of doing so, and copyediting can go more smoothly when a better-known style is used.

Status

Work toward a revised Z39.29, which will appear more like a style manual than the current standard, progressed during 1989 and 1990; a new standard may be ready in the early 1990s. The current version has been withdrawn by ANSI. The revision committee also consid-

---

8 Charles Davis, "Foreword," *Library Trends* 31, no. 2 (Fall 1982): 189.

ered the need for publicity, and the need to convince organizations and publishers to adopt the standard if it is to be of any use.

The problem continues to be motivation: publishers and writers have to be convinced that they stand to save money or time by using a different format for citations. Otherwise, Z39.29 will continue to be part of "the walking dead"—a standard that no one uses.

Z39.30-1982 (R1989)
Order Form for Single Titles of Library Materials in 3-Inch by 5-Inch Format

This standard establishes a standard 3 by 5-inch or 3 by 10-inch order form suitable for ordering one title. It is designed for use by libraries and those who supply forms to libraries. The standard may be used for serials and monographs, but is limited to single titles and does not allow for return information.

Details

The standard defines two sets of terms: those used in the standard that do not appear on the order form (purchaser, supplier, library materials) and those that do appear on the order form (title, author, edition, etc.). Definitions for items that do appear include the number of characters available for each element. For instance, the title can run to 87 characters, author to 57, publisher to 27, series name to 26, and special instructions to 78 characters.

After these definitions, the standard states four categories of data elements: item description, conditions of order, local data, and instructions to supplier. Dimensions are stated: 3 inches by 5 inches (*not* 75 mm by 125 mm), with an optional second 3 by 5-inch right-hand portion for custom imprinting. Color and number of copies are explicitly not stated; a sample filled-in form is included, as are three different versions of the blank form, suitable for copying and reproduction: a version suitable for typing, a version for continuous-form stock (suitable for computer printing), and the 3 by 10-inch version.

An appendix provides instructions for completing the order form; for example, "*Title*: Enter the distinguishing name of the material being ordered which forms a separate whole, whether issued in one or several volumes, units, or parts. The title field also includes the number of volumes, units, or parts in a multiunit title. 87 print positions."

Related Standards

Z39.30 refers to Z39.43-1980, *Identification Code for the Book Industry* (SAN), and cites ISBN and ISSN without referring to the actual standards.

Notes

The standard form is typical of those actually in use, and has the virtues of providing a checklist of data elements; for libraries that prepare orders on a typewriter, and that prepare a separate form for each title, the standard form should be helpful. The biggest drawback for such use is that the form makes no provision whatsoever for vendor reply: there are no specifications for back-of-form response areas, and the standard specifically excludes provision for vendor response.

For computer-produced orders, the form seems to have too many small data areas, and to provide many unnecessary labels that restrict flexibility. When RLG was designing an order form, it seemed clear that a computer-generated order should be as open as possible, so that space not needed for short or missing elements could be used for other purposes. For research libraries and some public libraries, spaces for descriptive data elements may not be long enough; based on our experience, the space provided for special messages is clearly insufficient. The inflexibility of the form makes the already small 3 by 5-inch area even smaller.

When standards such as this are proposed, it may be necessary to identify the intended beneficiaries. Libraries who prepare manual orders can certainly benefit from availability of an inexpensive standard form with sufficient specifications to ensure that enough information reaches the supplier. A statement of data elements that should be included in orders is also useful; a standard limited to such a list, as the Z39 standards on promotional material are limited to lists of data elements, would serve all libraries and all book suppliers.

A reasonable guess is that the primary benefit of Z39.30 comes from the list of data elements, not the form itself. Certainly, orders are more likely to be filled correctly and promptly if the supplier has proper information; as long as that information is unambiguously printed and legible, however, it seems unlikely that a supplier would favor a particular printed format, unless it made optical character recognition much easier, which this format does not. By including not only the data list but the form in the standard, Z39.30 narrows the possibilities for compliance. (To use RLG as an example, the 3½ by 7⅜-inch orders produced in RLIN include and conform to the data elements specified in Z39.30, but the form is entirely different; thus, even though RLG orders are high quality and follow the pertinent portions of the standard, the orders cannot be called standard.)

Status

The 1982 standard was reaffirmed in 1989 and will come up for review in 1994.

Z39.31-1976 (R1983)
Format for Scientific and Technical Translations

This standard states format requirements for translations of scientific and technical material, so that the translations will be useful for researchers, librarians, and others. It is intended for use by translators and those preparing translations for publication; it covers all translations, but does not cover abstracts of material in one language that are prepared in another language.

Details

The body of the standard includes five major sections: general forms of publication, particular forms of publication, presentation, translator's notes, and special features of the original text. Some of the points covered are as follows:

- **General forms of publication:** Any translation should be properly identified, including type of translation, substantive changes to the original, the translated title, its original context, place and date of publication, and name and address of translation publisher or source. The translator and language translated to may also be identified. The original should be identified by its original title (transliterated if necessary), location in original serial (if an article) with the title of the serial in the original language, name and affiliation of the author, and other elements.

- **Particular forms:** Specifications for identification are stated for books, conference proceedings, dissertations, cover-to-cover translations of periodicals, report literature, and patent documents.

- **Presentation:** Guidelines for typography, arrangement, tables, formulas, and illustrations are given, generally stating that the translation should follow the patterns of the original.

- **Special features:** Specific provisions for footnotes, captions, bibliography, symbols, units, and other areas finish out the standard.

Related Standards

Four other standards are cited as applicable in some cases: Z39.15, Z39.16, Z39.18, and Z39.23; these are summarized earlier in this chapter.

Notes

As with several other Z39 standards, Z39.31 provides a useful checklist for those preparing documents; it does not impose excessive overhead, and is designed to make translations more easily accessible. Although it will not assist the translation process, it should help researchers in locating translations and using them.

Status

The 1988 reaffirmation ballot resulted in one no vote and five yes votes with comments. The standard is scheduled for revision; as of this writing, there has been no activity on the revision. The standard might better belong in a handbook.

Z39.32-1981
Information on Microfiche Headings

Z39.32 recommends eye-readable headings for microfiche intended for use in libraries and information centers. It is limited to standard microfiche, and to headings actually created as part of the microfiche.

Details

The standard specifies positive polarity (dark letters on a clear background), type size at least 1.5 mm high (a very small type, roughly 4 point), and recommended content and arrangement. The heading consists of three areas: identification, document description, and sequential information. Elements that should be included in the document description area are specified, and some examples are given.

Related Standards

Z39.32 explicitly calls for use of the following ANSI standards where applicable: ANSI/NMA MS5, *Microfiche of Documents*, ANSI Z39.5, *Abbreviation of Titles of Periodicals*, ANSI Z39.29, *Bibliographic References*, the standard number standards Z39.9, Z39.21, and Z39.23, and the romanization standards Z39.11, Z39.12, Z39.24, Z39.25, Z39.35, and Z39.37.

Status

The standard is being revised; the initial ballot for a new version was scheduled for 1991.

Z39.33-1977 (R1988)
Development of Identification Codes for Use by the Bibliographic Community

Z39.33 is a standard for standards: a set of considerations for developing new standard numbers or standard codes. Its scope is limited to the bibliographic community and, naturally, to standard identifiers developed after adoption of the standard.

Details

The standard is concise, and calls for statements of scope and purpose, precise description of the proposed code format, and guidance for users. A set of general considerations and comments on composition and characteristics follow: for instance, the format of a code should be distinctive and should not duplicate other codes, codes should use check digits where appropriate, and there should be a code authority for any new code. A code identifier (e.g., "ISBN," "ISSN," "STRN") should be established for any new code.

Notes

Z39.33 has very narrow application: it is really only useful when developing new standard identifiers. Within that realm, it is a clear statement, although at least two of its points are arguable and not necessarily in line with existing standards or common desiderata: "4.4 Numeric representation should be used in applications where there is no compelling requirement for alpha or alphanumeric representation, since numerics are widely used and will facilitate the use of new code standards on a national and international scale"; and "5.1.3. The format of a code, as specified in its applicable standard, should be fixed, not variable." The second statement is ambiguous; the first makes it difficult to develop mnemonic codes.

One inclusion in Z39.33 appears directly aimed at National Union Catalog (NUC) codes: "4.6 If upper- and lowercase letters are to be used when displaying alphabetic code values, the case of the letters should be derivable by algorithm." The reason for this provision is unclear, but it and the call for fixed-length codes would both seem to rule out NUC codes as feasible standard institutional codes, despite their long history of successful use.

The recommendations for numeric characters or single-case alphabetics seem odd for a standard adopted as late as 1977. By that time, one would expect that all or nearly all machine processes would be equally able to handle alphabetic and numeric characters, and that the most of systems could handle lower-case and upper-case alpha-betics distinctly and with facility.

Z39.33 explicitly allows for mnemonic codes, stating that "any code constructed with mnemonic purposes should be fully explained and illustrated by examples." Still, it seems too restrictive in terms of real machine capabilities and the success of preexisting standards. Since only one new identification code (SAN: Z39.43) has been adopted since 1977, no clear indication of the value of this standard exists.

Status

Although this standard doesn't seem particularly useful, it apparently doesn't strike anyone as harmful either. It was reaffirmed without modification in 1988, and will come up for review in 1993.

Z39.34-1977 (R1988)
Synoptics [withdrawn]

This former standard[9] defines a concise form, called a "synoptic," in which the gist of a scientific or technical paper may be published in a primary journal. The synoptic (derived from synopsis) must be prepared by the author and must represent a full paper that is available at the same time. The standard is intended for use by authors and journals; its scope is largely limited to scientific and technical papers.

Details

Z39.34 is an extensive standard, including examples of actual synoptics taken from scientific journals. It defines a synoptic carefully: "a concise (usually two-page) first publication ... of those key ideas and results ... that are judged most important and most directly useful to others." The definition continues to require that a synoptic and

---

9 Withdrawn in early 1991, and included here as recent history.

the full paper be reviewed and accepted before either is published, that the full paper be available, and that the synoptic be no longer than "approximately one-third the length of the average full paper." A synoptic must contain an abstract (and is clearly differentiated from an abstract, letter, or note).

Detailed sections on parts of a synoptic, style and clarity, length, requirements for the full papers, and citation practices make the form and function of synoptics quite clear. An interesting small section, unusually speculative for the text of a standard, suggests that "if machine-readable systems are developed and employed for scientific papers, it may be possible to code the sections and subsections of a full paper in such a way as to permit the extraction of a synoptic from the full paper."

Related Standards

This standard refers to other Z39 standards for papers, abstracts, and references: Z39.16, Z39.14, and Z39.29.

Notes

Z39.34 had fairly narrow usage, as relatively few journals went to dual publication (where the synoptic appears in hardcopy and the full paper is available in microform or on request) or to strict publication of synoptics. The standard provided good, detailed guidelines for synoptics, and was straightforward to apply.

Status

The standard was reaffirmed in 1988, and would normally have come up for review in 1993. However, as a result of NISO's study of its future, a ballot to withdraw went out in December 1990, and it has been withdrawn.

Z39.35-1979
System for the Romanization of Lao, Khmer, and Pali

This standard allows names, titles, and other bibliographic fields in these languages to be rendered in the Roman alphabet. Scope for Pali includes 10 scripts. The standard is intended for all library and bibliographic uses.

Details

Z39.35 consists of character-by-character romanization tables for Lao, Khmer, and Pali, with two tables for Pali to cover the following scripts: Devanagari, Sinhalese, Burmese, Thai, Bengali, Khmer, Lao, Tua Tham/A, Tua Tham/B, and northern Thai. Figure 12.5 shows a portion of one of the tables.

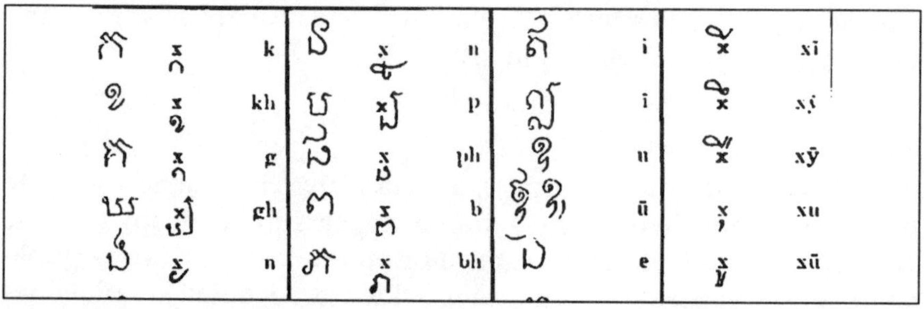

Figure 12.5: Portion of Lao Romanization Table

Notes

This standard was actually established by an ALA committee, the Descriptive Cataloging Committee of the Cataloging and Classification Section, Resources and Technical Services Division (RTSD: CCS: DCC), based on work from the Subcommittee on Technical Processes, Committee on Research Materials on Southeast Asia (CORMOSEA) of the Association for Asian Studies and the Orientalia Processing Committee of the Library of Congress. Since it is solidly based on work in the community, its wide use (within the community cataloging Lao, Khmer, and Pali materials) appears probable. On the other hand, since American libraries almost universally follow Library of Congress practice for romanization, it's not clear that the NISO standard has to exist as a separate document.

Status

This standard was being revised in 1989, but no recent activity has taken place. As with other romanization standards, it may be withdrawn in favor of the simple assertion that American libraries follow LC practice for romanization. ANSI has withdrawn the current standard for passing the 10-year limit.

Z39.37-1979
System for the Romanization of Armenian

Z39.37 provides a table of Roman equivalents for Armenian characters. It is applicable to all bibliographic uses.

Notes

This standard was forwarded to Z39 by RTSD: CCS: DCC, as was Z39.36. Unlike Z39.36, these tables differ from prior practice to some extent; those changes (from ALA/LC tables published in 1958) are

Character Number	Armenian		Romanization			
25	Չ	չ	Ch'	ch'		
26	Պ	պ	P	p	[B	b] [1]
27	Ջ	ջ	J	j	[Ch	ch] [1]
28	Ռ	ռ	Ṛ	ṛ		
29	Ս	ս	S	s		
30	Վ	վ	V	v		

Figure 12.6: Portion of Armenian Romanization Table

explained in the foreword. Figure 12.6 shows a portion of the romanization table.

Status

Some revision effort may be under way, although nothing has been reported recently. As with other romanization standards, Z39.37 may be a candidate for withdrawal. ANSI has withdrawn the current standard for passing the 10-year limit.

Z39.39-1979 (R1988)
Compiling Newspaper and Periodical
Publishing Statistics

This standard describes procedures for compiling and reporting statistics on newspapers and periodicals. It is intended for use by firms such as R.R. Bowker and other firms, libraries, and agencies that create or use publishing statistics. It specifically relates to statistics on first publication, that is, on new periodicals and newspapers. It excludes microform publications and the same categories of publications excluded from the related standards Z39.8 and Z39.40.

Details

Definitions of serials, newspapers, periodicals, and circulation are followed by sections on methods of enumeration, classification, and compilation. Some specific details: local or regional editions don't count as separate titles, but different language editions do; circulation figures should distinguish between paid-circulation, controlled-circulation, and free-circulation periodicals; statistics should be subdivided by language and frequency (and between newspapers and periodicals), and by subject, using the same 23 Dewey classifications used in Z39.8. Tables should be compiled annually. The standard parallels Z39.8, and should be as consistently used.

Status

The standard was reaffirmed in 1988 and will be up for review in 1993.

Z39.40-1979 (R1987)
Compiling U.S. Microform Publishing Statistics

This standard establishes simple statistical measures for microform publishing. It covers microform versions of books, pamphlets, dissertations, and the like, but excludes catalogs, advertising, timetables and the like, and publications for restricted readership.

Details

A set of definitions is followed by two report forms, one for original microform titles and one for republications. The definitions and the report forms make straightforward and consistent reporting possible. Categories include number of titles by category of publication, such as books, technical reports, and collections, and by microform format such as 16-mm roll and 105 by 148-mm fiche.

The two report forms are nearly identical; each contains 11 publication categories and 7 format categories plus grand total, making a total of 88 possible figures to be reported on each form.

Status

The standard was reaffirmed in 1987 and will be up for review in 1992.

Z39.41-1990
Book Spine Formats

This standard specifies information that should appear on the spine of a book and how it should appear. It applies to all books and is to be used by publishers and book designers.

Details

A page of definitions consists primarily of illustrations showing books with descending spine title, edge title, pillar spine title, and transverse spine title, and the 32-mm space to be reserved at the bottom of the spine for library use.

"Essential information" to appear on a spine includes author(s), title, series, and the library identification field (the blank space), which may contain the publisher's colophon or name. No preference is stated for descending spine (type that reads sideways if the book lies flat, cover up), pillar spine (upright letters appearing one to a line, reading top to bottom), or transverse spine (type in a line at right angles to the spine), or a mix of those. (Of the eight pages in the standard, the body of the standard is the last two.)

Notes

The standard is brief, clear, and modest in its requirements; most books appear to meet it. The most likely failure would be author or title lines extending into the bottom 32 mm of the spine; when this happens, it is probably through ignorance of the standard.[10] Colophons are most likely to appear at the bottom of the spine.

Status

A revised standard was approved in 1990 and should appear in 1991. It changes the wording slightly in some sections. Other than better provisions for handling right-to-left scripts such as Hebrew (the original standard was strictly left-to-right), the new version has one significant new provision: rather than reserving the bottom 32 mm for library identification, it specifies that area for publisher's colophon or name or for volume number, and reserves the 32-mm area *immediately above* for library identification. That's troublesome; on 24-cm (9-in.) spines, it's quite common for the author's name to extend into the bottom 64 mm of the spine.

---

10 A quick survey of books on hand showed only one, published by a very small library publisher, that put the authors' names within the bottom 32 mm.

Z39.43-1980
Identification Code for the Book Industry (SAN)

Z39.43 is a short, clear standard providing "a unique numeric identification for each address of each organization, in or served by the book industry, that is engaged in repetitive transactions with other members of this group, in order to facilitate communications among them." It establishes a six-digit number (plus check digit) sufficient to accommodate 999,999 addresses.

Details

The standard is designed for use by publishers, jobbers, bookstores, distributors, and libraries. R.R. Bowker assigned 278,000 numbers in the initial pass, with an additional 100,000 reserved for special use, leaving a pool of over 600,000 numbers. The standard establishes Bowker as the assignment agency. As with other numbering standards, an appendix specifies calculation of check digit for SAN.

Notes

When adopted, SAN seemed to be the agency identifier, but it was never widely adopted by libraries, although it does appear to be used by publishers, distributors, and bookstores. It's not clear whether SAN will ever extend significantly into the library community. On the other hand, its use within the book industry may justify its existence.

Status

A reaffirmation ballot in 1990 resulted in three votes to revise, specifically to change the name of the standard to *Standard Address Number*. A revised standard will probably be adopted in the early 1990s.

Z39.44-1986
Serial Holdings Statements

This standard specifies methods to identify, record, and display holdings information for serials at any of four levels of specificity. It only defines holding elements, but defines those for all serial publications in all physical formats. The standard supersedes the withdrawn Z39.42, serial holdings statements at the summary level, as it specifies summary and detailed holdings statements.

Details

This long (43 pages) and very detailed standard has eight textual sections and three appendixes. The eight sections provide explicit, carefully written details on data elements, their meanings, when required or recommended, and how they work together. Some areas:

- **Scope, principles, and guidelines:** Holdings should show what a library has, not what it lacks. Holdings should be linked to bibliographic records unambiguously, using any link desired. The standard is independent of cataloging systems, accommodates manual and automated systems, requires unique locational data but does not specify its construction, and does not require or recommend special typographic conventions other than punctuation. Four levels are defined:

  - **Level 1:** Serial identification and location;
  - **Level 2:** Adds date of recording, physical form, completeness, acquisition and retention policy, and local notes;
  - **Level 3:** Adds enumeration or chronology;
  - **Level 4:** Adds more detailed enumeration or chronology.

  The standard allows for composite statements (representing holdings at several locations within an institution) or copy-specific statements, and provides for compression of detailed level 4 holdings.

- **Glossary:** A detailed glossary covering more than 50 terms used in the standard.

- **Punctuation:** A minimal and unambiguous set of punctuation carrying meaning; for example, a comma indicates a break or gap in holdings, a semicolon indicates a break in publication.

- **Data areas and elements:** A table and set of guidelines for data elements, and areas containing those elements, for each of the four levels; for instance, the "status data area" includes date of report, type of holdings, physical form, completeness, acquisition status, and retention elements for levels 3 and 4. Each coded element (e.g., "type of holdings") has a code list; each element has an explanatory section.

- **Recording and display guidelines, by level:** Four sections, one for each level. Level 1 is relatively brief, level 2 even briefer (but incorporating level 1); level 3 quite long and detailed (and incorporating levels 1 and 2), and level 4 as long as the others combined (and incorporating levels 1 and 2).

The first appendix diagrams 11 examples of holdings statements at various levels to illustrate use of the standard. The second shows possible alternatives for correlating enumeration and chronology clearly, when such correlation is not inherent in the holdings level. The last appendix is a table of physical form designations in coded and text form, such as "hg" or "Microopaque" for microopaque microforms.

Notes

As stated, the standard could be implemented on its own in a manual system, but represents a fairly complex, if clearly defined, method for manual recording. In practice, implementation of levels 3 and 4 is dependent on good computer-supported systems. As a result, the fate of Z39.44 is closely linked to the USMARC holdings format. The two were developed in parallel, with significant changes in the holdings format being made when the original Z39.42 (summary) and proposed Z39.44 (detail) were merged into a single standard.

Levels 3 and 4 do provide clear and explicit forms for recording holdings, even when detailed holdings must be recorded. The standard at these levels does not appear fast or easy to apply, but is about as good as any other methods for recording detailed holdings. The complexities of the holdings format are directly based on the complexities of Z39.44 (and vice-versa).

In 1985, when the USMARC holdings format was still a draft document and Z39.46 was still a draft standard, I commented that it was "much too early to judge the general usefulness or likely use of

Z39.44; as with the Holdings Format, it is probably the best general solution available."

The *USMARC Format for Holdings and Locations* retained final draft status until quite recently, partly because a Z39 standard for nonserial holdings was still needed. As discussed below, that standard (Z39.57) was approved in 1989, and USMARC holdings is now an established format. It's still early to see how widely it will be used, but it and Z39.44 continue to be the best (and only general) known solutions for the complex serial holdings problem.

Status

Originally approved in 1986, this standard will be up for review in 1991.

Z39.45-1983
Claims for Missing Issues of Serials

This standard specifies data elements to be included in serial claims; an appendix suggests a preprinted form for such claims. The standard is limited to claims for missing issues on serial subscriptions; it excludes claims for monographs, invoices, and renewal notices.

Details

The standard itself consists of a series of data elements to be supplied by the claimant (library), such as title, publisher, pieces claimed, ISSN, and a supplier response section "to simplify the task of responding to the claim," based on the 16 responses that F.W. Faxon Company asserts account for 98% of supplier responses to claims.

The two appendixes include a preprinted blank claim form with notes on its design and use, examples of completed claim forms, and examples of computer-produced claim forms and video displays. The video display is clearly a typed printed form, in no way comparable to a video display; the computer-produced claim form is nearly as busy as the overly busy printed form.

Related Standards

Standards specifically used include ANSI X3.30, Z39.1, Z39.9, Z39.42, and Z39.43, ASTM E250-76 (*Recommended Practice for Use of CODEN*), and ISO 3297, the international version of ANSI Z39.9 (ISSN).

Notes

The recommended form, designed to be a preprinted form comparable to the ALA ILL form, is clear enough and could be used by almost any library. It is a classic multipart form with minimal space for a bibliographic description and 21 separate data areas on the top half, 18 on the bottom half. This standard's use is certainly limited by the deliberate decision to require separate forms for monographic and invoice claims, and by a design that restricts the amount of information that can be provided by demanding too many explicit slots for information.

As with Z39.30, the standard order form, Z39.45 suffers from including two different levels within a single standard. The list of data elements is sound and appears applicable to all claims, whether produced manually or by computer. The specified form is useful for manually produced claims as a prompting device, but appears unnecessary for computer-produced claims.

I believe that the requirement for a separate serials claim form is unnecessary complication. The standard is valuable as a list of elements that should be included in claims; its value in prescribing the layout of a claim form is much less clear.

Status

The 1988 reaffirmation vote resulted in two no votes and six yes votes with comments. As of now, the standard is awaiting revision, with no activity reported.

Z39.46-1983
Identification of Bibliographic Data on and Relating to Patent Documents

This standard specifies the minimum bibliographic data elements for the first page of a patent document and means by which those elements can be identified without knowledge of the language or patent laws involved. Scope is general to the bibliographic community.

Details

The standard itself consists of about 50 data elements, 18 of them required, and some rules for their use. Each data element is identified by an Internationally Agreed Number for the Identification of Data (INID) code, which is to precede the element in a circle or parentheses. INID codes are key to the standard, as they explicitly identify each bibliographic element without recourse to punctuation or language. Thanks to the codes, the standard need not (and does not) specify any order for data. It does allow for use in official gazettes, where INID codes are displayed in a representative specimen entry and omitted from individual entries following the same uniform pattern.

Examples of elements and INID codes: 11, "Number of the document"; 25, "Language in which the published application was originally filed"; 51, "International Patent Classification"; 72, "Name(s) of inventor(s), if known to be such."

Notes

Given the INID codes and their placement, the standard is clear and appears universally applicable. If, as the abstract states, "users of patent documents and patent gazettes often encounter difficulties in identifying the bibliographic data on or relating to patent documents," its widespread use would appear to alleviate those difficulties. Use of the standard appears to impose a small overhead on those filing patent documents: the bibliographic elements are clearly stated, and should be easy to provide. In practice, provision of the standard should also serve as a checklist for those preparing patent documents, to ensure that all needed identification elements have been included.

Status

The 1988 reaffirmation vote resulted in one no vote and two yes votes with comments. As of now, the standard is awaiting revision, with no activity reported.

Z39.47-1985
Extended Latin Alphabet Coded Character Set for Bibliographic Use (ANSEL)

This standard establishes a set of characters defined as proper extensions to the standard ASCII character set. Characters defined are generally those that were defined over a decade ago in "ALA Extended ASCII" and used in USMARC records for many years. Characters that required nonstandard code sequences in ALA Extended ASCII also require special code sequences in Z39.47, but the sequences required follow ANSI standards. Z39.47 is intended for use in USMARC records and similar interchange of bibliographic information.

Details

The standard includes two code tables, one for a seven-bit environment (in which the characters would replace normal ASCII, signalled by an escape sequence) and one for an eight-bit environment (in which the characters are the "high half" of the character set). The standard is not self-sufficient: rather than stating the escape sequence to be used (as in other Z39 standards, this one says that the escape sequences are "assigned by the ISO Registration Authority in accordance with procedures given in ISO 2375-1980." Thus, you would need more information than is contained in the standard in order to use it in most circumstances.

In addition to the two code tables (Figure 12.7 shows a portion of one of the tables), the standard includes a table giving the name

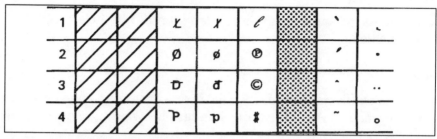

Figure 12.7: Portion of ANSEL Table

and an example of use for each character. It also lists the regular ASCII control and graphic characters.

Two appendixes show Latin alphabet languages and transliterated non-Latin languages using these characters and modifiers: the characters and modifiers used for each language, and, for each modifier or character, the list of languages in which it is used. So, for example, æ (the ae ligature), is used in Anglo-Saxon, Danish, Faroese, Icelandic (modern), Navaho, Norwegian, and transliterated Lao and Thai.

Notes

Z39.47 does establish most of the ALA extensions as standard ANSI extensions and adds a few more characters (e.g.,inverted exclamation, inverted question mark, and degree sign). The first few proposals for this standard also incorporated the limited set of superscript and subscript characters already in ALA Extended ASCII, as well as the three Greek letters—alpha, beta, and gamma. Those first versions would have made all accepted ALA Extended ASCII characters storable as single characters, and would have simplified storage and transmission of bibliographic data.

The final version took a more theoretically sound tack: standard escape sequences should be used for all superscripts, all subscripts, and all Greek characters. Thus it disregarded the practical situation that printing systems devised to support library needs do not typically support any superscripts, subscripts, or Greek letters beyond those in ALA Extended ASCII.

In fact, Z39.47 has never been properly implemented by any major U.S. MARC processing agency. The Library of Congress and, following their practice, most other MARC-handling agencies (including OCLC) use illegitimate escape sequences for superscripts, subscripts, and Greek letters, and use only the smaller set of special characters in ALA Extended ASCII. RLIN uses the character set approved by MARBI in the early 1980s, which resembles early drafts of Z39.47. Z39.47 is also at variance with the equivalent ISO standard; as it stands, it is problematic and unused.

Status

When this standard was balloted for reaffirmation in 1990, two members voted to revise or abandon the standard; another voted to reaffirm, but with comments. The standard has been revised and will be republished in the early 1990s.

Z39.48-1984
Permanence of Paper for Printed Library Materials

This standard sets criteria for uncoated paper that can be expected to last several hundred years under normal library use and storage conditions. It is intended for use by publishers and paper producers and to serve as a buying tool. Although primarily intended for publications that have some lasting significance, it provides useful information for any publication printed on uncoated paper.

Details

This standard addresses one of the most serious problems facing libraries today: the paper used during most of the nineteenth and twentieth centuries is falling apart. Specifically, acidic paper becomes brittle fairly quickly; as the foreword notes, "this embrittlement has made probable the loss of the original hard copy format of much of the published record from the 19th and 20th centuries." By defining standards for permanent paper and a symbol to identify use of such paper, the standard "seeks to encourage wider use of permanent paper...and to promote recognition of its need and acceptance by publishers and librarians."

Definitions of certain key terms are followed by minimum requirements: minimum pH of 7.5 (moderate alkalinity), folding endurance and tear resistance for various weights of paper, alkaline reserve, and the requirement that no unbleached pulp or groundwood be included in the paper stock. All requirements are stated with appropriate standard testing methods.

Adherence to Z39.48 is crucial to the future of printed materials in libraries; the standard carries instructions for showing such adherence. A statement that the standard has been met should appear, as should the trademarked symbol shown here. The statement and symbol should be on the verso of the title page and may be used elsewhere. The standard also recommends use of the symbol in advertising, and calls for adherence information to be included in Cataloging In Publication data as part of the ISBN qualifier.

Related Standards

Z39.48 refers to three TAPPI standards (Technical Association of the Pulp and Paper Industry): T-509, *Hydrogen Ion Concentration (pH of Paper Extracts—Cold Extraction Method)*, T-511, *Method for Folding Endurance of Paper (MIT Tester)*, and T-414, *Standard for Internal Tearing Resistance of Paper*. The standard also refers to the ASTM/ANSI standard D 3290, *Standard Specification for Bond and Ledger Papers for Permanent Records*..

Notes

The deterioration of books printed in the nineteenth and twentieth centuries is one of the great tragedies of publishing history: a substantial literature is destroying itself. The Library of Congress and other agencies are spending millions of dollars to try to maintain some of the damaged books and to microfilm those beyond hope; this standard can at least help to minimize future problems.

Z39.48 has been a considerable success in the few years since it was adopted. *Library Journal* occasionally runs an honor roll listing publishers that have signed up to use permanent paper for first editions. Several review media now note alkaline or permanent paper in their reviews (note that Z39.48 includes several provisions in addition to alkalinity). The compliance symbol and phrase turn up in increasing numbers of books. Several agencies are working for greater use of permanent paper; as of 1991, paper mills can produce alkaline book paper as inexpensively as acid paper and with less damage to the environment.

Publishers haven't always found it easy to assure compliance; for example, whereas G.K. Hall has used alkaline paper in its books for several years, it was only in 1990 that they were able to gain the assurance from their paper suppliers that allows them to use the symbol and compliance phrase on title leaves.

Status

While Z39.48 would normally have come up for review in 1989, revision actually began in December 1986, largely *because* Z39.48 has been both successful and very important. NISO established a committee to expand Z39.48 to encompass coated paper (the current standard deals only with uncoated paper). In 1988 the committee was also asked to review and revise the existing specifications for uncoated paper. The committee includes representatives from publishers and paper-making companies, as well as preservation specialists and librarians.

No published data exist on which to base permanence criteria for coated paper; thus, the committee first had to develop specifications for testing coated paper. The Mellon Foundation provided funding, and NISO contracted with the Institute of Paper Chemistry to perform tests during 1988. After reviewing the results of those tests, the committee requested more tests from the Institute, from Rochester Institute of Technology and from research laboratories at the Glatfelter Company and S.D. Warren Paper Company (two producers of permanent paper). Data from an ASTM testing program were obtained for comparison.

The original standard coupled tests for durability with tests that could indicate permanence, but the two are different attributes. An acid paper may be very durable before it yellows and becomes brittle; an alkaline paper that will last for centuries if stored properly may not withstand hard use (it may be permanent but not durable).

One aspect of the revision was to uncouple durability and permanence, in part because the permanence provisions could be determined fairly easily, whereas the durability provisions required testing of a sort not regularly carried out by paper makers. Thus, permanent paper could be reasonably assumed to be much more readily available than paper that could be certified for the current Z39.48. The key provisions for permanence are a specified pH level, a level of alkaline reserve, and lack of groundwood and lignin in the pulp; provisions for durability involve fold endurance and tear testing.

Coated paper consists of a paper core—which might be alkaline, neutral, or acidic—and a coating that is typically alkaline when applied. If the core paper is acidic, the coated paper is unlikely to be permanent, but there's no standard test for nonacidity of the core paper after it's been coated. Thus, a coated-paper standard must primarily rely on manufacturer certification.

A draft revision of Z39.48, with the new title *Proposed American National Standard for Permanence of Paper for Publications and Documents in Libraries and Archives*, was circulated for discussion at the end of 1989 and in early 1990. It is relatively short and clear. It establishes separate minimum requirements for uncoated paper and coated paper (all terms are clearly defined). The new requirements for uncoated paper include pH, tear resistance, alkaline reserve, and a limit of 1% lignin (rather than a restriction on groundwood and unbleached pulp); the folding endurance test is removed. Coated paper has the same requirements, except that the pH requirement for the core is slightly lower (neutral core paper with alkaline coating should be permanent), and the suggested method of confirming core paper pH is only an approximation. In addition, the tear resistance test requirements are based on the weight of the core paper, not the weight of the final stock.

Based on comments received on this draft, the committee made further revisions, stating a maximum pH, ordering more tests on the question of lignin's effects on permanence, and revising the method for determining pH of uncoated paper (when it is lightly coated). The draft standard went out for balloting in December 1990.

It is fair to assume that a new Z39.48, covering a wider range of paper stock and allowing easier certification, will emerge in the early 1990s, and that its use will continue to grow. It is one of NISO's great recent success stories, and one that serves libraries and archives now and will for centuries to come.

Z39.49-1985
Computerized Book Ordering

Two formats are established for computerized book ordering: fixed and variable-length. The standard is intended "for anyone who buys or sells books and has access to a computer," but appears better suited to bookstores and distributors than to libraries.

Details

Z39.49 is based on industry standards developed by the Book Industry Systems Advisory Committee (BISAC); the variable format is also based on ANSI Z39.2, but is not a MARC format, as it selects different options from Z39.2.

Each element in the fixed format is accommodated in the variable format, but the reverse is not true. An extensive data dictionary shows details of both formats, from "accompanying material" through "volumes in set."

The fixed format consists of a group of 80-character records, with specific tape density and blocking factor specified. Each record contains a tag and sequence number; a file includes a purchase order header record, several optional purchase order handling records, and one or more line item records for books ordered, followed by a purchase order control record providing totals for the order.

The variable format is a proper Z39.2 format, containing a 24-byte leader, directory, and tags. Unlike MARC, the directory consists only of tags and starting character positions: the length of a field is determined only by the field terminator. Also unlike MARC, there are no indicators in variable data fields, and subfield codes are upper-case alphabetic characters. The variable format is as detailed as a MARC format, and is quite flexible.

The most significant difference between Z39.49 and MARC is that the entire format, including content designation, is offered as an ANSI standard.

Status

This standard entered review in 1990. A reaffirmation ballot resulted in two negative votes, with four yes votes accompanied by comments. BISAC, maintenance agency for the standard, suggested some revisions and recommended dropping the variable format altogether. The fixed format is heavily used (although not within the library community); to BISAC's knowledge, no organization has ever implemented the variable-length version.

Furthermore, Electronic Data Interchange (EDI), using standards developed by X12, represents the norm for business use of electronic transactions. In 1990 the NISO Board endorsed the migration of NISO acquisition standards to ASC X12 formats. It is likely that a sharply truncated version of Z39.49 will be approved, including only the fixed-length version and referring to X12/EDI as a variable-length format.

Z39.50-1988
Information Retrieval Service Definition and Protocol Specifications for Library Applications

ISO 7498 establishes the Basic Reference Model for Open Systems Interconnection (OSI) as a way of organizing protocols for computer-to-computer linkages. OSI (as a reference model) does not itself represent a standard protocol; rather, it provides the framework for sets of standards.

Z39.50 is NISO's first standard within the OSI framework. It specifies a protocol to allow an application on one computer to query the database of another computer. The protocol specifies procedures and formats for intersystem submission of a search request, request for transmission of the result, responses to requests, access control, and resource control.

Details

The protocol provides a number of basic capabilities:

- After a communications session has been established (handled by other protocols), the originating computer may submit a search request that includes a query and parameters that determine whether the records resulting from the search are to be returned as part of the response.
- The target computer responds with a count of records identified and, possibly, some or all of the records.
- The originating computer may submit a request to transmit any number of the records, assuming that the selected records form an ordered set, which may be referenced by sequential position (e.g., records 3-10 of an 18-record set). Ordering is determined by the target computer.
- The target computer responds to one or more transmission ("present") requests, which may be followed by additional search requests, including requests that qualify earlier searches.

   Optional capabilities include the following:

- The originating computer may specify an element set name, specifying certain data elements to be transmitted instead of full records.
- The originating computer may provide a name for a result set and subsequently refer to it by name.
- The originating computer may delete a previously-named result set.
- The target computer may impose access control restrictions, demanding authentication before processing a request.
- The target computer may provide resource control, sending an unsolicited status report during processing, allowing the originating computer to decide whether to continue.

   A common type 1 format for queries (searches) is provided—although it is possible to use type 0 queries that don't follow the common format.

The standard is quite detailed but not detailed enough to be a complete implementation specification. Such detail would make it too narrow; as adopted, it should support a wide range of library computer-to-computer (system-to-system) linkages.

Notes

This standard emerged from the Linked Systems Project (LSP) and will be implemented far more widely than that initial computer-to-computer linkage. The protocol itself is independent of the content and format of data being searched and retrieved; it provides a solid basis for information retrieval within a library setting, regardless of the specific information being retrieved.

The standard defines the mechanism of a linkage, not the content. The content of a linkage agreement is defined by an implementation profile that will be registered with the Library of Congress (serving as the registration agency for Z39.50); such profile registration is the normal methodology for OSI application-layer standards. From the perspective of some who have been accustomed to dominant-agency and proprietary standards for data communication, this makes Z39.50 deficient: it doesn't spell out every detail.

Beginning in 1990, a group representing agencies already working on Z39.50 implementations has begun to meet to define a common implementation profile and work through the problems of implementing the standard. The group will be meeting occasionally and carrying out continuing discussions through an electronic mail list. The group will also establish testing procedures as implementations near completion.

This standard is fundamentally important for the future of library-to-library (and system-to-system) computer-based communications; it establishes a common ground through which searches and responses can take place. It has received favorable attention beyond the NISO community, as it represents a clear and very useful OSI standard.

Status

Z39.50 was adopted in 1988 and will come up for review in 1993.

Z39.52-1987
Standard Order Form for Multiple Titles
of Library Materials

This standard complements Z39.30, providing a form to facilitate ordering one or more titles of library materials.

Details

A specific form can be used to order one or more copies of one or more items or single issues or runs of a serial titles, and to request one or more copies of a single title as a gift or exchange. It is not intended to be used for computer-to-computer ordering, as a claim form, to be returned to report on status, to be returned to the supplier with returned items, with optical scanning equipment, as a substitute for a cover sheet, or as a cataloging record.

Definitions for each element include number of print positions; elements are broken down by category; the form is specified as 8½ by 11 inches "if form is bottom edge pasted" (with appropriate adjustments for bottom stubs or for continuous-form margins). All spacing is defined based on 10 characters per inch horizontally, 6 lines per inch vertically. The standard even specifies the typeface and size to be used for the preprinted form (Helvetica Medium, regular and light). The form itself appears as an appendix, with instructions for completing the form.

Notes

I find it nearly inconceivable that a NISO standard would go to such details as specifying 14-point Helvetica Medium caps for "PURCHASE ORDER NO." Like many earlier NISO standards, this one is totally lacking in argumentation; perhaps there's a reason that, say, 14-point Optima or 15-point Stone Sans or, to be radical, 14-point Palatino would somehow diminish the usefulness of the form, but I can't imagine what it would be.

The form itself is reasonable enough for libraries ordering relatively simple material (there's very little space for item description) and using a typewriter. The deliberate omission of backside spaces for vendors to provide a response makes it far less useful than some existing order forms, however.

I question the usefulness or advisability of NISO standards that specify the precise layout of business forms, although it's clear that some people feel them to be important. Perhaps book ordering has been so chaotic that this standard serves a real purpose, but specifying precise typefaces is absurd.

Status

The standard was adopted in 1987 and will come up for review in 1992.

Z39.53-1987
Codes for the Representation of Languages for Information Interchange

This standard essentially formalizes the list of language codes developed by the Library of Congress (working with the National Agricultural Library and National Library of Medicine) and published as part of the *USMARC Format for Bibliographic Data*.

As English is the predominant language in the United States (particularly for libraries and publishers), codes are based on the English names of languages. The standard does not distinguish languages from dialects or establish codes for programming languages.

The standard includes a brief, clear explanation, including explanations for the special language codes for miscellaneous, artificial (other), multiple and undetermined. After this is an alphabetic list of the codes (from *ace* for Achinese through *zun* for Zuñ), another list alphabetized by name of language; and the designation of the Library of Congress as maintenance agency.

Since USMARC is enormously successful, and since these codes are the ones used in USMARC, the standard will inherently succeed.

Status

Z39.53 was adopted in 1987 and will be up for review in 1992. Because it formalizes the de facto standard, it should survive as long as USMARC in its present form continues to be used.

dp[11] Z39.54-199x:
Proposed Standard for Environmental Conditions for Storage of Paper-Based Library and Archival Materials

This project began in 1984; its draft standards have appeared under two different numbers (a 1989 draft was numbered Z39.65). The area is a difficult one for several reasons: most variables are a matter of degree rather than kind; an elaborate, rigid standard can price many repositories out of the market or will simply be ignored; the best storage temperatures are too cold for users; relative humidity is very important, and current air-conditioning technology won't keep humidity in the ideal range without great expense.

The standard may be important; the development process has clearly been marked by contention. The committee has consulted with experts in the field, and has varied from too-short drafts to ones that are "much too long," in the words of the standard committee chair. A draft will be balloted in mid-1991.[12]

---

11 Here and elsewhere, "dp" stands for draft proposal.

12 dp Z39.55 was a proposed standard for computerized serials orders, claims, cancellations and acknowledgments. Because of the shift to X12/EDI standards, work on Z39.55 was suspended. It is possible that the number will be reused for a later development effort.

Z39.56-199x
Standard Serial Issue and
Contribution Identifier (SICI)

This standard defines the requirements for a variable-length code that provides unique identification of serial issues and the contributions contained in them. The standard identifier, SICI, is intended for use by all members of the bibliographic community; it could potentially be used as an unambiguous identification for online citation searching, interlibrary loan and other applications.

Notes

According to the foreword, work on this standard began in 1983 within SISAC, moving from there to NISO. That may be true, but work toward a serial article identifier actually begin before 1975. The June 1975 issue of *Journal of Library Automation* (*JOLA*) included a communication entitled "American National Standard Committee Z39 X/C34 on Code Identification of Serial Articles, Draft Code Proposal." That code, abbreviated SCISA, began with the ISSN and added four fixed-length segments to record date of an issue, one level of volume or issue identification, beginning page and a terminator; an optional variable-length portion contained subfields in which to record issue date, page fractions and the like.

That effort resulted in failure, but SCISA isn't all that far away from SICI. SICI includes ISSN, chronology, and enumeration. If the SICI is for contribution, the page number and title code (if more than one item begins on a page) follow. In any case, the SICI ends with a number identifying the version of the standard used, followed by a check character.

The old abandoned standard and the new proposal have different punctuation, and the methodology for identifying part of a page is different. Thus, "The Compaq Portable II," the second item on page 4 of *Library Systems* v. 6, no. 6, June 1986, would have a SCISA that displays as

SCISA*ISSN 0277-0288/19860600/0006/4$03 (6)$05 (2)

and a SICI that displays as
   SICI 0277-0288(198606)6:6P.4:CP;1-
where "-" is the not-yet-calculated check character, a modulus 37 character that could be 0-9, A-Z, or #.

The new version is certainly easier to read than the older one, has fewer optional elements, and has the security of a check character (an alphanumeric check character, somewhat unusual). Also, it doesn't expect users to figure out what the relative position of an item on a crowded page actually is. It is certainly the case that SISAC and those working on this standard feel that it will be useful.

The ISO has established ISO 9115: 1987, *Documentation—Bibliographic Identification (biblid) of Contributions in Serials and Books.* That standard serves much the same purpose in much the same ways; it is summarized in Appendix A. The biblid has not been widely used within the United States.

Status

A draft standard was circulated for ballot in 1987. A detailed five-page commentary accompanied the current version when it was balloted (May 1-August 1, 1990); the commentary, in a comment/response format, spoke directly to several dozen comments raised on the previous draft. Five NISO members voted against the 1990 draft; 12 others voted for it, but with comments. These comments are based on that draft; as of late February 1991, all negative votes have apparently been resolved, and the standard will be published in 1991 or 1992. It is not entirely clear that the published version will match the draft discussed here.

Z39.57-1989
Holdings Statements for Nonserial Items

The companion standard to Z39.44, this standard establishes rules, defines data elements, and sets forth display conventions to be used in preparing standardized records of holdings for nonserial items. Holdings can be prepared at four levels of specificity. The standard covers all formats of material.

Details

Most often, a nonserial item needs no more holdings information than item identification and location; that is, the most common nonserial item is a single-volume book. That simplicity can mask the complexity that nonserial holdings can take on; this long, clear standard, filled with examples, clarifies that potential complexity and completes the underlying standard definitions required to make the *USMARC Format for Holdings and Locations* fully workable.

The first of four levels includes item identification and institution code; sublocation identifier, copy identifier, call number, and date of report are optional.

The second level also requires date of report, physical form, completeness, acquisition status, and retention codes. Local notes may be added.

At the third level, types of holdings must be designated and some information on the extent of holdings must appear for multipart items. The fourth level increases the specificity of holdings, requiring that gaps in multipart items be explicitly stated.

Level 4 includes more specific enumeration; holdings may be compressed (e.g., v.1-3, the only format available at level 3) or itemized (e.g., v.1\v.2\v.3).

Item identification always represents the bibliographic item and may be any distinctive identifier—an RLIN or OCLC record number, an ISBN, even an author, title and imprint.

Most of the standard defines terms, spells out punctuation and other conventions, describes elements and their usage, and provides examples to show how it all fits together.

How explicit can a holdings statement be? One of the examples in the standard takes two pages of small type. A somewhat simpler example, for a kit entitled "Heart fitness," looks like this:

(SYS)720088
LOC Education Library — 19880000 — 14 stethoscopes + 7 backpacks + 14 heart fitness folios + 14 heart fitness charts + 50 orange dots + 100 red dots + 50 green dots + 3 erasable crayons — Note: In box; the 50 blue dots are missing.

Notes

At first glance, Z39.57 seems formidable, but it finally provides a common basis for recording holdings of complex nonserial items at a time when such items seem to be growing more complex. The standard makes USMARC holdings more workable, and should be useful to the library community.

Status

This standard, developed over six years, was approved in early 1989 and appeared in print in mid-1990. It will be up for review in 1994.

dp Z39.58-199x
Proposed Standard Common Command Language for Online Interactive Information Retrieval

When finally adopted, this draft standard will define a common command language that scholars and patrons can use across many different online catalogs and online databases, either as the default operating mode for each system or as a readily available alternate mode. CCL, the Common Command Language, can be extremely important to the future development and use of online information retrieval systems; that importance may explain the incredibly slow and frustrating path from initial development to final approval (which, as of this writing, still has not been achieved).

Details

Anyone who has ever used RLIN, its predecessor BALLOTS, or any of the derivative "West Coast group" of online catalogs (MELVYL, ORION, CARLYLE and others), or, more recently, EasyNet or EPIC, will recognize the CCL syntax: one-word commands (typically abbreviated to three or fewer characters), frequently followed by one or more specifications. DISplay 1-3 SHOrt; FINd AU eliot AND TI CATS; SHOw NEWs—these are all CCL commands.

The standard, although moderately long (the mid-1989 draft is 43 desktop-published pages), is relatively simple—a straightforward syntax; a set of definitions; detailed descriptions of the 19 commands; a formal syntactic description of CCL in Backus-Naur Form; a summary table of command names; a table of command operators, symbols, and punctuation; an illustration of the components of a complex FINd command; and examples of commands in use. Z39.58 conforms closely to ISO 8777; if the final version differs in any respects, there will probably be clearly stated reasons for the differences.

Notes

There are three problems with this proposed standard:

- Its conformance to ISO 8777 includes one or two choices that seem considerably less consistent than common American usage (e.g. MORE and BACK rather than the common FORWARD and BACK);

- The commands used may already be used for other purposes in current systems; since the requirements for conformance do not allow for explicit CCL mode and non-CCL mode, many systems will be prevented from compliance without major changes to existing functions;

- After *ten years* of development (including some inactive years in the early 1980s), and after more than one system has implemented CCL as it is understood, the draft has still not been adopted.

When I was preparing *Patron Access: Issues for Online Catalogs* (G.K. Hall, 1987) in 1986, I devoted three pages to the proposed Standard Common Command Language, noting that a March 1986 draft "with some revision, appears likely to gain approval as an American National Standard." As I wrote, "Such a model will ease the task of those patrons who use more than one library and may simplify design questions for new online catalogs." That second statement continues to be true, and I'm enough of an optimist to believe that the first is true, even if it does take five or six years from the March 1986 draft.

Z39.59-1989
Electronic Manuscript Preparation and Markup

This standard is an application of the Standard Generalized Markup Language (SGML), ISO 8879. The standard specifies the syntax of generic tags and provides predefined tags for commonly occurring manuscript elements applicable to a wide variety of manuscript preparation and markup applications. In essence, Z39.59 establishes ways to identify elements of an electronic manuscript so that computers can differentiate them.

Oddly, the standard is not currently available through NISO's publisher, although it carries an ANSI/NISO number. Instead, what is called "Version 2.0" is available for $100 from EPSIG, the Electronic Publishing Special Interest Group, a collaboration between OCLC and the Association of American Publishers devoted to spreading the word about Z39.59. The description that follows is based on the draft standard as it was approved at the end of 1988; clearly, NISO has not approved a Version 2.0 through any normal organizational processes.

Details

This extremely long standard—more than 150 pages in its final draft—begins with a lengthy application summary, continues with several appendixes showing how the standard works, continues with a brief formal syntax, and concludes with additional appendixes.

The first part discusses document structures, the basic concepts of generalized markup—basically, that the logical elements of a given document can be specified independently of the layout procedures required to produce the document, how the AAP standard implements generalized markup, the structure and definition of markup declarations, the role of predefined document type definitions, and the set of predefined element tags for this application.

Element tags can be as broad as <book> (for a book or monograph) or <chp> (for chapter) and as narrow as <aon> (acquisition/order number). An element is delimited by beginning it with the tag and ending it with the tag preceded by a slash.

Among other things, appendixes provide structural definitions for books, articles, and serials.

Notes

What does all this mean? For publishers, it potentially means considerably easier repackaging of manuscripts into different forms, since programs can deal with the logical entities involved and since layout becomes almost completely separated from the logical structure itself. A publisher could mount a manuscript as a searchable database fairly easily, once the encoding is done. Indeed, the foreword to the standard discusses its advantages for publishers, but never mentions any advantages for authors, however, some of whom may not be thrilled by the ease with which their work can be repackaged.

The frequent use of the phrase "AAP standard" within the text reveals a slight problem with the statement on the draft's cover, "Prepared by the National Information Standards Organization." It wasn't, not in any real sense; it was prepared at the behest of the Association of American Publishers (AAP), with funding from the Council on Library Resources; NISO approved the standard after some political maneuvering. The peculiar circumstances of the standard are reflected in the circumstances of its availability: it is the only NISO standard that NISO's supplier doesn't supply.

Some who have looked at the standard feel that its provisions unbalance the already uneasy relationship between publisher and author, giving publishers even more power. Of course, individual authors have not been part of NISO's constituency.

One interesting aspect of implementation is that, to date, it has been behind the scenes: that is, few publishers have asked their authors to insert these strange codes, but some publishers have inserted the codes into machine-readable manuscripts later.

When I was reviewing the standard in 1988, I assumed that several word processing programs would move fairly rapidly to support Z39.59 output as an option; that is, prepare the tagged manuscript based on the writer's use of a style sheet. To the best of my knowledge, that hasn't happened yet. It certainly hasn't with either of the dominant MS-DOS word processing packages, although it seems feasible with minor extensions of either Microsoft Word or WordPerfect.

Stepping back from a paranoid writer's perspective, I would note that many of us who work with modern word processing and desktop publishing programs are already quite familiar with the *concept* behind SGML; that is, that you should define logical aspects of a document while writing it, with the computer dealing with layout questions. That's how style sheets work, by and large; for PageMaker, the syntax for new styles is even roughly equivalent to SGML syntax. (For Ventura Publisher, the angle brackets are used for textual modifications such as boldface, superscript and typeface changes, but I had to double the brackets to get them to print in this Ventura-produced book.) It becomes quite natural to mark something as a second-level heading or a bibliography entry, without worrying too much about what that means in terms of the final printed product.

Chances are, this standard will prove both useful and beneficial, and chances are, it won't represent a burden on authors. The peculiar availability situation should be resolved, so that the standard fits properly within the NISO body, if that's really where it belongs.

Status

The standard would normally come up for review in 1994.

[Z39.60] ANSI/NISO/ISO 9660-1989
Volume and File Structure of CDROM
for Information Interchange

This international standard specifies the volume and file structure of CD-ROM (compact disc-read only memory) for the interchange of information between users of information processing systems. It is sometimes known as the High Sierra Group standard, because a group of CD-ROM manufacturers and other interested parties first assembled at the High Sierra Hotel & Casino in Stateline, Nevada (South Lake Tahoe) to formulate it.

I include this ISO standard in this chapter only because it was originally put forward as Z39.60 and approved on May 28, 1987 after a two-year development period. While NISO was processing the standard, the European Computer Manufacturers Association (ECMA) adopted a draft version as a regional standard and forwarded it to ISO for immediate processing as a draft international standard.

ISO 9660, the approved ISO standard, differs in certain respects from Z39.60 as approved, but serves the same purposes in (generally) the same manner. CD-ROM development must be international; it is in NISO's interest to have the two standards conform. In the end, NISO chose to withdraw Z39.60 (which was on the way to ANSI's board of standards review) and adopt ISO 9660 as an ANSI/NISO standard.

This process became even more peculiar because ISO 9660 was processed by ISO's TC 97 (information processing, now ISO/IEC JTC 1) rather than TC 46 (documentation). As a result, ASC X3 was the American body involved in the approval, and under normal circumstances, would have continuing responsibility in the area. As recounted in *Information Standards Quarterly* 1, no. 3 (July 1989), Paul Evan Peters (who is active in both NISO and X3) convinced X3 that CD-ROM standards belonged within NISO's area, since CD-ROM is essentially a publishing medium. (The underlying technological standards for CD-ROM are Philips/Sony licensed standards, since the two companies hold patents on CD technology.)

This standard, already used by most CD-ROM producers, may help to make this new publishing medium succeed. It will be enhanced by additional CD-ROM standards (i.e., Z39.68-199x) being worked on within NISO. NISO is also tracking activities in other organizations relating to CD-ROM standards.

Z39.61-1987
Recording, Use, and Display of Patent Application Data

This standard provides guidelines for recording, use, and display of patent application data in printed and computer-readable publications. It identifies the critical components of patent application data (which naturally varies from country to country, depending on the patent system) and places them into a single format.

Details

When an author must cite patent application data, a consistent format is important if the citation is to make sense. This standard sets forth such a format:

- A two-character country code for the application country, using Z39.27 or ISO 3166 codes, followed by a space;
- Two-digit calendar year in which the application was first entered, which may be part of the application number or may be supplied based on application date, followed by a dash (and converting Japanese year of the emperor to Gregorian date);
- Up to two letters for those application numbers that use letters;
- The numeric portion of the application number, excluding the year (if present) and any leading zeros, followed by a space;
- A code designating whether the application is for an inventor certificate or patent or for a utility model and, optionally, whether the application has special characteristics, followed by a space;
- Application date in form YYMMDD or, if the date would be ambiguous, YYYYMMDD.

This is really quite simple, and has the advantage of normalizing and identifying the many different nationally assigned patent application codes. Thus, for example:

- A Canadian application submitted November 23, 1981, and given the number 3899886 would have the value **CA 81-3899886 A 811123.**
- A French patent applied for March 10, 1978, and given the number 78 07074 would have the value **FR 78-7074 A 780310.**
- A United States patent division applied for January 25, 1984, and given the number 573,648 would have the value **US 84-573648 A2 840125.**

Status

This standard will come up for review in 1992.

dp Z39.62-199x
Proposed Standard for Eye-Legible Information on Microfilm Leaders and Trailers, and on Containers of Processed Microfilm on Open Reels

This draft standard would provide micropublishers and other agencies that produce reel microfilm with specifications and guidelines for the eye-legible information (i.e., information not requiring a microfilm reader) appearing on film leaders, trailers, and containers. It complements Z39.32, which deals with microfiche headings.

Details

The draft lists several standards and provides definitions, and goes on to specify several aspects of leaders and trailers: type size, romanization, treatment of numbers and punctuation, and content. For labels, the draft includes dimensions and placements, and analogous specifications to those for the leading and trailing targets.

Notes

All the examples use entirely upper-case type, presumably in a misguided attempt to improve legibility under adverse conditions, even though tests *consistently* show that upper-lower text is not only more readable but sharply more legible. Most of the standard provides guidelines rather than requirements; it sets a fairly minimal basis for workable labels.

Status

The most recent draft of this standard was balloted in early 1990. That vote resulted in four no votes and five yes with comments. It seems likely that the draft will be pursued, with additional changes eventually leading to an adopted standard.

Z39.63-1989
Interlibrary Loan Data Elements

To encourage clear and efficient communication between interlibary borrowers and lenders, regardless of the medium of communication, this standard defines the data elements to be included in requests and responses, and establishes which ones are mandatory or optional.

Details

The standard includes a structured order chart of the surprisingly large number of data elements involved, a glossary (the bulk of the standard) covering each element and stating whether it is recommended or mandatory, lists of data elements arranged by need level for each type of transaction, and, as an appendix, filled-out paper and electronic forms showing how the elements work together.

Notes

Since the standard is based on current practice, it should see wide use. It may help to standardize practice in newly developing electronic interlibrary loan (ILL) systems. Since incomplete ILL communications make the process much slower and more expensive, this standardization can result in significant savings for libraries (and, indirectly, borrowers). The ALA standard ILL form, which can include all Z39.63 elements, is widely available from library supply houses.

The standard was appealed by the Association of American Publishers on the basis that it did not sufficiently stress copyright compliance. That appeal was rejected by ANSI.

Status

The standard was adopted in 1989 and will be up for review in 1994. Given the furor over final adoption, the review should be a lively one.

Z39.64-1989
East Asian Character Code Set for Bibliographic Use (EACC)

This mammoth standard, almost all of which will be published as microfiche, establishes a computer coding structure for characters in Chinese, Japanese, and Korean (CJK) scripts. The code values take up three eight-bit bytes each.

Details and Notes

This character set was developed by the Research Libraries Group, Inc. for use in CJK support within RLIN, the Research Libraries Information Network. The character set, originally called REACC (RLIN East Asian Character Code), used the Chinese Character Code for Information Interchange (CCCII) as a structural model and incorporated all character graphics listed in four East Asian character sets. After developing the character set and implementing it within RLIN (with simultaneous adoption by the Library of Congress, which uses RLIN for CJK cataloging), RLG forwarded the character set for adoption by NISO. Figure 12.8 shows a portion of REACC/EACC.

REACC characters saw their first use within field 880 (alternate graphic representation) of MARC records representing bibliographic information in its original form. The standard was a demonstrated success even before adoption, with hundreds of thousands of CJK records created within RLIN, many later appearing in OCLC (which adopted REACC). This represents an important improvement in access to such bibliographic items, since transliteration of Chinese, Japanese, and Korean does not always result in uniquely identifiable entries.

The EACC coding structure is a three-dimensional coding scheme with 94 elements in each dimension (representing the 94 graphic spaces within the low-order or high-order halves of an eight-bit coding scheme. The EACC coding space consists of 94 planes, each of which has 94 sections; each section has 94 positions.

The EACC space is arranged into layers of six planes each. The first 12 layers show relationships between characters that are lexico-

Plane: 21				Section: 61		
	2	**3**	**4**	**5**	**6**	**7**
0		馱	騎	驥	髻	魄
1	餿	馴	騙	驢	髭	魏
2	餽	駁	驚	骨	鬃	魔
3	饅	駐	驀	骯	鬆	魘

Figure 12.8: Portion of EACC

graphically related, that is, variant forms of characters. Thus, variant forms of the same character will appear in the same section and position, but on different planes. For example, characters 224E41, 284E41 and 2E4E41 represent three variants of the same character.

The first publication of EACC includes 15,852 characters; additional ones will be added over time. The published standard will include the description of EACC in printed form, accompanied by microfiche reproductions of RLG-supplied pages showing the code and graphic representation for each character, in the form of tables for every section that contains any characters.

Status

The published standard should appear in 1991; it will come up for review in 1994. Note that Z39.64, important as it is, may be an interim step; RLG and a group of major computer and software manufacturers have established a group called Unicode, Inc., working toward refinement and adoption of Unicode, a universal character set employing two bytes (sixteen bits) per character and encompassing all known languages.

Z39.66-199x
Durable Hard-Cover Binding for Books

This standard describes manufacturing methods and materials that relate to the durability of the binding, including endpaper attachment and reinforcement, how leaves are bound together, rounding and backing, case-making, and casing-in.

Notes

The standard does not cover textbook binding or commercial library binding, both covered by existing industry standards. A conforming book must use permanent paper. The book block must be formed by machine sewing through the folds of signatures (the traditional sewn binding). The standard provides detailed specifications for each element involved, including test methods where appropriate.

Status

Work on this project began in August 1986. A late 1989 ballot resulted in two no votes, six yes with comments. Another draft, balloted in late 1990 and early 1991, resulted in approval. The description here is based on the last draft seen; the final standard, which will be published in 1991 or 1992, may differ.

Additional Standards in Development

As of this writing, three NISO standards committees are working on new standards not mentioned above.[13] The draft standards are at various stages of preparation; it is impossible to predict the final form and approval date for any of them, or, indeed, whether they will be adopted. Brief notes follow. Note that Z85.1, now administered by NISO, was fully described in Chapter 1.

---

13 Draft standards appeared earlier if their working Z39 numbers preceded the last adopted NISO standard.

dp Z39.67-199x: Computer Software Description

This standard is really a family of guidelines for specific aspects of computer software description: advertising; eye-legible data on packaging, on the carrier, or on title screen(s); accompanying materials; and bibliographic references. Each of the nine guidelines includes a list of data elements marked mandatory or optional. For example, working from a 1989 draft, the title screen should include the authors (if appropriate), title (mandatory), version statement (mandatory), publisher's name (mandatory) and address (optional, distributor's name (if applicable) and address (optional), copyright date or date of dedication to public domain (mandatory) and publication date (optional), series title (if applicable) and numbering (optional), and contractual/licensing provisions (if applicable). These are all sensible elements, but given the number of popular software packages that lack title screens altogether, the guidelines may not win universal acceptance.

The purpose and scope statement for the section discussed above explains that title screens are the primary source for information used in bibliographic records; "it is, therefore, essential that sufficient and accurate information appear on the title screen(s) to identify the software." True enough, but irrelevant for, say, most of Microsoft's programs or WordPerfect. Somehow, I doubt that either producer will seriously consider adding an intrusive title screen to serve the needs of libraries better, although I could be wrong.

One goal stated in the abstract is interesting but improbable: information shall be presented in such a manner that users will "be able to determine if the software package meets the users' needs and hardware capabilities."

A late 1989 ballot resulted in nine no votes and nine more yes with comments; fewer than half the NISO voting members voted yes without comments. Clearly, significant changes in this standard (or is it a set of guidelines?) will be necessary before it is approved. A second version will go out for ballot in 1991.

dp Z39.68-199x: Related Standards for CD-ROM and Other Optical Media

Standards Committee TT, formed to write standards building on ISO 9660, began its work in March 1989. The intent of the committee was to define the content and format of the publisher identifier, data preparer identifier, copyright file identifier, abstract file identifier, and bibliographic file identifier, all files specified in ISO 9660. In addition, the committee expected to identify data elements that should appear on disc labels, accompanying materials, and packaging for CD-ROM. A draft standard should appear for comment in 1991.

dp Z39.69-199x: Record Format for Patron Records

SC LL, Exchange of Circulation Systems Data, worked actively in the late 1980s to refine a proposed communications format for patron information—which does include provisions for privacy—and see how existing vendors' patron records would map into the proposed format. A draft standard was balloted beginning in November 1990. The group is also working on an interactive transaction communications format and a batch circulation format.

New Standards Committees

Several other NISO standards committees were approved in the late 1980s and 1990. Since NISO relies almost entirely on volunteer effort from relatively small organizations, the process of forming a committee and creating that first draft standard can be an arduous one. Newly formed committees include the following:

- SC MM, Environmental Conditions for the Exhibition of Library and Archival Materials; this committee met for the first time in November 1990

- SC QQ, Physical Preparation of Theses and Dissertations in Printed Form for Long-term Retention by Libraries and Archives

- SC RR, Adhesives used to Affix Labels to Library Materials

- SC SS, Information to be Included in Ads [etc.] for Products Used for the Storage, Binding or Repair of Library Materials

- SC XX, Abbreviations of Captions for Holdings Statements

Three other committees have been proposed but had not yet gone out for membership vote as of February 1991: CD-ROM interfaces, CD-ROM mastering, and guides to accompany microform sets.

Chapter 10 provides more information on likely future developments within NISO, probably charting the course of most standards development for the next decade.

Appendix:
Selected Standards from the
International Organization
for Standardization (ISO)

The International Organization for Standardization (ISO) has approved thousands of standards using a single numbering scheme. ISO publishes a series of standards handbooks "for easy reference and in order to make the International Standards more easily accessible to a larger public."[1] Available from the American National Standards Institute, they contain the full text of all current standards within a specified technical field. The original standards are photographically reduced for the handbooks, and the handbooks omit prefaces.

ISO Standards Handbook 1 includes standards from TC 46, information and documentation; TC 37, terminology (principles and coordination); TC 154, documents and data elements in administration, commerce and industry; and TC 171, micrographics and optical memories for document and imaging recording. A few standards in the handbook were prepared by TC 6, paper, board, and pulps; TC

---

1 International Organization for Standardization. *Documentation and information.* 3rd ed. Geneva, Switzerland: ISO, 1988. 1021 p. (ISO Standards Handbook 1). ISBN 92-67-10144-7.

42, photography; TC 68, banking and related financial services; and TC 130, graphic technology.

Five years ago, Standards Handbook 1 was a reasonably compact (522 pages), surprisingly inexpensive compendium of library-related standards. The current edition is almost twice as large and, at $156 plus $11 shipping, considerably more expensive. Still, it brings together many related standards in a convenient form.

ISO Standards with NISO Counterparts

The following ISO standards have related NISO standards (given after the name of the ISO standard), which may or may not be equivalent but are, in almost every case, more useful for American institutions. Sometimes, the ISO standard covers less ground than the Z39 standard; a few may be broader or more contemporary, or the NISO standards may have different provisions.

- ISO 4: 1984, *Documentation—Rules for the abbreviation of title words and titles of publications*; related to Z39.5

- ISO 8: 1977, *Documentation—Presentation of periodicals*; related to Z39.1

- ISO 9: 1986, *Documentation—Transliteration of Slavic Cyrillic characters into Latin characters*; related to Z39.24

- ISO 214: 1976, *Documentation—Abstracts for publications and documentation*; related to Z39.14

- ISO 233: 1984, *Documentation—Transliteration of Arabic characters into Latin characters*; related to Z39.12

- ISO 259: 1984, *Documentation—Transliteration of Hebrew characters into Latin characters*; related to Z39.25

- ISO 639: 1988, *Code for the representation of names of languages*; related to Z39.53

- ISO 690: 1987, *Documentation—Bibliographic references—Content, form and structure*; related to Z39.29

- ISO 999: 1975, *Documentation—Index of a publication*; related to Z39.4

- ISO 1086: 1975, *Documentation—Title-leaves of a book*; related to Z39.15

- ISO 2108: 1978, *Documentation—International standard book numbering (ISBN)*; related to Z39.21

- ISO 2146: 1988, *Documentation—Directories of libraries, archives, information and documentation centres, and their data bases;* related to Z39.10

- ISO 2384: 1977, *Documentation—Presentation of translations;* related to Z39.31

- ISO 2709: 1981, *Documentation—Format for bibliographic information interchange on magnetic tape;* related to Z39.2

- ISO 2788: 1986, *Documentation—Guidelines for the establishment and development of monolingual thesauri;* related to Z39.19

- ISO 2789: 1974, *International library statistics;* related to Z39.7

- ISO 3166: 1988, *Codes for the representation of names of countries;* related to and, effectively, supersedes the withdrawn Z39.27

- ISO 3297: 1986, *Documentation—International standard serial numbering (ISSN);* related to Z39.9

- ISO 5123: 1984, *Documentation—Headers for microfiche of monographs and serials;* related to Z39.32

- ISO 5426: 1983, *Extension of the Latin alphabet coded character set for bibliographic information interchange;* related but absolutely not identical to Z39.47

- ISO 5966: 1982, *Documentation—Presentation of scientific and technical reports;* related to Z39.18

- ISO 6357: 1985, *Documentation—Spine titles on books and other publications;* related to Z39.41

- ISO 8459-1: 1988, *Documentation—Bibliographic data element directory—Part 1: Interloan applications;* related to Z39.63

ISO Standards in Related Fields

Many of the ISO standards included in ISO Standards Handbook 1 deal with areas outside the coverage of this book. The handbook splits standards into six parts; of those, only parts 3 (character sets and transliteration) and 4 (library science and documentation) relate directly to the scope of this book.

Part 1, Vocabularies, has a number of glossaries or dictionaries, beginning with the somewhat self-referential ISO/R 1087: 1969, *Vocabulary of terminology.* Other standards in this section include five portions of ISO 5127, a dictionary for documentation and information, and five portions of ISO 6196, a dictionary for micrographics.

Part 2, Terminology (principles and coordination), includes seven standards (one, ISO 639, mentioned above) for aspects of terminology—developing dictionaries and transmitting terminology records:

- ISO 704: 1987, *Principles and methods of terminology*
- ISO/R 860: 1968, *International unification of concepts and terms*
- ISO/R 919: 1969, *Guide for the preparation of classified vocabularies (example of method)*
- ISO/R 1149: 1969, *Layout of multilingual classified vocabularies*
- ISO 1951: 1973, *Lexicographical symbols particularly for use in classified defining vocabularies*
- ISO 6156: 1987, *Magnetic tape exchange format for terminological/lexicographical records (MATER)*

Although some of these standards seem peculiar to me (particularly ISO 1951, with 24 pages of symbols to be used in dictionaries), that may stem from my inadequate background in the field.

Part 5, Documents in administration, commerce, and industry, includes ISO 3166 (noted above) and seven other standards:

- ISO 623: 1974, *Paper and board—Folders and files—Sizes*
- ISO 838: 1974, *Paper—Holes for general filing purposes—Specifications*
- ISO 4217: 1987, *Codes for the representation of currencies and funds*
- ISO 6422: 1985, *Layout key for trade documents*
- ISO 7372: 1986, *Trade data interchange—Trade data elements dictionary*
- ISO 8440: 1986, *Location of codes in trade documents*
- ISO 8601: 1988, *Data elements and interchange formats—Information interchange—Representation of dates and times*

Part 6, Documentary reproduction, is definitely of interest to American libraries and publishers involved in microfilming and related activities. Most of the standards in the section are outside the scope of the rest of this book (and of my ability to comment intelligently). It includes 21 standards in addition to ISO 5123, already mentioned:

- ISO R/169: 1969, *Sizes of photocopies (on paper) readable without optical devices*

- ISO 216: 1975, *Writing paper and certain classes of printed matter—Trimmed sizes—A and B series*

- ISO 435: 1975, *Documentary reproduction—ISO conventional typographical character for legibility tests (ISO character)*

- ISO 446: 1975, *Microcopying—ISO no. 1 mire—Description and use in photographic documentary reproduction*

- ISO 1116: 1975, *Microcopying—16mm and 35mm microfilms, spools, and reels*

- ISO 2707: 1980, *Micrographics—Transparent A6 size microfiche of uniform division—Image arrangements No. 1 and No. 2*

- ISO 2708: 1980, *Micrographics—Transparent A6 size microfiche of variable division—Image arrangements A and B*

- ISO 3272 (three parts), *Microfilming of technical drawings and other drawing office documents*

- ISO 3334: 1976, *Microcopying—ISO test chart no. 2—Description and use in photographic documentary reproduction*

- ISO 4087: 1979, *Microfilming of newspapers on 35mm unperforated microfilm for archival purposes*

- ISO 4331: 1986, *Photography—Processed photographic black-and-white film for archival records—Silver-gelatin type on cellulose ester base—Specifications*

- ISO 4332: 1986, *Photography—Processed photographic black-and-white film for archival records—Silver gelatin on poly(ethylene terephthalate) base—Specifications*

- ISO 5126: 1980, *Micrographics—Computer output microfiche (COM)—Microfiche A6*

- ISO 6197 (two parts), *Microfilming of press cuttings*

- ISO 6200: 1979, *Micrographics—Density of silver-gelatin type films*

- ISO 6234: 1981, *Bank operations—Authorized signature lists and their representation on microfiche*

- ISO 6243: 1981, *Micrographics—Unitized microfilm carrier (aperture card)—Determination of adhesion of protection sheet to aperture adhesive*

- ISO 6716: 1983, *Graphic technology—Text-books and periodicals—Sizes of untrimmed sheets and trimmed pages*
- ISO 6829: 1983, *Flowchart symbols and their use in micrographics*
- ISO 8126: 1986, *Micrographics—Diazo and vesicular films—Visual density—Specifications*
- ISO 9735: 1988, *Electronic data interchange for administration, commerce and transport (EDIFACT)—Application level syntax rules*

That leaves 19 ISO standards (not including those approved since 1988), each of which is summarized below.

ISO 18-1981
Documentation—Contents List of Periodicals

This standard provides a detailed specification for a table of contents. It is brief, clear, and follows typical practice for scholarly journals (but not for popular periodicals). It recommends that contents appear on the first page after the inside front cover, as well as appearing on the front or back cover.

ISO R30-1956
Bibliographical Strip

"The bibliographical strip is a concise summary of bibliographic reference data; it is printed at the foot of the front page of the cover of a periodical; it facilitates, on the one hand, the arrangement of periodicals and, on the other, the compilation of citations."

The bibliographical strip consists of abbreviated title, volume, issue, pagination, place of publication, and date.[2] The two-page recommendation includes one page of rules and one page of examples. This recommendation is not widely followed in the United

---

2 In the first edition I mistakenly equated the bibliographical strip with biblid, which is actually an entirely different construct specified by ISO 9115; see the last description in this chapter.

States; the bibliographical strip called for in the original Z39.1 was different in form and detail, and no longer appears in the standard.

ISO 215-1986
Presentation of Contributions to Periodicals

This four-page set of guidelines for authors and editors covers some of the same ground as Z39.18. Recommendations cover identification elements (title, author names and addresses; abstracts and date of contribution); main text (structure, contents list, numbering of divisions, notation, footnotes, citations, credits, bibliographies); contributions originally presented for a different application; illustrations and tables; copyright; annexes (appendixes); and errata. The guidelines are practical and straightforward within the context of other ISO standards.

ISO 832-1975
Documentation—Bibliographical References:
Abbreviations of Typical Words

This standard sets forth a brief set of rules for forming abbreviations of typical words in bibliographic references, and lists more than 1,200 words and abbreviations in 16 major languages. Words in the list range from "aantekening," abbreviated "aant.", to "Zwischentitel," abbreviated "Zwischent." The standard is 38 pages long, including a list in word order and one in abbreviation order. Two additional lists include more than 300 Cyrillic words and abbreviations.

ISO R843-1968
International System for the Transliteration of Greek Characters into Latin Characters

This brief standard includes a set of general principles, a one-page transliteration table, and one page of notes on special signs and retransliteration. No NISO equivalent standard currently exists.

ISO 2145-1978
Documentation—Numbering of Divisions and Subdivisions in Written Documents

This curious two-page standard establishes a method for numbering divisions and subdivisions of a book, article, standard, or other document. It specifies Arabic numerals with periods dividing levels. Each level is numbered continuously within a single occurrence of the next higher level. The standard even says how subdivision numbers are spoken: "when a division or subdivision number is spoken, full stops are not expressed"—that is, you say "part two one four" rather than "part two point one point four."

Although the standard is certainly reasonable, it also seems pointless. Is it possible that anyone deciding to number divisions and subdivisions, and further deciding to use only numerals, would not follow this pattern? For that matter, what advantage is there in using only numbers? A number "1.C.3.d.5" is surely easier to scan than "1.3.3.4.5," and probably easier to transcribe correctly. On the other hand, a pattern such as "1.3.3.4.5" is easier to assign mechanically.

Most modern outlining programs, and word processing systems that provide numbering, follow the ISO standard as the simplest method. Most likely, none of the program designers have ever considered the ISO standard as such. I can only wonder how much money and time was spent preparing it. NISO has not seen fit to prepare an American equivalent.

ISO 5122-1979
Documentation—Abstract Sheets in Serial Publications

Abstract sheets are pages divided into blocks, each block containing a detailed description of one article sufficient for documentation work. This standard specifies what should head such a sheet, what should be in each block, and how the sheet should be presented. Abstract sheets are uncommon in American periodicals; there is no equivalent NISO standard.

ISO 5427-1984
Extension of the Cyrillic Alphabet Coded Character Set for Bibliographic Information Interchange

This standard specifies a set of 42 graphic characters with their coded representations, presented as a graphic chart and a legend showing Cyrillic characters, codes, and comments. The character set expands the basic Cyrillic set (a Soviet [GOST] standard for Russian, registered as number 37 in the ISO International Register) to handle a wider range of languages and material, and is implemented through escape sequences. Figure A.1 shows a portion of the table.

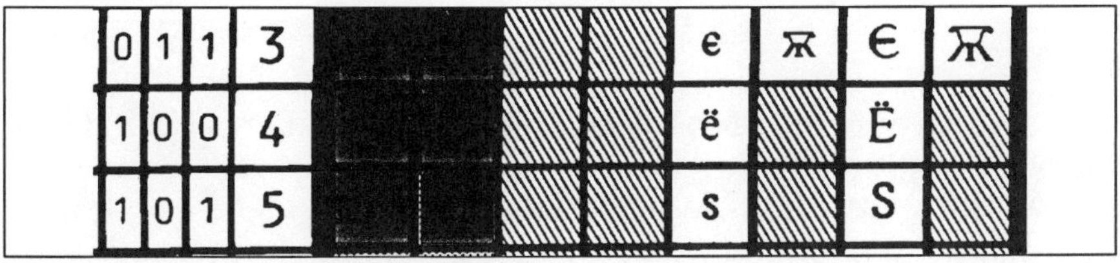

Figure A.1: Partial Cyrillic Code Table

ISO 5428-1984
Greek Alphabet Coded Character Set for Bibliographic Information Interchange

This standard specifies a set of 73 graphic characters to allow representation of Greek in machine-readable form. The graphic chart is accompanied by a legend giving position (machine encoding), graphic, name, and comments. Figure A.2 shows a portion of the table.

0 0 0	**0**				≪		N		ν
0 0 1	**1**			`	≫	A	Ξ	α	ξ
0 1 0	**2**			´	••	B	O	β	ο
0 1 1	**3**			••	••		Π	ℓ	π

Figure A.2: Partial Greek Code Table

ISO 5963-1985
Documentation—Methods for Examining Documents, Determining Their Subjects, and Selecting Indexing Terms

This standard is related to the ISO and NISO standards for indexes, and specifically deals with the process of assigning index terms. Four pages offer good advice on indexing practice (although it's a bit hard to think of the advice as constituting a standard); a fifth page offers a flowchart of the indexing operation using a thesaurus.

ISO 5964-1985
Documentation—Guidelines for the Establishment and Development of Multilingual Thesauri

This lengthy (61-page) standard builds on ISO 2788 (monolingual thesauri) to establish guidelines for creating multilingual thesauri that will be compatible across fields and languages. Multilingual thesauri present special problems, and the standard includes detailed discussions of those problems and how to solve them.

A quick reading suggests that ISO 5964 will prove extremely valuable to those facing the considerable challenge of building and maintaining multilingual thesauri. The group working to revise Z39.19, the American standard for thesauri, is explicitly dealing with monolingual thesauri, noting that ISO 5964 already exists and need not be duplicated within Z39.

ISO 6438-1983
Documentation—African Coded Character Set for Bibliographic Information Interchange

This standard defines a set of 60 graphic characters used in African languages, provides machine codes and suitable escape sequences to use the codes, and shows both a chart and a table giving the letters and names. Figure A.3 shows a portion of the chart.

0	0	0	0	0			Қ	ƙ	Ʈ	�
0	0	0	1	1				ƫ	Ʈ	ƫ
0	0	1	0	2	Ɓ	ɓ				
0	0	1	1	3	Ƈ	ƈ		ŋ	Ʊ	ʊ

Figure A.3: Partial African Code Table

ISO 6630-1986
Documentation—Bibliographic Control Characters

Bibliographic control characters, a concept unknown (to my knowledge) within American library automation, consist of a set of 15 control characters—that is, nongraphic characters in machine-readable form—to be used in cataloging, filing, and indexing. The characters extend the control characters provided in normal ASCII and its international counterpart, ISO 646.

These control characters can be used, for example, to set off strings of characters to be ignored in filing, to define subscript and superscript characters, or to set off strings of characters that are only included for sorting and filing purposes.

ISO 7098-1982
Documentation—Romanization of Chinese

This brief standard includes a section on general principles of conversion of writing systems, a section on principles for converting ideophonographic scripts such as Chinese, and a set of principles for romanizing modern Chinese using Pinyin transcription.

ISO 7144-1986
Documentation—Presentation of Theses
and Similar Documents

Intended for editors and authors, this eight-page set of guidelines includes some as vague (and essentially useless) as, "Margins shall be sufficient to facilitate binding and reproduction," and some as specific as "The typescript shall be of size A4 (210 mm x 297 mm)." The guidelines are all quite brief, cover many aspects of thesis preparation, and refer to quite a few other ISO standards. A two-page index provides detailed access to the brief standard. While much of the advice in the standard would be equally applicable for American theses, some would not; for example, A4 paper is nonstandard within the United States.

ISO 7154-1983
Documentation—Bibliographic Filing Principles

This eight-page standard "defines generalized bibliographic filing principles to be incorporated into the bibliographic filing rules of individual bibliographies, libraries, and documentation centres as well as those of entire nations or language groups.". It does not specify filing rules; rather, it sets forth a set of principles to be used in establishing filing rules.

ISO 7275-1985
Documentation—Presentation of
Title Information of Series

"To the documentalist or librarian series often present a number of complicated problems. The rules for the bibliographic description of series become correspondingly complex." This two-page standard describes the elements required to identify a series and its parts and gives rules for presenting and placing them.

The wording of a series title must distinguish it from other series; it should be uniform whenever it appears in the series; it should not be changed; and, if volumes are numbered, the numbers should follow the title. A series should carry an ISSN as well as the ISBNs that individual volumes may carry.

Except for the final provision, which does not seem applicable to series such as the one of which this book is a part (G.K. Hall's Professional Librarian series), the standard is sensible and easy to follow.

ISO/TR 8393-1985
Documentation—ISO Bibliographic Filing Rules (International Standard Bibliographic Filing Rules)— Exemplification of Bibliographic Filing Principles in a Model Set of Rules

Where ISO 7154 provides principles for filing rules, 8393, which is currently issued as a technical report because some ISO bodies are defining their filing rules, provides an actual set of rules. The 26-page report is fairly straightforward; its length is necessitated by the examples and notes required for it to be sensible. All terms used in the report are clearly defined; a long section providing principles for constructing filing sequences is followed by a relatively short set of filing rules; that is, handling the sequences once they have been defined. (For example, when two filing sections are identical to the end of the shorter section—e.g., "Rose" and "Rose aus Stambul"—the shorter one files first.) Most of the rules follow contemporary practice, with numbers filed before letters rather than being "filed as though spelled out." Except for distinguishing identical filing sections by type of filing area, most of the rules will produce the kind of sorted arrangement that readers might find intuitively obvious.

ISO 9115: 1987
Documentation—Bibliographic Identification (biblid) of Contributions in Serials and Books

This small standard "is intended to facilitate the identification of contributions in serials publications, and contributions in books containing separate works by different authors by means of a standard code called biblid." A biblid, which should appear on the first page of a contribution, is a standardized, unique, eye-readable identifier; it consists of an ISBN or ISSN, year (and issue, for serial), and pagination. Year need not always be recorded; it is surrounded by parentheses (which appear even if the year does not). No spaces appear within the code; thus, for example, my article "The Trailing

Edge, 6: The First Program for Your Second Personal Computer"
(*Library Hi Tech* 8, no. 2 [1990]: 95-111) would have as a biblid "**BIBLID
0737-8831(1990)8:2p.95-111.**"

The biblid has not been widely implemented in the United
States. NISO standard Z39.56, discussed in Chapter 12, is somewhat
similar.

Glossary

Definitions follow the usage in this book. All ISO members (as of 1989) are included for reference, even those not mentioned in the text.

ABNT: *Associação Brasileira de Normas Técnicas;* ISO member for Brazil. Charter member; secretariat for five technical bodies.

Accredited standards agency: Group that meets ANSI requirements for carrying out the process of developing and adopting voluntary consensus technical standards.

Active standard: Technical standard that is established before or at the same time as the relevant technology appears. Active standards are designed to prevent problems rather than to solve them.

AENOR: *Asociación Española de Normalización y Certificación;* ISO member for Spain since 1951; secretariat for 11 technical bodies.

AFNOR: *Association française de normalisation;* ISO member for France. Charter member; secretariat for 358 technical bodies.

AIA: Aerospace Industries Association.

AIChE: American Institute of Chemical Engineers.

ALA: American Library Association.

ANSI: American National Standards Institute; ISO member for the United States. Charter member; secretariat for 335 technical bodies.

ARL: Association of Research Libraries.

ASC: Accredited Standards Committee, a successor organization to an American National Standards Committee.

ASCII: American Standard Code for Information Interchange, ANSI X3.4; assigns standard meanings (control codes and graphics) to combinations of binary digits, to make computer communications feasible.

ASMO: Arab Organization for Standardization and Metrology, an Arab League standardization body.

ASMW: *Amt für Standardisierung, Messwesen und Warenprüfung;* ISO member for the German Democratic Republic (East Germany) since 1988; current status unknown.

ASTM: American Society for Testing and Materials.

BDS: *Comité de la qualité auprès du Conseil des Ministres;* ISO member for Bulgaria. Member since 1955; secretariat for one technical body.

BIS: Bureau of Indian Standards; ISO member for India. Charter member; secretariat for 22 technical bodies.

BISAC: Book Industry Standards Advisory Committee, a group that formulates industry standards within the book industry and, in some cases, proposes consensus standards to be processed through NISO.

BPS: Bureau of Product Standards; ISO member for the Philippines since 1968.

BSI: British Standards Institution; ISO member for Britain. Charter member; secretariat for 435 technical bodies.

BSR: Board of Standards Review. The ANSI board that verifies that organizations have achieved proper consensus. BSR does not review the technical content of standards; it reviews the legitimacy of the consensus.

BSTI: Bangladesh Standards and Testing Institution; ISO member for Bangladesh since 1974.

CAMAC: Computer-Automated Measurement and Control, a set of standards for traffic measurement and control embodied in ANSI/IEEE Camac.

CLR: Council on Library Resources. One of the funding agencies for ANSC Z39 (NISO's predecessor) from 1961 to the early 1980s.

CNLA: Council of National Library Associations. Secretariat for ANSC Z39 before it became NISO and became an independent corporation.

Community standard: Any technical standard other than an internal standard. Used in this book to refer to standards that have not become formal consensus standards.

Consensus: General agreement. In the standards field, consensus normally means that all critical objections by parties with stakes in a proposed standard have been resolved. It does not mean unanimity; a consensus standard can be adopted while negative votes remain.

COSQC: Central Organization for Standardization and Quality Control; ISO member for Iraq since 1974.

COVENIN: *Comisión Venezolana de Normas Industriales;* ISO member for Venezuela since 1959.

CSBTS: China State Bureau of Technical Supervision; ISO member for China since 1978; secretariat for three technical bodies.

CSK: Committee for Standardization of the Democratic People's Republic of Korea; ISO member for North Korea since 1963.

CSN: Federal Office for Standards and Measurements; ISO member for Czechoslovakia. Charter member; secretariat for 13 technical bodies.

CYS: Cyprus Organization for Standards and Control of Quality; ISO member for Cyprus since 1979.

De facto standard: Apparent standard arising through common practice without any formal agreement.

Defective standard: A technical standard that fails to serve the proper purposes of a standard.

by IEC or the ISO/IEC JTC 1. National standards organizations are members of ISO; unlike ANSI (which is an ISO member), most such organizations are governmental.

ISSN: International Standard Serial Number, a standard number used throughout the world to identify serial publications. Embodied in standard Z39.9.

ITINTEC: *Institutio de Investigación Tecnoloógica Industrial y de Normas Técnicas;* ISO member for Peru since 1962.

JBS: Jamaica Bureau of Standards; ISO member for Jamaica since 1974.

JISC: Japanese Industrial Standards Committee; ISO member for Japan since 1952; secretariat for 47 technical bodies.

JTC: Joint Technical Committee, as in ISO/IEC JTC 1.

KBS: Bureau of Standards; ISO member for South Korea since 1963.

KEBS: Kenya Bureau of Standards; ISO member for Kenya since 1976.

Licensed standard: Technical standard established by one or more agencies based on licensed use of protected (i.e., patented) processes or products. For example, the physical format and recording characteristics of compact discs are based on licensed standards established by Philips and Sony, holders of the underlying patents.

Minimum quality standard: A technical standard that establishes the lowest quality level considered acceptable for a product. The best minimum quality standards are performance standards, defining acceptability based on standardized tests.

MSSB: State Standards Board at the Council of Ministers of the Mongolian People's Republic; ISO member for Mongolia since 1979.

MSZH: *Magyar Szabványyügi Hivatal;* ISO member for Hungary. Charter member; secretariat for four technical bodies.

Naming standard: Any standard that establishes consistent naming conventions, including vocabularies and technical dictionaries.

NC: *Comité Estatal de Normalización;* ISO member for Cuba since 1962.

NISO: National Information Standards Organization, successor to ANSC Z39. NISO creates and maintains standards in the fields of libraries, publishing, and information science.

NNI: *Nederlands Normalisatie-instituut;* ISO member for Netherlands. Charter member; secretariat for 78 technical bodies.

NSAI: National Standards Authority of Ireland; ISO member for Ireland since 1951.

NSF: *Norges Standardiseringsforbund;* ISO member for Norway. Charter member; secretariat for 24 technical bodies.

ON: *Österreichische Normungsinstitut;* ISO member for Austria. Charter member; secretariat for 20 technical bodies.

OSI: Open Systems Interconnection, an ISO model for computer-to-computer communications.

Performance standard: A standard that defines a system or object by the end result, rather than by the means used to achieve that end. Some performance standards do include "means" requirements that are fundamental to successful performance.

PKNMiJ: Polish Committee for Standardization, Measures and Quality Control; ISO member for Poland. Charter member; secretariat for 10 technical bodies.

PNGS: National Standards Council; ISO member for Papua New Guinea since 1984; secretariat for one technical body.

Pseudostandard: Something that appears to be a technical standard, but is not. Examples include single names for several incompatible "standards," and standards that are actually internal practice for a single agent, thus subject to unilateral change.

PSI: Pakistan Standards Institution; ISO member for Pakistan since 1951.

Reactive standard: Standard developed because of perceived problems with existing situations—in other words, after the fact. Compare *Active standard.*

Romanization: Conversion of other alphabets or nonalphabetic scripts to Roman letters.

SAA: Standards Australia; ISO member for Australia. Charter member; secretariat for 35 technical bodies.

SABS: South African Bureau of Standards; ISO member for South Africa. Charter member; secretariat for nine technical bodies.

SAN: Standard Address Number. A standard number to identify addresses within the publishing industry (and, theoretically, libraries). Embodied in standard Z39.43.

SANZ: Standards Association of New Zealand; ISO member for New Zealand. Charter member; secretariat for two technical bodies.

SASMO: Syrian Arab Organization for Standardization and Metrology; ISO member for Syria since 1981.

SASO: Saudi Arabian Standards Organization; ISO member for Saudi Arabia since 1974.

SC: Subcommittee (in ISO Technical Committees) or standards committee (in NISO).

SCC: Standards Council of Canada; ISO member for Canada. Charter member; secretariat for 100 technical bodies.

SFS: *Suomen Standardisoimislitto*; ISO member for Finland. Charter member; secretariat for 12 technical bodies.

SII: Standards Institution of Israel; ISO member for Israel. Charter member; secretariat for five technical bodies.

SIRIM: Standards and Industrial Research Institute of Malaysia; ISO member for Malaysia since 1969; secretariat for three technical bodies.

SIS: *Standardiseringskommissionen i Sverige*; ISO member for Sweden. Charter member; secretariat for 102 technical bodies.

SISIR: Singapore Institute of Standards and Industrial Research; ISO member for Singapore since 1966.

SLSI: Sri Lanka Standards Institution; ISO member for Sri Lanka since 1967.

SNIMA: *Service de normalisation industrielle marocaine;* ISO member for Morocco since 1988.

SNV: Swiss Association for Standardization; ISO member for Switzerland. Charter member; secretariat for 56 technical bodies.

SON: Standards Organization of Nigeria; ISO member for Nigeria since 1972.

Specification standard: A standard that establishes a definition rather than a name, symbol or grade.

SSD: Sudanese Standards Department; ISO member for Sudan since 1973.

STRN: Standard Technical Report Number. An unusual standard number consisting of alphabetic, numeric and mixed segments. Embodied in standard Z39.23.

Symbol standard: A technical standard that defines symbols.

SZS: *Savezni zavod za standardizaciju;* ISO member for Yugoslavia since 1950.

TAPPI: Technical Association of the Pulp and Paper Industry.

TBS: Tanzania Bureau of Standards; ISO member for Tanzania since 1979; secretariat for one technical body.

TC: Technical committee (within ISO).

TCVN: General Department for Standardization, Metrology, and Quality; ISO member for Viet Nam since 1977.

Technical standard: An explicit definition that can be communicated, is not subject to unilateral change without notice and, if properly followed, will yield consistent results.

TESLA: Technical Standards for Library Automation Committee of the Library and Information Technology Association of the American Library Association (ALA LITA TESLA).

Test standard: A standard that specifies testing methodology.

TISI: Thai Industrial Standards Institute; ISO member for Thailand since 1966.

Transliteration: Conversion of characters from one alphabetic system to another.

TSE: *Türk Standardlari Enstitüsü;* ISO member for Turkey since 1956; secretariat for four technical bodies.

TTBS: Trinidad and Tobago Bureau of Standards; ISO member for Trinidad and Tobago since 1980.

UL: Underwriters Laboratories, Inc.

UNI: *Ente Nazionale Italiano di Unificazione;* ISO member for Italy. Charter member; secretariat for 66 technical bodies.

WG: Working group (within ISO).

Z39: American National Standards Committee Z39, predecessor to NISO. Formed in 1940.

Z85: American National Standards Committee on Standardization of Library Supplies and Equipment. Z85 only created one standard, Z85.1; its functions have since been assumed by NISO.

Additional Reading

The first edition of *Technical Standards* included a lengthy bibliography covering everything I consulted while preparing that book and, frankly, almost everything else in the technical standards field that I was able to locate during the process.

Looking back at the bibliography, I do not regard it as particularly useful. I'm well aware that any competent librarian armed with the tools of the trade can prepare a bibliography of current articles relating to technical standards; that bibliography will be more current and probably more comprehensive than anything I would include in this book.

The six books listed below include four very recent works in the field and two classics retained from the first edition. They differ in quality and currency; some combination of them will give you a broader perspective on standardization. Chapter 11 mentions some continuing sources of information on library standardization; articles also appear from time to time in the professional literature, although certainly not in profusion or in any predictable pattern.

Batik, Albert L. *A Guide to Standards*. Parker, Colo.: Albert L. Batik (available through ASTM), 1989. ISBN 0-9622523-0-1; $12 ($10 to ASTM members). 129 pp.

A brief (75 text pages, fewer than 25,000 words), readable, ASTM-oriented commentary on engineering standards. Clearly regards ASTM as more important than ANSI; wholly unaware of NISO. Not very useful, but an easy read.

Cargill, Carl F. *Information Technology Standardization: Theory, Process, and Organizations.* Bedford, Mass.: Digital Press, 1989. ISBN 1-55558-022-X (paperback). 252 pp. Index.

This book replaces *The World of EDP Standards*, which went through three different editions prepared and published by three different organizations. It's a very different book: somewhat less information on the organizations and their practices; much more theoretical and general discussion—more than half the book, in fact. Useful from an information technology viewpoint (i.e., primarily ASC X3 and related organizations), although I found much of the discussion muddled and unconvincing (e.g.,Cargill's question as to whether ANSI can survive the next decade) and sometimes misleading. He seems to think that any standards developer that isn't an ASC only does standards as a sideline. This is certainly not true, as in the case of ASTM. Read the first 125 pages and the last 20 or so for a very different discussion of standards than the book you're now holding; read the remainder as informative, brief commentaries on a range of organizations. I'm not sure all the commentaries can be trusted completely; he discusses NISO, but calls it ASC Z39 (NISO), with NIST as the secretariat. Five years after ASC Z39 became the independent organization NISO, that seems odd.

Hemenway, David. *Industrywide Voluntary Product Standards.* Cambridge, Mass.: Ballinger, 1975. 141 pp.

A good look at industry standards, with some emphasis on problems with standards and use of standards for anticompetitive reasons.

Library and Information Technology Standards: Papers Presented at the Second National Conference of the Library and Information Technology Association, October 2-6, 1988, Boston, Massachusetts. Michael Gorman, ed. Chicago, Ill.: American Library Association, 1990. ISBN 0-8389-7431-7. 90 pp.

A collection of nine speeches from two sessions at LITA's Second National Conference, half on developing standards, half on implementing them.

Standards Management: A Handbook for Profits. Robert B. Toth, ed. New York: American National Standards Institute, 1990.

This massive (8½ by 11 in., 505 pp.) handbook is, as the subtitle implies, directed at corporations. It includes several discussions of how to set up standardization programs and how they operate in various types of industries, provides profiles of company and national standards activities and ends with selected readings in company standardization and a small glossary. The book includes quite a bit of good information, but suffers from a fatal flaw: although it is explicitly designed as a reference, not for front-to-back reading, it has no index. It also lacks an ISBN or price notation; I believe it costs just under $100. Only a small fraction of the book is actually about consensus standards development; most of it deals with setting up and running standards groups within companies. Were it not for the lack of index, the book would be recommended reading for anyone in a corporation or very large organization.

Verman, Lal C. *Standardization: A New Discipline*. Hamden, Conn.: Archon, 1973. 461 pp.

A careful, exhaustive work on technical standards in theory and practice. Written from an Indian perspective, it tends to favor governmental involvement and imposed technical standards, particularly for developing countries. Given that very different perspective, this book is still probably the best overall perspective on standardization that I've seen.

Index

J

About the Author

Walt Crawford is a senior analyst in the Development Division of The Research Libraries Group, Inc. (RLG). He is active in the Library and Information Technology Association (LITA) of the American Library Association (ALA), serving on the LITA Board of Directors from 1988 to 1991 and as editor of the *LITA Newsletter* since 1985. He is also the founding editor of *Information Standards Quarterly*. Mr. Crawford has written several books in the Professional Librarian series.

This book is set in Zapf Calligraphic, a type family created for Bitstream, Inc. by Hermann Zapf. Zapf Calligraphic is one of a series of Bitstream typefaces optimized for digital typography. Zapf based the design on his own classic Palatino, a type family designed with an eye toward the early Renaissance.